D0056249

ALEXANDER THE GREAT
MURDER IN BABYLON

By the same author

THE GREEN STONE

THE EYE OF FIRE

KING ARTHUR – THE TRUE STORY

THE SHAKESPEARE CONSPIRACY

ROBIN HOOD – THE MAN BEHIND THE MYTH

THE SEARCH FOR THE GRAIL

ACT OF GOD

THE MARIAN CONSPIRACY

THE MOSES LEGACY

ALEXANDER THE GREAT
MURDER IN BABYLON

Graham Phillips

First published in 2004 by
Virgin Books
Thames Wharf Studios
Rainville Road
London W6 9HA

Copyright © Graham Phillips, 2004

ISBN 1 85227 134 5

Typeset by TW Typesetting, Plymouth, Devon
Printed and bound by CPD Wales

CONTENTS

DEDICATION

To Debbie, for saving my life

ACKNOWLEDGEMENTS

I would like to thank the following people for their invaluable help: Yvan Cartwright for fantastic IT support; Dr Harvey Germain and the staff at the Los Angeles County Regional Poison Center; Debbie Benstead, without whose help this book would not have been possible; my historical researchers Louise Simkiss and Kellie Knights; and Ian Allen, who painstakingly edited this work. Thanks to Mark Cockle for permission to use his wonderful photographs and to all at the Mary Evans Picture Library. I would also like to thank Andrew Collins for valuable background research and Sue Collins for extra support and insight. Finally, a very special thanks to my commissioning editor Kerri Sharp and to all at Virgin Books.
Graham Phillips
London 2004

For more information about Graham Phillips,
his books, and his research, please visit his website at
www.grahamphillips.net

WHO'S WHO

Aegus	Son of Alexander and Roxanne
Alexander	King of Macedonia and conqueror of the Persian Empire
Antipater	Governor of Macedonia and commander of European forces
Aristobulus	Military engineer
Arrian	Second-century Roman historian
Arridaeus	Alexander's brother and nominal successor
Artabazus	Barsine's father
Barsine	Alexander's concubine and mother of Heracles
Bessus	Persian governor of Bactria
Callisthenes	Court scribe executed by Alexander
Cassander	Eldest son of Antipater and eventually ruler of Macedonia
Chares	Alexander's chamberlain
Cleopatra	Alexander's sister
Clitus	Cavalry commander killed by Alexander
Coenus	Chief infantry general during the Indian campaign
Curtius	First-century Roman historian
Darius	Persian king and ruler of the Persian Empire
Diodorus	Sicilian historian who wrote in the mid-first century BC
Eumenes	Royal secretary
Hephaestion	Cavalry commander and eventually Alexander's deputy
Heracles	Son of Alexander and Barsine
Hieronymus	Chronicler and soldier in Macedonian army
Iollas	Son of Antipater and butler to Alexander
Kalyana	Indian priest who joined Alexander's court
Medius	Macedonian aristocrat and host at Alexander's final feast
Meleager	Macedonian infantry general
Nearchus	Admiral of the Macedonian fleet
Olympias	Philip's wife and Alexander's mother
Onesicritus	Macedonian officer and chronicler
Oxyartes	Roxanne's father
Parmenion	General in the armies of Philip and Alexander

Pausanias	Philip's chief bodyguard and his assassin
Perdiccas	Cavalry commander and vizier – regent after Alexander's death
Pharnabazus	Barsine's brother
Philinna	Wife of Philip and mother of Arridaeus
Philip	King of Macedonia and Alexander's father
Philostratus	Second-century Roman historian
Philotas	Cavalry commander executed by Alexander
Plutarch	Greek biographer who wrote around AD 100
Ptolemy	Alexander's chief bodyguard and later king of Egypt
Puru	Indian king defeated by Alexander
Roxanne	Alexander's first wife, queen and mother of Aegus
Seleucus	Commander of the Hypaspistes and later ruler of the eastern empire
Spitamenes	Bactrian rebel leader
Statira	Persian princess and Alexander's second wife

1. THE FINAL BANQUET

In 323 BC Alexander III, king of Macedonia, ruled a dominion that stretched from the Balkans to the Himalayas and from Egypt to the Caspian Sea. It was the largest empire the world had yet seen. Possibly the most brilliant soldier in history, Alexander had led a small and poorly equipped European army on a campaign of over 32,000 kilometres to conquer the mighty Persian Empire. Originally from Iran, the Persians held sway over a domain that also included all of what are now Iraq, Afghanistan, Syria, Jordan, Israel, Egypt and most of modern Turkey. In addition, he even went as far as to conquer part of India. It had taken him twelve years and he was still only 32. With such an astonishing achievement to his name, it is little wonder that history would know him as Alexander the Great. However, Alexander may have been the undisputed master of much of the known world, but he was a slave to destiny. He did not die a warrior's death in battle, but expired as helpless as a baby in his own bed.

In the summer of 323 BC, Alexander had finished his conquest of the Persian Empire and returned to Babylon: the greatest city on earth. Situated on the banks of the River Euphrates, in what is now central Iraq, the city was to be the capital of the new empire that Alexander intended to expand still further. However, his conquering days were over. On the night of 1 June, Alexander was holding a memorial banquet to honour the death of a close friend. Suddenly, late that evening, he was seized with intense pain and collapsed. Alexander was taken to his bedchamber where, after suffering agony, convulsions and delirium, he eventually fell into a coma and died.

The death of Alexander the Great is one of history's most enduring mysteries. What caused this strong young ruler of half the known world to die so unexpectedly at the very height of his power? Historians have proposed malaria, typhoid and alcohol poisoning as possible causes of death, but none of these completely matches the symptoms described. There have also been those who have suggested murder, but until now no one has seriously investigated the possibility. There was no official allusion to assassination at the time Alexander died, but his successors had good reason to avoid raising the question of regicide. Alexander had been considered a living god and such a suspicion would have seriously damaged the credibility of the generals who took over the empire after his death. However, according to Hieronymus of Cardia, one of

1

Alexander's officers who wrote a personal account of his reign, Alexander's mother Olympias went to her grave believing that her son had been poisoned by someone at the feast that night. Was the Queen Mother right? Was Alexander the Great really assassinated?

Orthodox historical opinion tends to discount assassination, contending that those present at the feast had everything to lose by the death of their powerful, unifying leader. However, the more I read the historical accounts of Alexander's life, the more I became convinced that over half a dozen of the guests that evening had ample motive for murder. Although there is no longer a body to examine, five separate accounts have survived giving details of the king's death. Modern forensic examination of the symptoms they record now provides compelling evidence that the cause of death could only have been poison.

In the real-life historical detective story that follows, a fascinating trail of clues, preserved for over two thousand years, leads us finally to discover who killed Alexander the Great.

Before examining the circumstances surrounding Alexander's death, we should first put the time of his demise into a global, chronological perspective. The year of his death, 323 BC, was over a thousand years since the reign of the Egyptian pharaoh Tutankhamun, but over two centuries before the birth of Julius Caesar. It was around a hundred years since the height of Athenian culture in Greece, but some three hundred years before the building of the Roman Coliseum. On the religious front, it was around a thousand years since the time of Moses, almost two and a half centuries after the birth of Buddha, and some 228 years after the birth of the Chinese sage Confucius. It was over three centuries before the birth of Christ and almost nine hundred years before the birth of the prophet Mohammed. When Alexander sat down to his last banquet in Babylon, Rome was a prosperous city, but it was still some half-century before it would start to build its empire; and on the north coast of Africa, the city of Carthage (in modern Tunisia) was the most prosperous trading centre in the Mediterranean. The Iron Age had spread throughout Western Europe, where Celtic tribes had settled in areas such as Britain, France and Spain; while at the same time, from Arabia, the Nabateans had migrated west and had founded the rich city of Petra in what is now southern Jordan. Western civilisation had only just come into direct contact with India but it was still completely unaware of the advanced culture of China. The Macedonians knew little about the Germanic peoples of Scandinavia and the Baltic, who were moving progressively south, and, of course, absolutely nothing about the Olmec civilisation in Central America that had existed for almost a thousand years. This, then, was the world at the time Alexander died.

Alexander may have been a Macedonian but, for all intents and purposes, he was a Greek king. Macedonia, in southeast Europe, lay just to the north of Greece and over the years it had completely adopted Greek culture. So also had Sicily, the islands of the Aegean and much of what is now Western Turkey. In 323 BC, Alexander intended that Greek civilisation should be embraced by his entire new empire in Asia. However, this was something that he never lived to see.

Unlike many events in ancient history, the details of Alexander's death have been preserved. Five people present at the ill-fated banquet were to write accounts of the events: Ptolemy, Alexander's bodyguard, Nearchus, his admiral, Eumenes, his secretary, Chares, his chamberlain, and Aristobulus, his military engineer. Although the original accounts no longer survive, they were cited by a number of writers from the later Roman Empire whose works have been preserved. These were Diodorus, a Sicilian historian who wrote in the mid-first century BC;[1] Plutarch, a Greek biographer who wrote around AD 100;[2] and Arrian, a Roman historian who wrote in the first half of the second century AD.[3] Additionally, there survive an anonymous Latin work known as the *Historia Alexandri Magni* ('The History of Alexander the Great') dating from around AD 250,[4] and the work of Justinus, a Roman historian who lived in the late second century AD.[5] It is from these classical writings that the circumstances surrounding Alexander's death can still be gleaned.

Although Alexander is said to have fallen sick on the seventeenth day of the Macedonian month of Daesius – 1 June, according to the modern calendar – there is some disagreement about where and precisely when Alexander first became ill. Diodorus' account of Alexander's life is contained in two volumes of his work, the *Universal History*. According to Diodorus, the banquet was a funeral feast for Alexander's friend and senior minister Hephaestion, who had died some months earlier. The funeral was being held late because Alexander had sent a deputation to consult with an oracle of the god Ammon in Egypt about the nature of the funeral and to ask if Hephaestion could be deified.

It was at this time that Philip, one of those who had come from Egypt, came bearing a response from [the oracle of the god] Ammon that Hephaestion should be worshipped as a god. Alexander, who was pleased that the god [Ammon] had confirmed his own belief, was himself the first to sacrifice [animals] to that god, and staged great festivities ... After the funeral, the king ordered many entertainments, but as it so seemed that he was at the height of his power and great fortune, Alexander's life was cut short by fate which allowed him no further time to live.[6]

In Arrian's account of Alexander's death, in his work *The Campaigns of Alexander*, the author fails to give a specific reason for the feast, but he does add a few more details.

Alexander had finished the festivities and celebrated the customary sacrificial rites in gratitude for both his success and in memory of his friend [Hephaestion]. After which he was advised by certain seers that he should distribute wine and the meat from the sacrificial animals to his troops and followers of the army and to feast himself. There followed a night of dinning and drinking when, according to some accounts, Alexander decided to leave his friends at their revels and retire to his bedroom to sleep. As he left, he happened to meet Medius who was a close companion and in the king's confidence and Medius asked him to come and continue drinking at his own table ...[7]

The Medius mentioned in the passage was a Greek army officer who acted as Alexander's adjutant and personal assistant. In Arrian's account, Medius seems to have arrived late at the feast and persuaded Alexander to stay later than he intended. However, in Plutarch's version of events, in his *Life of Alexander*, the banquet was more of a drinking binge that had actually been organised by Medius.

At the request of Medius he went to hold high revel with him; and here, after drinking all day, he began to have a fever.[8]

In the *Historia Alexandri Magni*, Medius is again mentioned, but here the adjutant is responsible for having organised a proper funeral feast, rather than a drinking party:

And when Alexander had received the embassy from Ammon, he sent word that Medius of Larissa should prepare a great dinner to honour Hephaestion ...[9]

In Justinus' work, *Philippic History*, Medius is also the host, but Alexander does not become ill until after the banquet when he retires to the man's home.

> As he [Alexander] was leaving the banquet, Medius, a Thessalian, proposing to renew their revelling, invited him and his attendants to his house.[10]

What, then, were the real circumstances in which the feast was held and where exactly was Alexander when he first became ill? As three of these sources fail to mention the reason for the celebration and the two that do specifically say that it was to honour Hephaestion, we can safely assume that the banquet – or drinking party, as Plutarch has it – was held as part of Alexander's friend's funeral proceedings. Medius was clearly the host, as four of the sources specifically refer to him. This would make sense, as it was the adjutant's job to organise such festivities. However, it seems most unlikely that Alexander went back to Medius' house after the banquet, as Justinus contends. Alexander was in the heart of what had been the Persian Empire and his life was constantly under threat. As such, the banquet would almost certainly have been held within the secure confines of the Babylonian royal palace. It is most improbable that Alexander would have left the building to wander the city in the middle of the night and then end up at his adjutant's house, or, as Plutarch suggests, held the celebration in Medius' home. Justinus and Plutarch may have wrongly assumed that, as Medius was hosting the celebrations where Alexander fell ill, the king must have become sick in the man's house.

There is no discrepancy in these sources as to why the banquet was held and, apart from Justinus, they all agree that Alexander first fell sick at the feast itself. It is safe to assume, therefore, that the banquet was to honour Hephaestion and that Alexander became ill at the event, which probably took place in the royal palace. However, there are two very different versions of the symptoms Alexander exhibited when he first became ill.

According to the *Historia Alexandri Magni*, late in the evening, Alexander started showing signs of growing unease and began pacing around the room. After what appears to have been half an hour or so, his condition became acutely worse:

> Alexander again sat down beside Medius and, with his hands trembling, complained that it was as if a heavy yoke were upon his

neck. When he stood again to drink to Heracles, he shouted with pain as if struck through the stomach with an arrow.[11]

Heracles was the Greek name for the mythical hero more famously known by the Roman version of his name, Hercules. The reference here of a toast to the hero confirms the date of the feast, as the traditional day of Heracles' death was celebrated each year by the Macedonians on the seventeenth day of Daesius – 1 June. In fact, Diodorus, in his work, specifically refers to the commemoration of Heracles' death during his account of Alexander's sudden pain.

To commemorate the aniversary of the death of Heracles, he drank much unmixed [strong] wine. Finally he downed a large beaker in a gulp, he shrieked aloud as if struck by a violent blow.[12]

Justinus also refers to the sudden, stabbing agony, but adds that pain soon spread through Alexander's entire body.

Taking up a cup, he suddenly uttered a groan while he was drinking, as if he had been stabbed with a dagger, and being carried half dead from the table, he was excruciated with such torture that he called for a sword to put an end to it, and felt pain at the touch of his attendants as if he were all over with wounds.[13]

The other two accounts differ considerably from these first three, portraying Alexander's initial symptoms as being more gradual and less violent. Arrian says that Alexander did not become really ill until he actually went to bed.

The *Royal Diaries* record that he drank at Medius' table until he left, bathed, and went to sleep. Soon after, however, he arose again and once more returned to drink with Medius and continued until late into the night. Then, after he bathed again and ate a little more, he went to sleep, with the fever already upon him.[14]

Plutarch also portrays Alexander's initial symptoms as milder and, aware of the accounts of Alexander's sudden and unbearable pain, he even went so far as to claim they were invented.

[Alexander] was attacked with a fever, which seized him, not as some write, after he had drunk of the bowl of Hercules, nor was he taken with any sudden pain in his back, as if he had been struck with a lance, for these are the inventions of some authors who thought it their duty to make the last scene of so great an action as tragic and moving as they could.[15]

So which version of events is correct? Was Alexander seized with sudden and severe pain as the first three accounts assert, or was it a less spectacular fever, which these authors dramatised, as Plutarch purports? To answer this, we need to examine the sources that each author used. Although, throughout their works, these writers used a variety of ancient historical documents that still survived, and often use the same material as each other, for their accounts of Alexander's death they each used a different testimony from one of the five witnesses present at the banquet. The first three witnesses, who evidently described Alexander's acute pain, appear to have been reliable.

The account of Alexander's death in the *Historia Alexandri Magni* was taken from the work of Chares of Mytilene, Alexander's chamberlain. He was a Greek, originally appointed as head of the royal household, but towards the end of the war with Persia, impressed by the man's learning and his eloquent manner with words, Alexander also appointed him as his official biographer. After Alexander's death Chares retired to the Greek island of Lesbos where he wrote ten books, dealing mainly with the private life of the king. As Chares appears to have been an honest writer, dealing candidly with Alexander's personality (even his negative traits), and he had no political affiliations with any of Alexander's successors, his account of Alexander's death is generally considered to be trustworthy.

The same seems to be true of Aristobulus, the source for Diodorus' account of Alexander's death. Aristobulus was an old but astute man who served as Alexander's military engineer, building such constructions as catapults, fortifications and bridges. After Alexander's death he lived in Egypt, where he compiled his memoirs. As he was 84 when he wrote and had played no part in the power struggles that followed Alexander's death, there is no obvious reason for him to have invented anything concerning his account of Alexander's illness.

Justinus' account, too, appears to have employed an objective source. His work on Alexander's life was taken exclusively from a book by the Roman historian Pompeius Trogus, who wrote in the early first century AD. Trogus' original work only survives in

7

fragmentary form. Nevertheless, from what still exists, we learn that his source for the later part of Alexander's life had been the admiral Nearchus. Not long after Alexander's death, Nearchus retired to write a book about the foreign countries he had visited during the war with the Persian Empire, ending with a description of Alexander's last days. As far as we can tell, like the previous two witnesses, Nearchus had no obvious motive for inventing the manner of Alexander's death.[16]

These three sources all give pretty much the same account of the initial symptoms that Alexander suffered. Why, therefore, do the other two differ so dramatically?

In his version of events concerning Alexander's death, Arrian specifically cites the *Royal Diaries* as his source. These were the official court records kept by Eumenes. Eumenes had been an officer in the army of Alexander's father Philip and had continued to serve with Alexander during the war with Persia. However, by the end of the campaign, Eumenes was an old man and, although he held an honorary commission in the cavalry, he now served as Alexander's secretary and chief scribe. When Alexander died, these records were seized by Alexander's chief minister Perdiccas, who used them in an attempt to authenticate his claim to the throne. Many of his contemporaries accused Perdiccas of tampering with these records and altering some of them for his own ends. What exactly was accurate and what had been falsified in the *Royal Diaries* is difficult to tell, but their authenticity concerning Alexander's illness is clearly open to question. Sudden and acute pain is often a symptom of poisoning and the last thing Perdiccas wanted was anyone believing that Alexander had been assassinated: claiming to be his successor would make him a prime suspect. Perdiccas had every reason to alter the diaries to portray Alexander slipping quietly into a fever.

Plutarch's source concerning Alexander's death is equally suspect. He took his account from the eyewitness Ptolemy. Ptolemy was about ten years older than Alexander but had been his friend from childhood, and throughout much of Alexander's reign he served as his chief bodyguard. Although he had never distinguished himself as one of Alexander's commanders, Ptolemy rose to prominence shortly after the king's death. For seventeen years he served as governor of Egypt, but in 306 BC, with Alexander's empire having fragmented, he proclaimed himself Egyptian pharaoh. Shortly after, he wrote a narrative of the whole of Alexander's life, in which he often depicts himself in a more significant role than other contemporary writings report. For example, Ptolemy has himself playing a heroic role in the battle of Issus in 333 BC, whereas all the other sources fail to mention it. It is generally agreed amongst historians that Ptolemy's work is a reliable source concerning Alexander's life, apart from when the author is personally involved in events. There could be no more important event at which Ptolemy was present than Alexander's death. Not only had he attended the banquet where Alexander fell ill, but he was also the chief bodyguard and so ultimately responsible for keeping his king alive. If Alexander was assassinated, then Ptolemy had failed miserably to do his job. Such stigma was hardly fitting for a pharaoh of Egypt; particularly one who had founded a dynasty that would not end until the death of Cleopatra in 30 BC. Even if Plutarch himself did not falsify the account of Alexander's illness, then his Egyptian copyists certainly had every reason to portray Alexander as dying from natural causes. As such, any classical historian, such as Plutarch, who used Ptolemy's work as his source for the symptoms of Alexander's fatal sickness, would have to accuse the other witnesses of dramatising events.[17]

When everything is taken into consideration, the first three accounts of Alexander's initial symptoms seem to have been taken from reliable eyewitness testimony. It appears that Alexander first became agitated, before starting to shake and complaining of stiffness or discomfort in the neck. Soon after, he experienced an intense pain, seemingly in the area of the stomach. As two of the accounts liken the pain to a wound inflicted by a sharp weapon, we can suppose that Alexander described it as a stabbing pain. In fact, the pain was so intense that it made him scream. Immediately, Alexander collapsed and had to be carried from the table, although he was still conscious. The pain, it seems, quickly spread to his entire body and he suffered extreme discomfort wherever he was touched.

Unlike the descriptions of the initial symptoms, there are no major disagreements between the accounts concerning Alexander's condition after he was taken to his bed. Diodorus tells us that Alexander continued to get worse during the night.

When his servants put him to bed they attended him closely, but the pain grew worse and the physicians were called. None of them were able to do anything to help and Alexander's great and acute discomfort continued unabated.[18]

Diodorus gives no specific details, but the *Historia* says that Alexander spent the night suffering what appear to have been repeated convulsions, followed by periods of delirium and unconsciousness.

Throughout the night the king would writhe and shake upon his bed, then he would become still. At other times he would ramble with meaningless words, speaking as it seemed with spirits around his bedchamber.[19]

Plutarch not only refers to the delirium, but also an intense thirst.

In the rage of his fever and a violent thirst, he took a draught of wine, upon which he fell into delirium.[20]

The following day Alexander's condition improved, although he was still too ill to leave his bed unaided. According to Arrian:

The day after he was carried on his bed to perform his religious duties at the temple as usual . . . From there he was carried to the river [Euphrates], and ferried across to the park on the opposite bank, where he bathed and rested.[21]

According to Plutarch, 'he slept in the bathing-room all day on account of his fever'.[22] (Bathing was the usual way to attempt to alleviate many ailments.) Alexander appears to have been left by himself in the bathing-room as, according to the Historia, 'he bade his attendants to leave him alone in darkness, as he was distressed at both their presence and by the light'.[23]

The following day, Alexander's condition had vastly improved. Plutarch tells us that he was even able to move around, play dice and was eating again:

He bathed and removed into his chamber, and spent his time in playing at dice with Medius. In the evening he bathed and sacrificed, and ate freely.[24]

The sources agree that for the next couple of days Alexander continued to get better. By the fifth day he was even planning a new campaign and issuing orders to his officers. However, soon after, Alexander took a dramatic turn for the worse. According to the Historia:

As if a knife had been thrust in and turned beneath his stomach, the pain returned and the king was beside himself with agony and again he fell into fits and delirium.[25]

There appears to have been some confusion as to when exactly this happened. Justinus says that it was the sixth day after Alexander's illness began, making it 7 June; by Arrian's reckoning it was the following day; while Plutarch says it was the day after that. Nevertheless, they all agree that somewhere between 7 and 9 June Alexander had relapsed into a far worse condition than before. According to Plutarch, Alexander's generals decided that their king was close to death and decided to visit him one last time.

On the twenty-fifth [day of Darius – 9 June] he was removed to his palace on the other side [of] the river, where he slept a little, but his fever did not abate, and when the generals came into his chamber he was speechless and continued so the following day.[26]

According to Arrian, although Alexander was unable to speak, he was still conscious.

He lay speechless as the men came in, yet he struggled to raise his head, and in his eyes there was still a look of recognition for each as they entered.[27]

The *Historia* gives pretty much the same account.

He recognised his officers and raised his head to speak to them, but could utter no word. From that moment until the end he spoke no more.[28]

Justinus also says that Alexander was unable to speak. However, he was able to sit up and give Perdiccas his ring.

Being unable to speak, he took his ring from his finger, and gave it to Perdiccas, an act which tranquillized the growing dissension among his friends; for though Perdiccas was not expressly named his successor, he seemed intended to be so in Alexander's judgment.[29]

For another day Alexander lingered on, his breathing becoming more laboured, until he fell into a coma and died the following evening. The traditional date of Alexander's death is 11 June, although it could have been a couple of days earlier if Justinus is right, and a day or so later if Plutarch is to be believed.

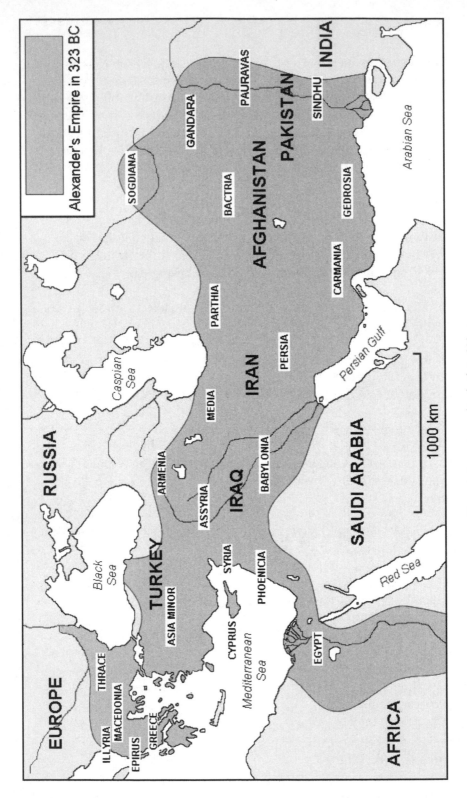

Alexander's empire on his death in 323 BC.

Alexander the Great had been the most successful soldier in history and his empire had been the largest the world had ever seen. However, his end was no warrior's death and what happened to his body was hardly the kind of obituary he would have hoped for. As Alexander had died without publicly naming an heir, his generals spent the best part of a week arguing over his successor. Plutarch tells us that during this time Alexander's body was unceremoniously left to lie in a storeroom somewhere. Strangely, although it should have begun to decompose in the hot Babylonian summer, the body remained preserved.

> During the dissensions among the commanders, which lasted several days, the body continued clear and fresh, without any sign of such taint or corruption, though it lay neglected in a close, sultry place.[30]

Alexander's body was eventually despatched to a tomb that had been prepared in Macedonia's religious capital of Aegae. However, once it arrived in the Syrian city of Damascus, it was hijacked on the orders of the new Egyptian governor Ptolemy and taken back to Egypt to be buried in Alexandria. However, the precise location of the tomb has been long forgotten.

So how did Alexander die? Modern science could probably discover much from his remains, but unfortunately his tomb has never been found. We are left, therefore, with the eyewitness testimony alone from which to postulate a verdict.

The most popular theory for the cause of death has been malaria. Alexander had travelled to a part of India where malaria was common, and some of his symptoms do indeed match the disease. With malaria, the patient experiences chills which cause shaking, as Alexander is said to have done, and they develop a high fever, which comes and goes every few days for a week or so. Alexander is described as initially having a fever, which then abated until he relapsed a few days later. Malaria can also induce delirium and periods of unconsciousness, which Alexander also seems to have suffered. And in cases where malaria is fatal, the cause of death is usually a ruptured spleen: an agonising condition that would result in excruciating pain in the area of the stomach, such as described in Alexander's case. For years, malaria was widely accepted by historians as the cause of death, until a tropical-disease specialist, Dr James Maynard of London University, examined the accounts of Alexander's fatal illness in the 1970s. He concluded that,if the ancient reports were reliable, then Alexander could not have died from malaria.

Dr Maynard seriously doubted that Alexander had suffered a ruptured spleen. If his spleen had ruptured when he was struck down with pain at the banquet, as the malaria theory supposed, then the pain would not have subsided overnight and abated for some days, as the sources report. Alexander would have been in persistent agony until he died from internal haemorrhaging. Moreover, the pain would have been on the left side of the stomach and not beneath it, as described. The other way that malaria victims can die is when diseased blood cells clog the brain tissue of the patient. Dr Maynard found no evidence that Alexander had died in this way either, as the condition would have been accompanied by severe headaches, which are not mentioned once by any of the sources. In fact, Dr Maynard was certain that Alexander could not have contracted malaria at all.

Malaria is a disease carried by certain mosquitoes that can infect a person with a bite. These mosquitoes live in jungle and tropical locations, but not in desert regions such as central Iraq where Alexander died. However, two years earlier, Alexander had been in an area of India where malaria was common. Nevertheless, Dr Maynard seriously doubted that Alexander could have contracted the illness there. The disease can remain dormant in the bloodstream for anything up to ten months from the time of the initial exposure. Someone who fails to exhibit symptoms after that time is probably not infected, and certainly not after two years. Bouts of malaria, perhaps lasting some days, can and do recur, so it is possible that Alexander had previously suffered from the illness since he left India. However, Alexander's life from the time he was in India is well documented and there is no report whatsoever of a previous illness of this kind.[31]

With the malaria diagnosis in question, in 1998 a team from the University of Maryland in the USA suggested that Alexander had died of typhoid. Typhoid causes chills, high fever and delirium, from which Alexander appears to have suffered. However, so do many other illnesses. What convinced the team that he had specifically died of typhoid was the description Plutarch gives of the state of preservation of Alexander's body after his apparent death. One symptom sometimes associated with typhoid is a condition known as ascending paralysis: muscle paralysis that starts at the feet and moves slowly up the body. Patients with this condition can eventually appear dead and, in the days before modern medicine, some unfortunate victims of typhoid were even buried before they had actually died. As Plutarch reported that Alexander's body failed to show any signs of decomposition for days, the team proposed that the king had been suffering from paralysis caused by typhoid and was actually still alive.[32]

However, the typhoid theory failed to address many of the symptoms and circumstances associated with Alexander's death. To begin with, typhoid is caused by *salmonella typhi* bacteria, which are transmitted by food or water contaminated by an infected person, or by sewage containing the germs. As such, there would almost certainly have been an epidemic of the disease when Alexander fell sick. However, there is nothing in any of the historical accounts to suggest such an outbreak in Babylon at the time. Secondly, *salmonella typhi* is an intestinal bug which causes severe diarrhoea and abdominal pain. Besides the fact that diarrhoea is not mentioned in the historical accounts, Alexander's pain is reported to have been in the area of his stomach and not his bowel, which would have been the area of discomfort if he had had typhoid. In fact, the University of Maryland team proposed that Alexander's stabbing pain suggested that he had died of a perforated bowel, which is often the cause of death in cases of typhoid fatality. Even if the sources are wrong about the location of Alexander's pain, a perforated bowel would have left him in constant agony until he died, rather than recovering for days as the accounts all describe.[33]

Perhaps the most obvious possible cause of Alexander's death to consider is alcohol poisoning. He is reported as having been a heavy drinker, and on the day he was taken ill Alexander had been consuming large quantities of strong wine. Intense pain in the area of the stomach is a symptom of alcohol poisoning and unconsciousness is inevitable. Alexander did suffer stabbing pains in his stomach and was unconscious shortly after. If Alexander had suffered from the toxic effects of alcohol to the point where he was in excruciating agony, as is reported, then the lining of his stomach would have been so inflamed that he would also be vomiting violently and would not be able to hold down food or liquid for many hours or even days. If Alexander was a chronic alcoholic, as has been suggested, then this condition would be extremely serious. Unable to hold down any alcohol, he would soon suffer from dangerous withdrawal symptoms.

Serious alcoholics suffer severe withdrawal symptoms known as delirium tremens, or DTs for short. Unless the alcohol intake is lessened gradually, or substituted by modern drugs, the person experiences fevered agitation, extreme anxiety, delirium, hallucinations and severe trembling. Moreover, delirium tremens also include grand mal seizures that sometimes lead to death. All of these, or similar symptoms, seem to have been suffered by Alexander. However, as DTs occur because the body has been denied the alcohol it has become dependent upon, they do not begin until enough alcohol has left the system – usually not for

24 hours or more. Even with an extremely high metabolism, DTs would not occur until at least six hours after the last drink; and even then they would be the less severe effects, such as anxiety, agitation and some shaking. The more extreme conditions – delirium, hallucinations and seizures – would not occur until many hours later. However, Alexander was suffering from all these symptoms the night he was taken from the banquet. In fact, the trembling and agitation are recorded while he was still drinking. Whatever Alexander was suffering from on the night of the banquet it was not DTs, and alcohol poisoning itself would not cause such symptoms. Alcohol poisoning either results in complete unconsciousness or a state of stupor in which the nervous system is dangerously sedated for hours: the victim is in precisely the opposite condition to one that would produce the writhing seizures and delirium which Alexander is said to have suffered. In fact, the major effect of alcohol poisoning is continual vomiting. Death often results from the victim choking on their own vomit or, in the days before intravenous drips, from dehydration. Even though Plutarch does say that Alexander suffered a violent thirst on the night he was taken ill, not once does he or any of the other historical sources mention vomiting or even nausea as one of Alexander's symptoms.[34]

Whatever really killed Alexander has never been successfully explained. Indeed, it seems to have been a mystery to Alexander's contemporaries, as no particular illness was officially named at the time the king died. However, some years later there were suspicions that Alexander was murdered. Justinus records that some of Alexander's friends considered that drink was responsible for his death but, for some reason, he dismissed the possibility in favour of assassination. In fact, Justinus goes so far as to suggest a cover-up by Alexander's successors.

> His friends reported that the cause of his disease was excess in drinking, but in reality it was a conspiracy, the infamy of which the power of his successors threw into the shade . . . He was overcome at last, not by the prowess of any enemy, but by a conspiracy of those whom he trusted, and the treachery of his own subjects.[35]

On what evidence Justinus was basing these allegations is unknown, but he could have read the work of Hieronymus of Cardia who evidently referred to the suspicions of Alexander's mother, Olympias, that her son was poisoned. Hieronymus was a soldier who had served with Alexander, and his memoirs still survived in Justinus' day. In fact, copies were still in existence some half a century later when the *Historia* was compiled, as it cites Hieronymus concerning Olympias' belief that someone had murdered her son.

> Upon a story told to her in Pella [the capital of Macedonia], Olympias believed that her son had been poisoned. Whoever had committed so grievous a crime, she seems not to have known, for it is said she killed many who were innocent in her search [for the culprit].[36]

Plutarch, in his account, also states that Olympias came to believe that someone had killed Alexander.

> At the time, nobody had any suspicion of his being poisoned, but upon some information given six years after, they say Olympias put many to death.[37]

Who exactly provided Olympias with the information, what it was and why it so convinced her that Alexander was murdered is as much a mystery as the cause of Alexander's death. Whatever Olympias was told, she obviously regarded it as proof that Alexander had been poisoned. However, the information clearly did not include the name of the supposed culprit. Nevertheless, Olympias' suspicions seem to have started fingers pointing at various suspects, as the historical sources even name some of them. Plutarch, for instance, refers to suspicions that Antipater, one of Alexander's generals was responsible, and that he had been encouraged by the renowned philosopher Aristotle, who was alive at the time.

> But those who affirm that Aristotle counselled Antipater to do it, and that by his means the poison was obtained, cite one Hagnothemis as their authority.[38]

Who this Hagnothemis was is unknown, as he goes unrecorded elsewhere, but he may have been the same person who informed Olympias of a plot. Justinus also mentions suspicions that Antipater was responsible and refers to rumours that his youngest son Iollas, who was the royal butler, administered the poison into Alexander's wine at the banquet.[39] Olympias clearly considered Iollas a suspect at one point because Plutarch says that she desecrated his grave after he died.[40] However, she obviously decided that he was not the guilty party as she continued to pursue others. Another man she seems to have suspected was Medius, as Arrian says that suspicion was also attached to him. As the person in charge of the festivities where Alexander fell ill, he would have been an obvious suspect. Nevertheless, Olympias eventually rejected him as the culprit too, and appears to have turned her attentions to Antipater's eldest son Cassander. Diodorus suggests that Cassander eventually murdered Olympias around 316 BC because she had accused him of the murder.[41] However, it appears that Olympias died still uncertain as to the identity of the person who was supposed to have killed her son. According to the *Historia*:

> The queen mother [Olympias], it is said, had good and sound proof that poison had been administered to him [Alexander], and that the assassin had been present at the revel [the banquet] as all the food and all the drink had been well tasted [tested by a food taster] earlier that evening and had since been guarded. Though she put many to death and levelled accusations, the culprit, if indeed there was one, was never exposed for the deed.[42]

Was Olympias right – had Alexander really been poisoned by someone at the banquet that night?

One reason why the possibility of assassination has been largely ignored by modern historians is that they have tended to rely on Plutarch, who not only dismissed the allegations of murder but also portrayed Alexander's illness as a naturally occurring fever. Additionally, as he cited the *Royal Diaries* as his source, Arrian's depiction of Alexander's condition as a gradual fever has also been regarded as evidence negating the likelihood of poisoning. However, as we have seen, both these authors' sources, Ptolemy and Eumenes, cannot be accepted as reliable, objective witnesses concerning the initial symptoms Alexander suffered. Each of the other three accounts, for which there is no obvious reason to doubt the integrity of their sources on the matter, are quite specific about the violence of Alexander's condition: one which would be consistent with various types of poisoning.

Nevertheless, the main reason why it has been generally accepted that Alexander died of natural causes is a sound one. Namely, that there appeared to be no actual evidence to the contrary. However, when I confronted forensic experts with the reports of Alexander's fatal illness, it transpired that there was, in fact, every reason to believe Alexander had been poisoned.

SUMMARY OF CHAPTER ONE

Alexander died suddenly of a mysterious illness at the age of 32. The cause of death has remained a mystery, but it does not seem to have been one of the natural illnesses once suggested.

- On the night of 1 June 323 BC Alexander was holding a funeral feast in the city of Babylon for his friend and deputy Hephaestion. Suddenly, late that evening, he was seized with intense pain and collapsed.
- Unlike many events in ancient history, the details of Alexander's death have been preserved. Five people present at the ill-fated banquet were to write accounts of the events. Although the original accounts no longer survive, they were cited by a number of writers from the later Roman Empire whose works have been preserved: Diodorus, Plutarch, Arrian, Justinus and the anonymous author of the *Historia Alexandri Magni*. It is from these classical writings that the circumstances surrounding Alexander's death can still be gleaned.
- The initial symptoms were agitation, tremors, aching or stiffness in the neck, followed by a sudden, sharp pain in the area of the stomach. He then collapsed and suffered acute and excruciating agony wherever he was touched. Alexander also suffered from an intense thirst, fever and delirium, and throughout the night he experienced convulsions and hallucinations, followed by periods of calm. In the final stages of the condition he could not talk, although he could still move his head and arms. Ultimately, his breathing became difficult and he fell into a coma and died.
- The three popular theories concerning the cause of Alexander's death – malaria, typhoid and alcohol poisoning – can now be discounted. Malaria is carried by mosquitoes that live in jungle and tropical locations, but not in desert regions such as central Iraq where Alexander died. Two years earlier, Alexander had been in an area of India where malaria was common. Nevertheless, the disease cannot remain dormant for this period of time. Alexander's life from the time he was in India is well documented, but there is no report whatsoever of a previous illness of this kind. Typhoid is transmitted by food or water contaminated by bacteria, and causes epidemics not just a single case. There is nothing in any of the historical accounts to suggest such an outbreak in Babylon at the time Alexander died. The main effect of alcohol poisoning is continual vomiting, but not once do any of the historical sources mention vomiting or even nausea as one of Alexander's symptoms.

- As Alexander was at the height of his power, only 32 years old and in previous good health, his mother Olympias suspected that he had been poisoned. The historical sources refer to information she obtained that convinced her that she was right. Unfortunately, they do not reveal what this evidence was or the name of the murderer.

2. FORENSIC OPINION

If I was going to discover what really killed Alexander the Great then I needed an expert opinion. Having a friend who worked for the police in California, I asked him if he could suggest someone who might be of help and he put me in touch with Dr Harvey Germain, a forensic pathologist attached to the Los Angeles Police Department. When Dr Germain examined the list of Alexander's symptoms, he could suggest no single disease that would account for them all, although he did propose that the patient could have been suffering from more than one naturally occurring ailment. Nevertheless, he immediately suspected foul play. If he was confronted with a report of someone dying in this way, he told me, he would certainly want to examine the body. To start with, there were a number of poisons that would cause precisely the illness as described. However, what concerned him most was what is said to have happened to Alexander's corpse after death.

Apparently, Alexander's body strangely failed to show any signs of decomposition for some days. According to Plutarch, after Alexander died, 'his body continued clear and fresh, without any sign of such taint or corruption, though it lay neglected in a close, sultry place'.[1] The team from the University of Maryland suggested that Alexander had not actually been dead, but was in a state of paralysis caused by typhoid. However, as we have seen, if the reports are accurate, Alexander cannot have been suffering from typhoid. Indeed, if Alexander had been suffering from muscular paralysis of any kind – enough to make him appear dead – then he could not possibly have survived in that state for more than a day or two without intensive care. In fact, Alexander's body failed to show any signs of decay for six days. There survives a second, independent account of the preservation of Alexander's body, by a Roman historian who wrote about Alexander's funeral. Curtius Quintus Rufus was a Roman politician who compiled a history of Alexander's reign around AD 33.[2] His work, *The History of Alexander*, does not include details of Alexander's illness, but it does mention what happened after he died:

> Although Alexander's body had lain in the coffin in sweltering heat for six days, there was no evidence of decay when the Egyptians and Babylonians came to embalm it.[3]

Curtius cites Aristobulus, the military engineer, as his source, a man who, as we have seen, appears to have been a reliable witness. If Alexander's body had remained preserved for this amount of time under the conditions described, Dr Germain told me, then somehow bacteria had been prevented from starting the process of decomposition. There could be only two causes: radiation, which could be discounted in the fourth century BC, or a lethal dose of a toxic substance that pervaded the corpse. For a proper opinion, Dr Germain suggested that I consult the Los Angeles County Regional Poison Center at the University of Southern California. When I did, they confirmed Dr Germain's view that the corpse's state of preservation could only have been caused by large amounts of a toxic substance in the body's system. It seemed, if Plutarch's and Curtius' reports were accurate, that Alexander the Great had to have been poisoned.

Ironically, the bizarre preservation of Alexander's body had been reported by the sceptical Plutarch – the very man who had led historians to ignore the possibility of assassination for so long. After two thousand years, had he unwittingly added credence to the suspicions of Alexander's mother, who believed that her son had been deliberately poisoned? The question now was, what had poisoned him?

The Poison Center told me that there are certain animal toxins that might produce the symptoms described. However, as they are obtained from creatures that live in the African rainforest, south of the Sahara, and in Central and South America and in Australia, all of which were unknown to the people of Europe, the Middle East and western Asia during Alexander's time, they could be ruled out. There were, though, three mineral poisons that would have been available that might have caused some of the symptoms described; these were mercury, arsenic and antimony.

Mercury is found in cinnabar ore and was obtained by the ancient Greeks from deposits in Italy. Because mercury is an unusual metal that is liquid at room temperature, it was highly prized by the Greeks, who believed it had magical properties, and it was even kept in ceramic phials, which were used as currency. At high doses, mercury causes tremors and seizures, such as those Alexander suffered, ultimately leading to coma and death. However, mercury is an accumulative poison and in smaller doses it was even used as a medicine in ancient times. The quantities necessary to produce the acute effects Alexander experienced would have made it completely impractical as a murder weapon: the blobs of silvery metal would not dissolve in wine and would be noticeable in food. Alexander could have been gradually poisoned by mercury over time, but there are no reports of the symptoms he would then have suffered for some weeks, such as tingling sensations in the limbs, slurred speech, blurred vision and headaches.[4]

Arsenic is found naturally in rock, often near gold deposits. In ancient times it was used as a pigment and would have been available to someone in Alexander's court. Severe arsenic poisoning causes stomach pains, contractions of the limbs, spasms and convulsions, followed by coma and death. Again, these were symptoms exhibited by Alexander. Arsenic is a well-known poison, often used in popular mystery novels. However, like mercury, its effects are cumulative, and it would take an impractical amount of the substance to bring on an acute condition. Alexander was certainly not being administered arsenic over a long period of time, in the way that arsenic is usually used as a murder weapon, as he would have suffered a gradual decline in health, including headaches, vomiting and weight loss, none of which is reported.[5]

The last possible mineral poison was antimony, a silvery-white metal that is found in many kinds of rocks and was used in ancient times as a cosmetic. If ingested in sufficient quantity it produces symptoms similar to acute arsenic poisoning. However, once again, it is an accumulative toxin and the large amounts necessary to produce immediate and severe effects would also make it impractical for use as an instant poison. Antimony is known to have been used as a murder weapon in ancient times, as it mimics the symptoms of other diseases. However, it would have to be administered over time, resulting in a gradual deterioration of the victim's condition before the more severe effects became evident, such as long-term headaches and vomiting, which again are not mentioned.[6]

We were left, therefore, the Poison Center told me, with vegetable toxins. There are different categories of poisonous plants and trees, but only three would produce sudden, acute reactions, such as Alexander suffered, where no previous clinical signs were evident. The first two are cyanogenic glycosides (such as sorghum and parts of the cassava plant) and cardiac glycosides (such as foxgloves and oleander). However, these could be ruled out in Alexander's case. Cyanogenic glycoside poisons immediately affect respiration and Alexander is not described as having initial breathing difficulties: besides which the victim becomes flushed and then blue as the body is deprived of oxygen. Again, such dramatic symptoms are not once described. In fact, the chemical involved in cyanogenic glycoside poisoning is cyanide, and anyone who is poisoned by enough cyanide to cause an acute reaction would be dead in minutes.

Cardiac glycosides, as the name implies, affect the heart, leading to cardiac arrest. None of Alexander's symptoms suggests a heart attack; besides which, the patient would experience chest pains, and not pain in the area of the stomach, as described.[7]

The only other group of vegetable toxins that could have caused Alexander's acute symptoms come from plants containing alkaloid poisons, such as larkspur, mandrake and hemlock. These plants, shrubs and trees contain nitrogen-bearing chemicals that especially affect the nervous system, causing shaking limbs and muscle pains in the back or neck before the victim experiences severe agony and seizures.[8] The *Historia Alexandri Magni* describes both Alexander's 'hands trembling' and that he 'complained that it was as if a heavy yoke were upon his neck', before he was struck with pain and collapsed.[9] The most potent of these neurotoxins, as they are called, also cause inflammation of the extremity nerves, leading to intense discomfort when the victim is touched. According to Justinus, when Alexander was carried from the table where he collapsed, 'he was excruciated with such torture that he called for a sword to put an end to it, and felt pain at the touch of his attendants as if he were all over with wounds'.[10] Most of the alkaloid poisons cause stomach pain, and many produce seizures, delirium and hallucinations; all of which are described in Alexander's case. However, the list of poisons that could have killed Alexander could be shortened considerably because many of the alkaloid toxic plants also produce severe vomiting and intense headaches that are not reported. In fact, it could be shortened even further because some of these plants, such as mandrake, also contain chemicals that quickly cause sedation, and so would counteract the violent seizures Alexander suffered. Finally, the list could be brought down to only five plants that could cause the symptoms described and would have been available in the Middle East, southern Europe or western Asia. These were aconite, hemlock, henbane, thorn apple and belladonna. If the Poison Center was right, then one of these plants was responsible for Alexander's death.

Aconite is a tall, slim-stemmed plant with a beautiful blue blossom that is native to the mountain slopes of Europe, and in Alexander's time was also found growing in high places across western Asia as far as the Himalayas. All parts of this deceptively pretty plant are poisonous, especially the roots and seeds. In fact, it is one of the most poisonous plants in the world and in ancient times its toxin was used for coating spears and arrowheads. The Roman naturalist Plinius describes how aconite was often used for criminal purposes by being put into the victim's food or drink. The Greeks were also well aware of the toxic properties of aconite, as in Greek mythology the poison in this plant was deadly foam that dripped from the mouth of Cerberus, the gatekeeper of hell. Aconite poison is a quick-acting toxin and symptoms appear almost immediately, which include violent stomach pains, convulsions and delirium, followed eventually by coma and death.[11]

Hemlock is an unpleasant-smelling weed with a hollow stem and small white blossoms that look somewhat like parsley. All parts of the plant are extremely poisonous and it is native to Europe. In ancient Athens hemlock poisoning was employed as a means of execution and was used on the Greek philosopher Socrates when he was found guilt of heresy. The effects of hemlock poisoning are progressive, beginning with trembling limbs, followed shortly after by violent and painful convulsions. Eventually, the victim becomes partially paralysed, then comatose, and death ultimately results from respiratory failure. All these symptoms match those described in Alexander's case.[12]

Henbane is a tall, foul-smelling weed with large, pale, jagged-edged leaves. The leaves and stem are covered with tiny hairs and the bell-shaped flowers have mustard-yellow petals with dark purple veins. Henbane produces a huge amount of seeds – up to half a million per plant – yet as few as ten are enough to poison a child, and thirty would kill a healthy adult. All parts of the plant are poisonous and, if eaten, even small amounts cause delirium, violent seizures and trembling limbs; in larger quantities it can lead to a slow and painful death. Even when absorbed through the skin, henbane toxin can kill, and, in Shakespeare's *Hamlet*, Hamlet's father is murdered by a distillation of henbane being poured in his ear. Henbane is widely distributed throughout Europe and western Asia and in ancient times is recorded as a poison in Babylon, Egypt, Persia, Greece and Rome. The smoke from the dried and burning plant produces delirium and in Greece it was used to induce visions; but even this was dangerous and resulted in many recorded deaths. So infamous was the poisonous henbane that in Greek mythology its leaves were used to crown the dead.[13]

The thorn apple, or jimson weed as it is also known, is an unpleasant-smelling bush that grows about a metre tall and produces white funnel-shaped blossoms and a spiny, green fruit. It was known throughout Asia and the ancient Persians used its seeds as a hallucinogenic drug to induce what were believed to be mystical visions. However, it was extremely dangerous, as it could only be used in this way in very small quantities. All parts of the plant are extremely toxic and it is recorded by a number of classical writers, who refer to it being a popular murder weapon as it achieved an immediate poisoning effect.

The affected person quickly develops tremors, followed by intense pain, convulsive delirium, hallucinations and finally paralysis, coma and death.[14]

The belladonna plant stands over a metre tall, with large, dark-green leaves, bell-shaped purple flowers and shiny black berries. All parts of the plant are poisonous in the extreme, so much so that it has gained the common name deadly nightshade. It is native to Europe and western Asia and has been recorded as being used by a number of famous murderers in ancient times. The Roman empress Agrippina, for example, was accused of using belladonna to poison her husband, the Emperor Claudius, in AD 54. The symptoms of belladonna poisoning include uncontrollable shaking, intense stomach pains, convulsions, delirium, hallucinations and finally paralysis and death. These deadly properties were so infamous that the Greek name for the plant, *atropa*, came from the mythical Atropos who cut the threads of life.[15]

If the toxin from one of these plants did poison Alexander, which appears to have been the case, then it was probably in his wine. Some of these toxins could be absorbed through the skin, or administered in a cut or by a poisoned dart. However, in Alexander's case, it must have been ingested because of the violent pains in the area of his stomach, which would not have occurred if the poison had entered his system intravenously. The toxins from nearly every part of these plants have a strong, bitter taste, and the traditional method of administering such poisons was in wine. Unmixed wine, such as Alexander is described as drinking at the banquet, also has a bitter flavour that would adequately mask the poison's taste. The question is, did this poison get into Alexander's drink, or possibly food, by accident or was he deliberately poisoned?

If the food or wine had somehow been contaminated by accident then we would expect others at the feast to also have been poisoned, but this was clearly not the case. The most damning evidence that it was quite deliberate, however, is that Alexander appears to have been poisoned twice. A lethal dose of any of these poisons would usually kill the victim within 24 hours; otherwise the toxin would begin to leave the system. If they survived that long they would remain sick and weak for some days but would probably recover. Alexander began to recover and two days after the banquet he was no longer in pain, and was even playing dice and eating again. He remained weak for the next few days, but no longer appears to have been critically ill. However, between four and six days later, depending on the account, he was taken acutely ill once more. The reoccurrence of the illness seems to match the first, with the intense stomach pains – 'as if a knife had been thrust in' – followed by convulsions and delirium – 'again he fell into fits and delirium'.[16] This time his condition was so bad that Alexander's generals decided that they should visit him for the last time. Within 24 hours he was partially paralysed, then comatose and finally dead. If Alexander was poisoned, then for the same thing to have happened to him twice – and to no one else – almost certainly points to deliberate poisoning.

A lethal dose of alkaloid poison from the plants we have examined can vary depending on factors such as the age and previous health of the victim. Alexander was young and strong, and by all accounts in good health prior to the banquet on 1 June 323 BC. Also, he was a heavy drinker, and alcoholics can build up a resistance to certain poisons. Alexander could well have tolerated the dose of a toxin that would usually prove fatal. It seems that, whoever the poisoner was, they failed to kill him on the first attempt and were forced to strike again. This, as we shall see, can help us narrow down the list of suspects. However, before we examine who might have killed Alexander, we can first make an informed guess as to which particular poison might have been used.

One of the five plants, henbane, can probably be eliminated because it has a particularly strong and unpleasant smell that would make it noticeable, even in unmixed wine. As a poison it is usually applied to an abrasion on the skin of a sleeping victim or one that is already too ill to notice. The thorn apple also has a foul smell that would make it an impractical murder weapon in this particular case. Of the three plants left on the list, belladonna is by far the most likely cause of Alexander's death. Although it, too, has a foul smell when first cut, once dried it is completely odourless. What makes belladonna the most probable murder weapon is that, unlike the other plants being considered, it causes certain specific symptoms that Alexander appears to have experienced.[17]

One of the first symptoms of belladonna poisoning is a dry mouth, which causes intense thirst. This is precisely what Alexander suffered from on the first night of his illness. According to Plutarch, 'In the rage of his fever and a violent thirst, he took a draught of wine, upon which he fell into delirium.'[18] Such a thirst could have been a result of excessive drinking, although if it had been due solely to alcohol then it is unlikely to have come on until a number of hours later, once the body had become dehydrated.

The references to fever, not only by Plutarch, but also by Arrian, also suggest belladonna poisoning. Fever could be a way of describing any incapacitating illness, especially if delirium is involved, although strictly speaking fever means a high temperature, which would usually be caused by a bacterial or viral infection and not as a reaction to a toxin. However, belladonna is among the few poisonous plants that do cause fever (in the strict sense of the word) and results in the victim becoming hot and sweaty.

The symptom that seems to exclusively suggest belladonna among the shortlist of poisons, however, is that it eventually affects the vocal cords, rendering the victim incapable of speech.[19] All but one of the accounts of Alexander's death refer to him being conscious but unable to speak. According to Plutarch, 'when the generals came into his chamber he was speechless and continued so the following day'.[20] Arrian also refers to the same event: 'He lay speechless as the man came in, yet he struggled to raise his head'.[21] The *Historia* also says that Alexander was conscious and able to move, although he was unable to speak: 'He recognised his officers and raised his head to speak to them, but could utter no word. From that moment until the end he spoke no more.'[22] As does Justinus: 'Being unable to speak, he took his ring from his finger, and gave it to Perdiccas'.[23]

It seems, therefore, that Alexander's mother had been right all along in believing that her son had been murdered. She also seems to have been right about the fact that he was poisoned by someone who was present at the banquet. The alkaloid toxins from each of the five plants on the list all produce symptoms well within the hour. Although many people could have had access to Alexander the second time he was poisoned, at the banquet he became ill late in the evening and so whoever poisoned him had to have been present. Unfortunately, Olympias went to her grave not knowing who murdered Alexander. However, with what we know from the historical sources, we can now compile a list of likely suspects.

SUMMARY OF CHAPTER TWO

The strange state of preservation of his body after death indicates that he had died from large amounts of a toxic substance. The only poisons that are known to cause the symptoms Alexander suffered cannot have got into his system by accident.

- According to Plutarch and the Roman historian Curtius, Alexander's body failed to show any signs of decay for six days after death, even though it was kept in a hot, sultry place. The fact that it did not begin to decay for six days well and truly rules out the possibility of Alexander mistakenly being thought dead because of paralysis. If

Alexander's body had remained preserved for this amount of time under the conditions described, somehow bacteria had been prevented from starting the process of decomposition. There could be only two causes: radiation, which could be discounted for that era, or a lethal dose of a toxic substance that pervaded the corpse. If Plutarch and Curtius' reports were accurate, then Alexander the Great had to have been poisoned.

- The only known poisons that produce the symptoms from which Alexander is recorded to have suffered are alkaloid vegetable toxins. Coming from plants, shrubs and trees, these nitrogen-bearing chemicals especially affect the nervous system, causing shaking limbs and muscle pains in the back or neck before the victim experiences severe agony and seizures. Most of the alkaloid poisons cause stomach pain, and many produce seizures, delirium and hallucinations; all of which are described in Alexander's case. However, the list of poisons that could have killed Alexander can be shortened considerably because many of the alkaloid toxic plants also produce severe vomiting and intense headaches, which were not reported in his case.

- The list can ultimately be brought down to only five plants that could cause the symptoms described. These were aconite, hemlock, henbane, thorn apple and belladonna, none of which Alexander is likely to have consumed by accident. If any part of the banquet refreshments had been accidentally contaminated then it is likely that others would have suffered too.

- The most damning evidence that it was quite deliberate, however, is that Alexander appears to have been poisoned twice. A lethal dose of any of these poisons would usually kill the victim within 24 hours; otherwise the toxin would begin to leave the system. If they survived that long they would remain sick and weak for some days but would probably recover.

- Alexander began to recover and two days after the banquet was no longer in pain, and was even playing dice and eating again. He remained weak for the next few days, but no longer appears to have been critically ill. However, a few days later he was taken acutely ill once more. The reoccurrence of the illness seems to match the first, with the intense stomach pains followed by convulsions and delirium. If Alexander was poisoned, then for the same thing to have happened to him twice – and to no one else – almost certainly points to deliberate poisoning.

3. MOTIVE AND OPPORTUNITY

Murder investigation is always about motive, means and opportunity. A list of suspects is compiled of those who had the opportunity to commit the murder – normally people who could have been present at the scene of the crime – which can then be shortened to include only those who had a motive to kill the victim at the time he died. Finally, it comes down to establishing if any of the remaining suspects uniquely had the means to commit the crime; in this case, to obtain the poison used. We need, therefore, firstly to decide who had the motive and opportunity to murder Alexander. Before we do, however, we should examine why Alexander decided to host the private banquet that offered the assassin the opportunity to strike. It all began with an event some months earlier that seems to have sent the increasingly despotic Alexander over the edge into virtual insanity.

During the last year of his reign, Alexander appears to have become mentally progressively unbalanced, and in the end he was close to being psychotic. If a date could be put to the time Alexander finally seems to have lost his grip on reality it would be during the late autumn of 324 BC. The war was at last over and, having finally conquered the Persians and now ruling the greatest empire the world had ever known, Alexander summoned ambassadors from every corner of his dominion to attend a conference in the city of Ecbatana, in what is now northern Iran. During a banquet to entertain the guests, Alexander's lifelong friend and chief minister Hephaestion fell ill and died. No one knew what actually killed the man but, as he was only in his early thirties and had previously been in the best of health, Alexander suspected that he had been poisoned. Alexander was devastated by the death of his closest friend and flew into a rage and threatened to kill all the ambassadors if the culprit could not be discovered. When Hephaestion's physician tried to explain that the man had died of a naturally contracted fever, Alexander went berserk and tried to throttle him with his bare hands. Eventually, Alexander's bodyguards managed to restrain him and he collapsed to the floor, wailing like a child. He was taken to his bedchamber, where he remained for three days, refusing to eat or to see anyone.[1]

When Alexander recovered from his hysterical mourning, he decided that the gods were to blame – the Persian gods.[2] The main Persian religion was Zoroastrianism and Ecbatana was the Zoroastrians' holy city, said to be the burial site of the religion's founder, the prophet Zarathustra. Alexander ordered that a monument to the prophet that stood in the centre of the city be torn down and replaced by a statue of a lion, his own personal emblem. Alexander had previously shown tolerance to foreign religions but now he began a wholesale persecution of the Zoroastrian faith. A Zoroastrian text known as the *Book of Arda Viraf* refers to him desecrating temples, outlawing religious practices, executing priests and ordering the *Avesta*, the holy book of Zoroastrianism, to be burned. Moreover, it actually names Alexander as the incarnation of the Persian devil Guzastag.[3]

Zoroastrianism taught that there was a supreme god, Ahura Mazda, 'the wise lord', who had created goodness and the world, and that evil was created by a devil known as Angra Mainyu, 'the hostile spirit'. It was Zoroastrian belief that at the end of days Angra Mainyu would be incarnated as a demon known as Guzastag, 'the accursed', who was represented in Zoroastrian art in the form of a lion.[4] Alexander's desecration of the prophet's monument was sacrilege enough, but the fact that he had erected a statue of a lion in its place was the worst form of blasphemy. Moreover, it was taken as a sign that Alexander was the devil personified. The Zoroastrian priesthood immediately put out a contract on Alexander's life, offering not only gold but everlasting life to anyone who would kill him. In effect, this was the first known example of a religious fatwa being issued against anyone in history. Alexander should have been deeply concerned about this turn of events. After all, he was surrounded by thousands of devout Zoroastrians. Instead, he laughed at the threat to his life. Alexander had decided he was immortal. He had long believed that he was the spiritual son of the supreme Greek god Zeus, but now he concluded that he was a god himself. As a living god, he could do whatever he pleased and he decreed that the Persians and the rest of the world should start worshipping him, or else. Hephaestion's death had clearly unhinged the once pragmatic Alexander.[5]

There can be no doubt that the burdens of command had gradually been wearing away at Alexander's mind, and the death of his closest friend had been the final straw in what we would now call a mental breakdown. However, Alexander was the most powerful man in the world and no one could do a thing about it. Alexander could act out his crazed delusions as he wished and his next such whim was to make Hephaestion a demigod. Determined that he would be reunited with his friend in the afterlife, Alexander decided that he, too, should be deified. Earlier in his reign, Alexander had visited a temple to the Egyptian god

Ammon. Deep in the deserts of Egypt, at the oasis of Siwa, the temple was the seat of an oracle who had impressed Alexander with his prophecies and insights. Ammon was the chief Egyptian deity, and the Greeks and Macedonians believed that this was simply the Egyptian name for Zeus. Believing that this oracle had a direct line to the supreme god, Alexander sent a deputation to consult him about Hephaestion's deification and the manner of his friend's funeral. However, the journey would take some months and Alexander decided to move on to Babylon; when the deputation returned they could meet him there.[6]

Over the next few months, as word spread throughout the empire that Alexander demanded to be worshipped as a god, it was not only Persians who were furious at such blasphemy but also Greeks and Macedonians. Every Greek and Macedonian town had its own local deity, and the troops in Alexander's army had their own regimental gods. These were the gods that the common people and soldiery prayed to on a daily basis and to which they believed they owed their health, wellbeing and prosperity. By decreeing that idols of these gods should be replaced by effigies of himself, Alexander had the entire Hellenistic world fearing that some great catastrophe would befall it if their leader wasn't stopped.

In the spring of 323 BC, Alexander arrived in Babylon, the cultural capital of the ancient world. Here, he immediately ordered that the main Persian temple in the city be rebuilt and consecrated as a shrine for his own worship. Greatly disturbed by Alexander's actions, an astrologer came to visit the king and told him that he was in grave peril. According to Arrian, the man implored Alexander to leave Babylon immediately, as his life was in danger if he stayed. It didn't take a clairvoyant to realise that most of Babylon's inhabitants now wanted him dead. Nevertheless, Alexander shrugged the warning aside. He was a god and no one or nothing could harm him.[7]

Once in Babylon, Alexander decided that the city was to be the new capital of his empire – an empire that he intended to enlarge. Alexander's plans were now no less than to conquer the entire world. Summoning his generals, he announced that in the south they would march into Arabia; in the west they would attack Carthage, and in the north they would invade Italy. Much of Alexander's army was sick of the endless fighting – it had been going on for eleven years. Alexander had promised that he only intended to conquer the Persian Empire, and the army had fought long and hard so that he could realise this ambition. Just as they thought it was all over, their king was now planning a war on three fronts that even a military genius like Alexander could not possibly hope to win. The Greeks and Macedonians had shed their blood to establish Alexander's empire; all they wanted was to return home to enjoy the spoils of war. It was now not only religious fanatics who entertained ideas of assassinating Alexander, but also some of his military commanders.[8]

Suspecting that Alexander had lost his reason, some of his generals asked a group of Babylonian priests to perform a ritual to help him recover. At the end of May, the rite was carried out in Alexander's stateroom, which involved a young slave-boy sitting in Alexander's throne. It seems that the belief was that the unfortunate slave would take on the evil possessing the king. When Alexander heard what had happened, he mistakenly thought that witchcraft was being used against him to place another on his throne.[9] It is not recorded what happened to the priests or the unfortunate youth, but Alexander's belief in his own divinity now turned to outright paranoia. According to Plutarch, he spent the next few days involved in rituals to protect himself.

> When once Alexander had given way to fears of supernatural influence, his mind grew so disturbed and so easily alarmed that, if the least unusual or extraordinary thing happened, he thought it a prodigy or a presage, and his court was thronged with diviners and priests whose business was to sacrifice and purify and foretell the future.[10]

However, at the beginning of June the deputation that Alexander had sent to Siwa to consult the oracle returned with the news that Ammon had permitted Hephaestion to be venerated as a demigod. Once more, Alexander had one of his acute mood swings and became deliriously excited. In fact, according to Plutarch, he began sacrificing animals to Zeus (the Greek version of Ammon) and drinking himself stupid to celebrate.

> But upon some answers which were brought him from the oracle concerning Hephaestion, he laid aside his sorrow, and fell again to sacrificing and drinking.[11]

This, then, was Alexander's state of mind when he ordered the ill-fated banquet to be held on the night of 1 June 323 BC. The feast was to honour Hephaestion and only a select group of guests were invited. There may have been wider political and religious motives for many people to have wanted to kill Alexander but, as we shall see, a number of those present at the banquet had their own personal motives to assassinate the king. Alexander should have been well aware of the danger and should never have held such a banquet, let alone one in which there was evidently only a single bodyguard in attendance. It seems his madness had made him throw caution to the wind.

Half of Alexander's empire probably wished him dead but, with his elite bodyguard, there would usually be little chance of anyone surviving an attempt to kill him with a sword, knife, arrow or spear. However, the possibility of poisoning was always a very real threat. As lethal poisons generally produce noticeable symptoms within an hour of ingestion, most kings in ancient times had slaves specifically to taste their food around an hour before consumption and Alexander was no exception. Constant fear of assassination had led to tight security measures before royal feasts, and Alexander's palaces even had a special chamber adjoining the banqueting hall where the food and drink was tested. Once considered safe, it remained here, under guard, and no one outside the banqueting area had access to it again. Alexander's acute condition – the sudden pain in the area of the stomach and the convulsions shortly after – shows that he was poisoned by one of the alkaloid toxins, all of which produce symptoms well within the hour. We can safely assume, therefore, that, as the queen mother Olympias suspected, whoever poisoned Alexander had to have been inside the banqueting hall on the evening of 1 June.

Fortunately, contemporary accounts were written to reveal exactly who was present at the feast. From the beginning of his reign, Alexander had an eye on posterity and employed scribes to write down nearly everything he did and said. Two of them, Eumenes and Chares, were present at the banquet and, accordingly, full accounts were made of who was there. Quoting Chares, the *Historia Alexandri Magni* tells us that Alexander had eleven guests and that there were a further nine other people in attendance.[12] It does not name all of these people but the others can be discovered from the works of Arrian (taking his account from Eumenes), Justinus (quoting the admiral Nearchus) and Plutarch (citing Ptolemy). We can, therefore, compile a full and accurate list of the twenty people who were present.

It was a small and intimate affair and the guest list included only Alexander's brother, his three consorts and his seven most senior officers. Additionally, there were also his two scribes, his bodyguard, his physician, his butler, three Macedonian servants and his adjutant who acted as host and master of ceremonies. One of these twenty people appears to have been the murderer, but we can safely remove many of

35

them from the list of likely suspects. We can eliminate the three servants because, as royal slaves, they would have been under pain of death to assure the king's survival. The same is also true of the chief bodyguard Ptolemy and the physician Philip. If either of them had intended to kill Alexander, the feast would have been an extremely stupid time to have tried it, unless they were prepared to be put to death if they succeeded. As it turned out, they did survive Alexander's death; only because, before he died, Alexander specifically ordered that they be allowed to live. It was a lucky break that none of them could have expected. The same is also true of Medius, the adjutant. Although Olympias seems to have suspected him at one point, it would have been idiotic for him to poison the king at a banquet that he had personally organised.

It is also highly unlikely that either of the scribes, Eumenes and Chares, had any reason to kill their king. In fact, they had every reason to want him to remain alive. Scribes usually led rather dull lives, and few could expect to make much money from their work. Both these men had been living a prestigious and eventful life in Alexander's entourage and were making a relative fortune. Alexander was the exception among monarchs of the time for employing such people in his court. Who could say that any new king would continue to want their services?

There were eleven actual guests at the banquet but some of these can also be ruled out. As we have seen, although he became severely ill, Alexander began to recover before suffering a relapse the day before he died. The murderer, it seems, initially failed to kill the king and had to try again a few days later; sometime between 7 and 9 June, depending on the account. This means that the assassin had to be someone who was still close to Alexander at that time. Four of the guests – Nearchus, the head of the Macedonian navy, the financier Cleomenes, Aristobulus, the military engineer and Peithon, the governor of Media – were no longer anywhere near the royal palace when Alexander appears to have been poisoned for the second time.[14] From the historical sources we know that Nearchus was preparing the navy for Alexander's new war and Aristobulus was with him; Cleomenes had been sent to Susa, in southern Persia; and Peithon was on his way back to Media in what is now the north of Iran. Remarkably, considering the fact that only a few days earlier Alexander had been in fear of his life, of the eight possible suspects that remain, each appears to have had an obvious motive to murder him.

There is no way of knowing for certain, but the banquet was probably held in the most magnificent palace in the ancient world – the Hanging Gardens of Babylon. Before its invasion by the Persians in the sixth century BC, Babylon was the capital of Babylonia; roughly, what is now Iraq. The largest city on earth, it had been the seat of the biblical king Nebuchadnezzar who, in 597 BC, conquered Jerusalem and returned home with thousands of Jewish slaves. Here, these unfortunate prisoners were forced to build the so-called Hanging Gardens. One of the most remarkable palaces in history, it was a huge pyramidal structure, as high as a fifteen-storey apartment block, with a series of open, tiered balconies, thickly planted with flowers, shrubs and trees from all over the known world. The entire complex was irrigated by some kind of sophisticated hydraulic system, but how it worked is still a mystery to archaeologists, historians and modern engineers.

We can imagine the scene when, just after sunset on 1 June 323 BC, as the palace was cooled by the evening breeze that blew across the River Euphrates, the small group of guests began to arrive. Soon after, the festivities began with Alexander proposing a toast to Heracles and to Hephaestion; announcing that, as his dead friend was now a demigod, he was certain to meet him again in the afterlife. As he raised his cup to drink, Alexander could have had no idea quite how soon this would be. Indeed, the poison was probably secreted in this very vessel. Like most alkaloid toxins, the poisons from suspect plants have a distinct and unpleasant taste. The ideal mask for the bitter flavour would have been the wine, which at the time was a tart concoction with a sharp, vinegary taste.

The wine was served by the royal butler Iollas who, as in the traditional murder mystery, turns out to be a chief suspect. Iollas' father was Antipater, one of Macedonia's top generals who had helped secure Alexander the throne by mustering the army behind the young king during the civil turmoil in the early years of his reign. In Alexander's teens, Antipater had been the boy's mentor, tutoring him in the martial arts and treating him in many ways like his own son. Indeed, as he had shared a close personal friendship with the boy's mother Olympias, some even suspected that he was Alexander's true father. When Alexander set off to conquer the Persian Empire in 334 BC, Antipater remained behind as governor of Macedonia and Olympias stayed with him. No specific details survive concerning their relationship but, over the years, it appears to have gone sour, as Olympias began sending despatches to her son accusing Antipater of conspiracy. For a long time Alexander ignored the allegations, attributing them to personal squabbles, but, on his return to Babylon, he decided to summon Antipater to court to answer the charges. Antipater, however, refused to go, claiming that he needed to remain in Europe, as he feared a rebellion in Greece. Instead, he sent his son Cassander as an emissary to explain his absence and to refute Olympias' allegations. Most of the historical resources mention suspicions some years later that Antipater was behind Alexander's death,[15] and Justinus refers to rumours that Cassander was sent with a contingency plan to assassinate Alexander if he failed to convince him of his father's innocence.[16] If the rumours were right, Cassander's younger brother Iollas was ultimately instructed to poison the king.

The seven other suspects were all guests at the banquet, which would probably have been eaten in the traditional Greek style, with the diners seated informally on couches around a low central table, similar to the familiar feasts of later Rome. We can imagine, therefore, the scene of the crime with the main protagonists reclining around their king, any one of whom could have surreptitiously slipped the poison into Alexander's wine.

One of those seated closest to the victim would have been his brother Arridaeus, a man who was the exact opposite of Alexander. The surviving busts and statues of Alexander show him to have been an athletic, muscular man with rugged good looks. In complete contrast, Arridaeus was thin and puny with a bony, ashen face and small, beady eyes. Alexander was a brave, natural-born warrior, whereas Arridaeus was timid and shy. Arridaeus was actually the elder of the brothers by two years and should, by right, have been king. However, the army had refused to accept Arridaeus, considering him both weak and mentally incompetent, choosing Alexander in his place.[17] While Alexander was off conquering the world, Arridaeus remained behind at home under the domineering influence of the queen mother Olympias where he became the laughing stock of Macedonian society. Arridaeus appears to have suffered from some kind of periodic psychological disorder, possibly schizophrenia or manic depression, but he was certainly not feeble-minded. As children, he and Alexander were tutored by the famous Greek philosopher Aristotle, and the ancient historian Plutarch records that Arridaeus was an intelligent and accomplished student.[18] Arridaeus had not seen Alexander for ten years until shortly before the feast, when he arrived unexpectedly in Babylon as an envoy from Olympias. It is quite possible that, harbouring bitter resentment of his brother for depriving him of the throne and abandoning him to a life of public humiliation and ridicule, Arridaeus seized this first opportunity in years to take his revenge.

If tradition was observed, at the banquet on Alexander's right there sat his queen, Roxanne. Along with Cleopatra and Helen of Troy, she was famous in the ancient world for her overwhelming beauty. Ancient historians describe her large dark eyes, her smooth olive skin and the shiny black hair that fell to her waist. Coming from the Sogdiana Mountains in what is now Afghanistan, Roxanne first met Alexander four years earlier when she was only sixteen. Her father was a local chieftain who surrendered to the Macedonian army and, as a gesture of peace, offered his daughter to Alexander as a bride. Alexander had had many such offers after previous victories, but had never before accepted one of them as a wife. This time, however, he fell immediately in love with Roxanne and, by all accounts, the feeling was mutual and the couple were happily married.[19]

Roxanne was not only beautiful; she was also vivacious and had a sense of humour that was popular with almost everyone. She was intelligent too. She already spoke Persian and Greek and, when she accompanied Alexander during his campaign into India, she learned the local language fluently in six months. For over three years, she had been the darling of Alexander's court. Then, just a few months before the feast, Alexander had taken a second wife: another sixteen-year-old, Statira. The historical sources all record that Roxanne was insanely jealous of this new bride, giving her a possible motive to murder her husband in revenge.[20]

Statira was young and pretty, but her personality was no match for Roxanne. We can imagine Roxanne casting cutting, sarcastic remarks at the girl during the banquet, as Statira glared back at her, arrogantly looking down her nose at someone she considered her social inferior. Roxanne had come from the rough end of the Persian Empire. She was merely the daughter of a mountain chief, whereas Statira was a royal princess, the daughter of the dead Persian king Darius III. Ten years before, she had been captured as a child when her father's western army was defeated in Turkey. When Darius died in 330 BC, Statira was taken to the Persian city of Susa where she was brought up as a Macedonian-style princess. She seems to have been a queen in waiting, for when Alexander returned from India he decided to marry the girl and make her his second wife.[21] It seems to have been a political marriage so that together the royal couple could produce an heir and found a new Persian–Macedonian dynasty. If Statira bore Alexander a son, any son Roxanne might bear him would no longer have a chance of succession. This gives Roxanne an additional motive to murder her husband. Statira, however, may have beaten her to it, and killed Alexander herself. Another rumour that the ancient sources record is that, even as a child, Statira vowed she would one day avenge her father's death.[22]

Roxanne and Statira were not the only women in Alexander's life who attended the banquet that night. Long before he met either of them, his lover had been Barsine. Although she was eight years his senior, Alexander had fallen for Barsine when he met her in Turkey at the beginning of his campaign.[23] Her father was a senior Persian aristocrat and, when the Macedonian army had swept through her homeland, she was captured as spoils of war. It seems that Alexander saved her from rape by his troops and kept her for himself. Barsine unquestionably came to love Alexander and remained his concubine for five years, although, for reasons unknown, he never married her. Barsine bore Alexander his only son and the boy, Heracles, was the nearest thing he had to an heir.[24] However, when he met and married Roxanne in 327 BC, Barsine left Alexander's side and returned home. Being dumped for a girl less than twice her age would have been heartbreaking enough, but the fact that Alexander did what he had never done for Barsine and made Roxanne his queen added insult to injury. Barsine stayed in Turkey during the remainder of the campaign, but just a few weeks before the feast Alexander summoned her to Babylon so that he could see his child for the first time in years.[25] Now, here she was at the banquet with every reason in the world to wish her former lover dead. We can imagine her staring bitterly over at Roxanne, knowing that she was the girl she had been jilted and humiliated for, and then looking across to Statira, with whom Alexander intended to found a dynasty. If Barsine was the murderer, then her motive may have been revenge. Alternatively, she may have taken the opportunity to kill Alexander in the hope of securing her son the throne, before it was too late.

The scribe Eumenes records that about halfway through the evening Alexander flew into what had become a customary drunken rage. Perdiccas, his 38-year-old second-in-command, had dared to question the wisdom of the new campaign Alexander was planning.[26] He was a brave man for having done so: Alexander's officers had long ago learned to keep quiet. Alexander had once respected the counsel of his men, but, as his victories mounted and his power grew, he had become increasingly intolerant of even the slightest criticism. It began five years earlier when, at a victory celebration in Afghanistan, the drunken Alexander had run a lance through his deputy Clitus during a petty argument, killing the man on the spot.[27] Since that time, Alexander had executed, on a whim, no less than a dozen senior officers on the slightest suspicion of disloyalty. Indeed, two of Perdiccas' predecessors had died in this way. His immediate predecessor, however, was Hephaestion, who had died unexpectedly seven months earlier and Perdiccas had only been appointed as his replacement because better men were either dead, in prison or had been exiled.

Perdiccas was a brave but by no means outstanding soldier and his appointment was clearly expedient and temporary. There can be little doubt that he was well aware of the fact, as Alexander had openly contemplated replacing him with his admiral Nearchus. It was not a matter of if, but when and how Perdiccas would go. Alexander's drunken rage at the banquet that night must have been a vivid reminder to Perdiccas that his end might come at any moment, on the point of a spear. As Alexander had not named an heir, and his only son was illegitimate, then, as second-in-command, Perdiccas was the logical choice of successor should Alexander die. If Perdiccas had designs on absolute power, then he had to kill Alexander – and soon. In fact, to take Alexander's life may have been the only way to preserve his own.[28]

Perdiccas was not the only senior officer at the banquet that night with a motive to slip poison into Alexander's wine. Seated near the king was the veteran general Meleager, whose motive for the murder may have been survival – the survival of the entire Macedonian army. Somewhere around sixty years old, Meleager had originally served in the army of Alexander's father King Philip, and had risen through the ranks to become the overall commander of the Macedonian infantry. Unlike the other guests, Meleager came from a humble, farming background in the Balkan Mountains, where for generations the populace had suffered repeated raids of plunder by the Persians. To Meleager and his men, Alexander's campaign to conquer the Persian Empire was something of a crusade. For twelve long years, the 20,000-strong Macedonian infantry had extracted their revenge, fighting battle after battle, everywhere from the Mediterranean to the Arabian Sea, never losing once.

However, as the war dragged on, Meleager and his men must have watched horrified, as their leader became more and more a Persian-style king. Now that the war was over, Alexander had made the Persian city of Babylon the capital of his empire, and he had taken to dressing like a Persian monarch by wearing a long coloured robe and a golden diadem for a crown.[29] Worst of all, he was turning his back on the army that had made it all possible. Just a few months earlier, he had demobilised half his infantry and replaced them with a Persian force trained to fight in the Macedonian way. Incredibly, three-quarters of Alexander's soldiers were now Persian and, when the Macedonian infantry protested, he threatened to deploy the Persians against them and had thirteen officers executed for mutiny.[30] Now that Alexander was planning a new war, he intended to send the entire Macedonian infantry home. Within a few weeks, their replacements would be arriving from southern Iran. If the Macedonian infantry wished to survive, Alexander had to go. There can be little doubt that at least some of Meleager's officers would have urged their commander to kill Alexander the first chance he had.

The final suspect is a sinister figure. The most feared man in the Macedonian army, Seleucus was the commander of the elite shield bearers. This 6,000-strong heavy-infantry contingent was the royal guard; something like the praetorians of the later Roman emperors. They also acted as a kind of military police force whose purpose it was to maintain discipline in the Macedonian and allied armies. Moreover, they were Alexander's crack terror troops, sent in to combat civil disorder or quash Persian resistance.[31] In many ways, they were the Waffen-SS of the day and Seleucus was their Himmler.

Seleucus' origins are somewhat mysterious, although he appears to have begun life in the Macedonian army as a Greek mercenary. About the same age as Alexander, around 33, he was tall and slim with boyish good looks. He was, however, a quiet, brooding man who seldom involved himself in trivial conversation. We can imagine him, therefore, sitting quietly alone at the banquet, observing the scene with scheming eyes.

Of all Alexander's officers, Seleucus was the best placed to seize control in a military coup, as his soldiers were now barracked inside Babylon, whereas the infantry and cavalry were still camped outside the city. Indeed, in the civil war that followed Alexander's death, Seleucus was by far the most successful protagonist, taking control of nearly all of what had been the Persian Empire. His dominion became the Seleucid Empire, named after him, and lasted for almost two and a half centuries until it was conquered by the Romans. On the evening of 1 June, Seleucus did indeed have reason to contemplate Alexander's assassination. Fearing that they had gained too much influence, Alexander had a habit of replacing senior officers between campaigns. The conquest of the Persian Empire was over and Alexander was already planning his new war: a reshuffle in the high command was almost inevitable. In June 323 BC, if Seleucus had his eyes on Alexander's crown, it may have been a case of now or never.[32]

By mid-evening, Alexander finished his tirade and instead began pacing nervously around the room. 'It was as if the king knew that some dreadful fate awaited him,' wrote Ptolemy, his bodyguard, some years later.[33] He was right. Sometime around nine o'clock, Alexander dropped his cup, screamed, bent double with pain and collapsed to the floor. Rambling incoherently, apparently in a state of delirium, he was carried to his bedchamber by Ptolemy and Medius. Alexander the Great, conqueror of half the known world, would never walk again.

Historical hindsight affords us a wider perspective than Alexander would have had at the time, allowing us to see the danger he was in. · Nevertheless, it still seems strange that he should have freely dined with so many potential assassins. In the end, Alexander's worst enemy may have been his own crazed arrogance. He had come to believe he was a god – and gods do not die. It is doubtful that he considered that any of his entourage could – or would have the guts to – try to kill him. However, he was wrong. One of them clearly did. But which one?

In search of the solution to this ancient murder mystery, we need to examine the suspects in turn. Interestingly, each of their stories is a crucial part of the greater story of Alexander's remarkable life. We start at the beginning, when Alexander's father prepared the Macedonian army for its eventual conquests. These remarkable military accomplishments were made possible by one man – Antipater. Our first suspect was not even present at the banquet, but, if guilty, murdered Alexander by proxy in the form of Iollas, his son.

SUMMARY OF CHAPTER THREE

Of those who were present at Alexander's final feast on 1 June 323 BC, there are eight suspects who all had a potential motive and also the opportunity to have poisoned the king then, and for a second time a few days later.

- Murder investigation is always about motive, means and opportunity. A list of suspects is compiled of those who had the opportunity to commit the murder – people who could have been present at the scene of the crime – which can then be shortened to include only those who had a motive to kill the victim at the time he died. Finally, it comes down to establishing if any of the remaining suspects uniquely had the means to commit the crime – in this case, obtain the poison used.
- The feast at which Alexander first fell ill was a small and intimate affair and the guest list included only Alexander's brother, his three consorts and his seven most senior officers. Additionally, there were also present two of his scribes, his bodyguard, his physician, his butler, three servants and his adjutant Medius, who acted as host and master of ceremonies.
- If Olympias was right, then the person who poisoned her son was actually present at the feast on the night of 1 June. We can accept this

43

as a logical assumption as all the food and drink would have been tasted before being brought into the banqueting room. However, although he became severely ill, Alexander began to recover before suffering a relapse the day before he died. The murderer, it seems, initially failed to kill the king and had to try again on 10 June. This means that the murderer had to be someone who was still close to Alexander on that date. This narrows down the list of suspects, as a number of them are known to have been elsewhere by this time.

- There are eight suspects who all had a potential motive: his three consorts, three of his senior officers, his brother and his butler. Barsine was Alexander's concubine whom he had jilted for the younger Roxanne; Roxanne herself had suffered humiliation when Alexander had taken a new wife, the Persian princess Statira. Statira also had a motive to murder her new husband as he had subjugated her country and was responsible for her father's death.

- The two most senior officers, Meleager and Perdiccas, both had reason to kill Alexander as he had imminent plans to replace them, and the commander of the royal guard, Seleucus, was ideally placed to benefit from a military coup. Alexander's older brother Arridaeus should by rights have been king, but had been passed over for Alexander and may have harboured a grudge for years. Finally, the butler Iollas may have been acting under instructions from his father Antipater, governor of Macedonia, who, although not present in Babylon, had been accused of conspiracy by Alexander.

4. ANTIPATER – PRELUDE TO CONQUEST

Little is known of Antipater's early life other than the fact that he was the son of a Macedonian nobleman. He is first recorded in 368 BC, at the age of 31, when he was an officer in the army of the Macedonian king, Alexander II. At the time, Macedonia was a small and insignificant kingdom on the world stage. Roughly 350 kilometres from east to west and 200 kilometres from north to south, it covered an area no bigger than modern Scotland and was about the same size as the state of South Carolina. Macedonia lay immediately to the north of Greece and, although an ethnically distinct country, over the years it had absorbed much of Greek culture and even spoke its language. Greece had reached a zenith of civilisation a century earlier but was now a collection of independent, declining states surrounding major cities, such as Athens, Sparta and Thebes (not to be confused with Thebes in Egypt). Nevertheless, these small city-states were still far more powerful than the kingdom of Macedonia and were a constant threat to its existence. More sophisticated, better armed and organised, the Greeks already occupied large tracts of what had once been southern Macedonia.[1]

Greece, however, was not the only menace facing Macedonia. The beginning of Antipater's military career saw some of the darkest days in the ancient country's history. Alexander II was forced to fight repeatedly against incursions from Illyria to the west and Thrace to the east, which each moved relentlessly in on Macedonian territory. Illyria, what is now northern Albania, was about the same size and population as Macedonia, while Thrace, modern Bulgaria and most of Turkey north of the Sea of Marmara, was over three times bigger. Luckily for the Macedonians, these countries were made up of various tribes who often quarrelled with each other, preventing either of them from seizing the initiative to fully conquer their neighbour. However, in the same year that Antipater first appears in history, an event took place that was eventually to change Macedonian fortunes and ultimately lead to the empire of Alexander the Great.

In 368 BC, the city-state of Thebes in southeastern Greece, the strongest military power in Europe, annexed southeastern Macedonia, taking Alexander II's ten-year-old brother Philip back to Greece as a hostage.[2] Royal hostages were taken and exchanged all the time in the ancient world as the usual way of endorsing an armistice, peace treaty or truce. However, this seemingly trifling event was to change the course of Macedonian decline, prove a disaster for Greece and create a major turning point in world history.

During his three-year captivity in Thebes, Philip was treated well and, although accompanied by guards, he was free to wander the city. As such, the talented young boy was able to observe Theban martial training and its military techniques. Shortly before Philip's arrival, the Greek military tactician Epaminondas had reorganised the Theban army into the greatest in Greece. Epaminondas was a military genius; he broke with convention and developed completely new tactics. Previously Sparta, in southwestern Greece, was the most powerful Greek state, but with Epaminondas' new army the Thebans decisively defeated them at the battle of Leutra in 371 BC. By the time Philip arrived, Thebes was successfully conquering much of the Peloponnese Peninsular and he was able to observe first-hand exactly how Thebes put an end to Spartan military dominance and firmly established itself as the strongest state in Greece. This was a mistake the Thebans would eventually pay for with their blood.[3]

In 365 BC, another of Philip's brothers came to the Macedonian throne and negotiated the boy's release. When he returned home, Philip discovered that the new king, Perdiccas III (not the Perdiccas who was at Alexander's feast), was in even greater trouble than his older brother, who had died of natural causes. The country was on the brink of collapse with Thrace and Illyria poised to put an end to its existence. However, by some miracle the country held together for the next few years: more due to Thracian and Illyrian internal quarrels rather than anything Perdiccas did.[4]

Sometime around 360 BC, Antipater was appointed commander of the garrison in the Macedonian capital of Pella. Left in charge of the capital while Perdiccas was away fighting, Antipater first became properly acquainted with the twenty-year-old Philip. Immediately, he was impressed by the young man's intelligence and was fascinated by his remarkable memory. Philip told Antipater many stories of his time in Thebes and described in astonishing detail the military training and tactics he had observed there. No doubt, he had been relating such accounts for years, but no one appears to have grasped the importance of what he had to say. Unlike Perdiccas, who had taken little notice of his brother's tales, Antipater quickly realised their significance. If Macedonia could reorganise its army along Theban lines, it would stand a fighting chance against its enemies. When the king returned home to re-equip his forces for an ill-conceived counteroffensive to free north-western Macedonia from Illyrian control, Antipater tried to persuade him to wait and adopt some of the Theban military techniques Philip had described. Perdiccas may have been fond of his younger brother, but he put little credence in what he considered to be fanciful tales. No matter how Antipater attempted to demonstrate that Theban strategy would work, his advice fell on deaf ears. Perdiccas was impatient to attack the Illyrians, who were preoccupied with internecine, tribal wars, and in 359 BC he left Pella at the head of his army and marched into disaster. A few weeks later, Antipater received the news that Perdiccas had been killed and 4,000 of his soldiers had been wiped out in a single battle.[5]

Philip was still only 21 when the king died, but he was appointed regent to Perdiccas' infant son and successor Amyntas. However, Macedonia faced imminent attack on all fronts and the generals knew that they needed a capable and undisputed ruler, and Philip was able to persuade his generals to accept him as king. They may not have known much about him, but a 21-year-old leader was better than a baby. Philip soon proved himself far more competent than either of his older brothers. He was a brilliant diplomat and political strategist: he needed to be, as there were a number of Macedonian nobles who did not accept Philip's right to rule and two pretenders to the throne were a serious threat to his reign. One of these had fled to Thrace, where he hoped to muster support to seize the throne in return for Macedonian land. Learning of this, Philip bought off the Thracian king and persuaded him to put the Macedonian pretender to death. The second pretender was far more dangerous as he was supported by the Greek Athenians, who supplied him with arms and manpower. With Athenian support for his rival, Philip would stand little chance against him in battle. Cleverly, Philip made a treaty with Athens, offering them the Macedonian coastal city of Amphipolis if they would abandon his enemy. This they did and the second pretender was defeated.

Philip now had to tackle the Illyrian threat in the northwest, and once again the new king demonstrated his shrewd diplomatic manoeuvring. To the immediate south of Illyria, in what is now southern Albania, was Epirus. Like its northern neighbour, Epirus was divided into various tribes, the greatest of which were the Molossians. In 358 BC Philip made an alliance with the Molossians, offering them support to overcome their tribal foes. This not only effectively neutralised any threat from Epirus as a whole, it gave Philip an ally to fight the Illyrians. In little more than a year Philip had cleverly removed all internal threats and firmly established himself as king. He was now ready to concentrate on plans to regain the Macedonian land that his predecessors had lost to their foreign foes.[6]

The Macedonian and western Persian empires at the time of Alexander's accession in 336 BC.

Philip was a diplomatic mastermind, but he knew the importance of delegating responsibility. His urgent priority was to reorganise the army in the way that his brother had refused to do. He realised that Antipater understood the Theban military methods better than he did himself and was the most appropriate person to implement such reforms. Rather than attempt to do all the work, Philip appointed Antipater as one of his two most senior generals and instructed him to restructure the army.[7]

The most significant change to the Macedonian forces was the introduction of the phalanx. The phalanx, meaning 'foot companions', consisted of infantry soldiers in a densely packed formation, each carrying a *saris* – a lance six metres long. These soldiers, wearing helmets, breastplates, steel-ribbed skirts and armoured shin pads, also carried a solid, round shield. Each phalanx consisted of 1,500 men, sixteen ranks deep, carefully spaced so that the breastplate, helmet and shield of each man would serve as communal armour. Drilled to turn quickly in any direction and plunge the point of their spears into the bellies of the enemy, whether advancing on infantry or holding their ground against cavalry, the phalanx bristled like a huge porcupine and was extremely difficult to penetrate with the weaponry and tactics of the time.

The men of the phalanx not only needed to develop considerable strength to wield such long spears, they also required discipline and co-ordination previously unknown in the Macedonian infantry. Drilling was hard and long and may have led to mutiny had it not been for Antipater persuading Philip to use what remained of the royal treasury to pay these men as full-time, professional soldiers. Until this time, most of the Macedonian infantry had been pressed into service as and when required, and received little in return other than their rations and whatever booty they could seize from the enemy. The cavalry, on the other hand, had been made up mostly of higher-ranking citizens who could not only afford a horse but had the spare time to practise their fighting skills. Nevertheless, this too was reorganised along Theban lines to work with the infantry as part of a cohesive force. In the past, the cavalry and infantry fought almost like two completely separate armies, engaged in their own particular type of battle. Now, the cavalry were formed into units known as *hetairoi*, meaning 'companions'. These 1,800-strong divisions would be used to drive a wedge into enemy forces before the infantry advanced, or would counterattack from behind the phalanx. Another advantage of the six-metre spears of the phalanx was that, when the back ranks held them vertically, they obscured the manoeuvring and even the whereabouts of the troops behind. The cavalry could therefore often outflank the enemy with a surprise attack.[8]

Until this time, the Macedonians had employed little in the way of siege technology, as for years they had been on the defensive. Now, Philip's plans to regain Macedonian territory would require forces that could besiege and take fortified strongholds and destroy city walls. Antipater therefore established a new unit of engineers to build and use siege engines such as the Thebans possessed. These siege engines consisted of a battering ram sheltered within a protective framework that could be rolled up against timber stockades, mud-brick walls or city gates. Under the cover of the armoured roof, the metal-tipped ram could safely be used to smash away defences. If the walls were built from stone, then a larger siege engine could be used: one with an armoured structure built above the battering ram and resembling a fortified tower. Protected inside, troops could climb up ladders and prepare to attack. When wheeled up against the walls, archers from the top could fire down on the walls and a ramp lowered from the top of the tower allowed attackers to storm the enemy battlements.[9]

Antipater, however, did not only copy the Theban war machine, he came up with important modifications of his own. Perhaps the most spectacular was the introduction of artillery. Catapults, the first long-range missile weapons, had been invented by the warlord Dionysius of Syracuse in Sicily in 399 BC. These catapults hurled large stones against walls from a distance, minimising the danger to attackers while slowly crumbling the defences. Also, the stones fired against the wall built up at its base, forming a rough assault ramp into the breach. By the second half of the fourth century BC, such weapons were standard in the armies of the Greek and Middle Eastern world. However, in 359 BC, they were still virtually unknown outside Sicily. At some point Antipater must have visited the island because he knew of the weapon and hired a Sicilian engineer to build them for the Macedonian army.[10]

Antipater's most significant innovation, however, and seemingly his own idea, was the introduction of the world's first military police force. The Macedonian army had a royal guard, known as the Hypaspistes – the 'shield bearers' – a thousand-strong unit of heavy infantry whose job it was to protect the king in battle. Although small in number, they were already full-time soldiers and the most highly trained in the Macedonian army. Antipater increased their number threefold and gave them the additional task of maintaining order and discipline among the other troops. In the past, if a battle appeared to be going badly, the day might be lost prematurely by soldiers running away. With the newly empowered shield bearers watching their every move, the men of Philip's army now knew that they stood a better chance of survival if they stood and fought.[11]

The year after his ascent to the throne, Philip was ready to free northwestern Macedonia from the Illyrians and his new army was tested for the first time in battle. It was still some years from being perfected and its numbers were still relatively small. Nevertheless, the Illyrians were utterly defeated and three-quarters of their army – 7,000 men – lay dead on the battlefield. Philip also moved north into Paeoina and Agriania – Macedonian territories which had declared independence some years before – and brought them back under Macedonian control. By 357 BC, Philip's domain had more than doubled in size.[12] The Greek Epaminondas may have invented this new type of warfare and Philip may have observed it, but it was Antipater who realised its significance and practically implemented the considerable changes that were necessary to improve the Macedonian army. Moreover, Antipater's innovative military police were the cement that held the entire enterprise together. In short, Antipater ensured Macedonian survival, and created the means by which his country would one day become the most powerful on earth. This was the blueprint for the army that Alexander the Great would later use to conquer much of the known world.

With the expulsion of the Illyrians, Philip was determined to free southern Macedonia from the Greeks who still occupied most of the southeastern part of the country, including much of its Mediterranean coastline and its important seaports. Philip's new army may have succeeded decisively against undisciplined tribes, but the Greeks were still more than a match for the Macedonian forces, which needed more time to be fully trained. However, much of Philip's army was tied up policing the newly acquired provinces in the north and defending the eastern and western borders. Although Illyria and Thrace may no longer have been in a position to defeat Macedonia on the battlefield, they were still able to harass its borders and they constantly tied up large numbers of troops. Philip needed to free up as many of these men as possible so that they could receive further training, and he came up with a brilliant but simple solution. He managed to negotiate non-aggression pacts with all his immediate neighbours. It may only have been a short-term solution, but it gave Philip the extra time he required. He lulled his enemies into a false sense of security by strengthening loyalties through a series of political marriages and ended up with a virtual harem of foreign wives.[13]

Philip married Audata, the daughter of a powerful Illyrian chief, as a sign of an end to hostilities with Illyria. He married Meda, a Thracian princess, as a gesture of goodwill to his eastern neighbours. He married Phila, the daughter of a Macedonian noble who was a possible rival for the throne, and he married Myrtale, the daughter of a Molossian chief, in order to cement his alliance with Epirus. He even married two women from northern Greece, as a symbol that he intended to live in harmony with the Greeks. Philip had everyone believing that he wanted no more land and only wished for peace. They could not have been more wrong, as the Illyrians were the first to discover in 356 BC when the Macedonian army swept through the region, seizing over half of the country in a few short weeks.

At first, it is difficult to see why Philip should have attacked Illyria. He had already driven them from Macedonian soil and they had little in the way of resources. However, they did have something he desperately needed – manpower. Philip does not appear to have had his sights set on a Macedonian empire at this time, but to drive the Greeks from his soil he needed more fighting men, and to free them from the land he needed slaves. He got all he needed from his Illyrian conquest.[14]

Philip had just won his decisive victory over the Illyrians when he received two pieces of news that he interpreted as good omens for his planned campaign against the Greeks. On the same day, he learned that one of his wives, Myrtale, had borne him a son and that a chariot he had entered in the Olympic Games in Greece had been victorious. To mark the occasion, he decided to give his wife the Greek name Olympias. The son, he named after his oldest brother, Alexander. This was the boy who would one day be the man the world would know as Alexander the Great.[15]

Philip may not have been in Pella for the birth but Antipater was. While the king was leading his troops against the Illyrians, Antipater had remained behind to continue overseeing the training of new recruits. It is apparently from him that a story was later circulated concerning portents that surrounded Alexander's birth. Some claimed that the story was invented later, to show that Alexander was destined for greatness, while others, including Olympias, swore that it was true. Plutarch later wrote a full account, not only of the portents at the birth but also at the time Alexander was conceived:

> The night before the consummation of their marriage, she [Olympias] dreamed that a thunderbolt fell upon her body, which kindled a great fire, whose divided flames dispersed themselves all

about, and then were extinguished. And Philip, some time after he was married, dreamed that he sealed up his wife's body with a seal, whose impression, as he fancied, was the figure of a lion . . . the meaning of his dream was that the queen was with the child of a boy, who would one day prove as stout and courageous as a lion.[16]

According to Plutarch, when Philip later discovered that his wife was indeed pregnant, confirming the interpretation he had been given of his dream, he became convinced that her dream had meaning too. However, none of his astrologers or soothsayers could offer an interpretation. Philip therefore sent an envoy to consult the oracle of Apollo at Delphi in Greece. The Delphic Oracle was a priestess who was believed to commune with the gods, foretell the future and offer divine advice. Apparently, the oracle did not directly reveal the meaning of Olympias' dream, but told Philip that he should honour one god above all others – the god Zeus, the supreme deity in the Greek pantheon. Evidently Philip had no idea what to make of this, but Olympias interpreted the oracle's words to mean that her unborn child was the son of Zeus who had been infused in her body by the thunderbolt in her dream.[17]

Plutarch goes on to relate what was said to have occurred on the day Alexander was born:

> Alexander was born on the sixth day of Hecatombaeon [20 July] . . . the same day that the temple of Diana at Ephesus was burnt . . . [Ephesus was in Asia Minor, the ancient name for the Asian part of what is now Turkey] The temple took fire and was burnt while its mistress [the high priestess] was absent, assisting at the birth of Alexander. And all the Eastern soothsayers who happened to be then at Ephesus, looking upon the ruin of this temple to be the forerunner of some other calamity, ran about the town, beating their faces, and crying that this day had brought forth something that would prove fatal and destructive to all Asia.[18]

The fate of Asia was thus seen to be in the hands of the newborn child who would grow to be a mighty conqueror. How much of these stories are true is open to question, but Olympias later convinced her son of them. Alexander grew up believing that omens and portents had surrounded his conception and birth and that he was destined for greatness; he eventually came to believe he was the son of a god.

After Alexander's birth, Philip returned home and, finding Antipater's army ready for action, prepared to march against the Greeks. However, he appointed his other senior general, Parmenion, as commander of the force and ordered Antipater to remain in Pella. Philip's decision at first appears strange. Parmenion was a battle-hardened veteran and had commanded Philip's armies in the Illyrian campaign. Nevertheless, Antipater was the greater strategist, and by far the more experienced with the new type of army he had personally trained. Philip's reason for leaving Antipater behind could only have been that he needed him to continue to build his forces in case the first expedition failed. The king, it seems, had no intention of leaving fate in the hands of the gods.

In late 356 BC, Parmenion led the army of around 10,000 men into southeastern Macedonia and within the year he had driven out not only the Athenians but also an entire army from mighty Thebes. The capture of the city of Amphipolis in the region, which Philip had surrendered to the Greeks when he came to power, was a crucial nexus point in Macedonian history. Before this time, Philip seemed to have had no plans to build an empire; his intentions had been merely to reunite Macedonia and expel all foreigners from within its historical borders. During the Athenian occupation of Amphipolis, gold and silver had been discovered in nearby Mount Pangaeus and the new mines were an almost inexhaustible source of finance for any future campaigns. Within a short time, Philip decided to use his new wealth to create a Macedonian empire. Even though parts of southern Macedonia were still under Greek control, he began to make preparations to invade Greece itself.[19]

Three years later, Philip finally led his army into Greece and by 352 BC he was firmly in control of Thessaly in the north of the country. In fact, he advanced as far south as the Thermopylae Pass, occupying almost half the landmass of the Greek peninsular. However, here the Macedonian army halted as the pass was strongly defended by a Greek alliance made up primarily of Athenians and Spartans who had united to oppose the invasion. With the war in Greece reaching a standstill, Philip turned his attention back to his homeland and by 348 BC had driven out the last of the Greeks on Macedonian soil. Attacking the region of Chalcidice in the far southeast of his country, he razed 31 Greek-occupied cities to the ground and carted off their citizens as slaves.

By 346 BC Philip was ready to march into southern Greece, but problems nearer to home forced him to temporarily abandon any plans for further invasion. The Macedonian king had to spend the next few years securing his borders. With the Illyrians and Thracians again harassing northwestern and eastern Macedonia, some of the tribes of

Epirus grasped the opportunity and attempted to seize Macedonian land. Philip managed to pacify the region, but no sooner had he done so than the Greeks in Thessaly rebelled. Once he had put down this uprising, the king decided that he would put an end permanently to the problems that had led to trouble in the first place – the constant border threats posed by Illyria and Thrace. He assembled two large armies and invaded both these countries, and by 339 BC they were firmly under his control.[20]

During much of these campaigns, Antipater had remained in Pella where he struck up a close personal friendship with Philip's wife Olympias. He also began to take a keen interest in her son, the teenage Alexander. In fact, no one played a greater role in shaping Alexander's early life than Antipater. Although Philip had an older son, Arridaeus, by one of his Greek wives, Philinna, the boy was considered mentally incompetent and the king had named Alexander as his heir. Antipater realised the dangers Macedonia faced if Philip should die in battle, and that a strong and capable new king would be essential to hold the country together. He therefore spent as much time and effort preparing Alexander for his future role as he had done reorganising the army. Antipater trained the young prince in the martial arts and taught him all the military tactics he knew. Alexander learned quickly. Even at this early age, the boy showed all the signs of a military genius, and showed a keener grasp of warfare than even his father. Philip had a remarkable mind; he wisely delegated the right responsibilities to the right men, and he had proved himself to be a brilliant diplomat and political strategist. However, Antipater realised that Alexander might well exceed his father as a warrior. He grasped the full significance of the military strategies he was being taught, and Alexander was a born soldier for the field.[21] The athletic young man excelled with the sword, bow and spear, and he quickly became an expert horseman. In fact, he appears to have been what today we would call a horse whisperer. Plutarch records an unusual anecdote of Alexander taming a horse when his father returned home after conquering Illyria and Thrace.

> Philonicus the Thessalian brought the horse Bucephalus to Philip, offering to sell him for thirteen talents. But when they went into the field to try him, they found him so vicious and unmanageable, that he reared up when they endeavoured to mount him, and would not so much as endure the voice of any of Philip's attendants. Upon which, as they were leading him away as wholly useless and intractable, Alexander, who stood by, said, 'What an excellent

horse do they lose for want of address and boldness to manage him!'

Philip at first took no notice of what he said; but he heard him repeat the same thing several times, and saw he was much vexed to see the horse sent away. 'Do you reproach,' said he to him, 'those who are older than yourself, as if you knew more, and were better able to manage him than they?'

'I could manage this horse,' he replied, 'better than others do.'

'And if you do not,' said Philip, 'what will you forfeit for your rashness?'

'I will pay,' answered Alexander, 'the whole price of the horse.'

At this the whole company fell laughing; and as soon as the wager was settled amongst them, he immediately ran to the horse, and taking hold of the bridle, turned him directly towards the sun, having, it seems, observed that he was disturbed at and afraid of the motion of his own shadow; then letting him go forward a little, still keeping the reins in his hands, and stroking him gently when he found him begin to grow eager and fiery, he let fall his upper garment softly, and with one nimble leap securely mounted him, and when he was seated, by little and little drew in the bridle, and curbed him without either striking or spurring him.

Presently, when he found him free from all rebelliousness, and only impatient for the course, he let him go at full speed, inciting him now with a commanding voice, and urging him also with his heel. Philip and his friends looked on at first in silence and anxiety for the result, till seeing him turn at the end of his career, and come back rejoicing and triumphing for what he had performed, they all burst out into acclamations of applause; and his father shedding tears, it is said, for joy, kissed him as he came down from his horse, and in his transport said, 'O my son, look thee out a kingdom equal to and worthy of thyself, for Macedonia is too little for thee.'[22]

Philip was evidently so impressed by Alexander's command of horses that he gave him his first commission, and put him in charge of a cavalry unit. The king had to spend some months in Pella recovering from an injury he received in battle, and while at home was able to watch his son prove himself to be an equally good commander of men. In 338 BC, when he mustered the largest army he had ever assembled to finish off his conquest of Greece, Philip placed Alexander, still only eighteen, in overall charge of an entire cavalry division.[23]

What followed was an all-or-nothing campaign, as the Greek states had united to put together an even larger army than Philip's. Their army, under Theban command, was 37,000 strong, compared to Philip's 32,000 men. On 2 August 338 BC, the two armies met at Chaeronea in central Greece where, for the first time, Philip deployed his military tactics on the home ground of the very people he had learned them from. It was here that Alexander proved his bravery, leadership and military genius to the world. According to Diodorus, it was Alexander who saved the day. Evidently, for a long time the outcome of the battle was unclear, until Alexander led a charge that secured a Macedonian victory.

Both armies were ready at daybreak and the king placed his son Alexander, who was still young but nonetheless brave and quick-thinking, on one wing. Alexander was with the best commanders, while Philip was at the head of the elite corps which were the best men he had. Other units, he deployed where the fighting required.

The outcome of the battle was in question for a long time and many were killed on both sides, so that victory could have gone either way. Then Alexander, keen to show his father his skill, and bettered by no other in courage, and also with some of the best troops at his side, succeeded in breaking the front line of the enemy forces and, killing many, he struck those who opposed him into the ground ... The bodies piled up, until finally Alexander and his company forced their way through the enemy ranks and put their opponents to flight.[24]

All of Greece, apart from Sparta in the far south of the country, was now in Macedonian hands and Philip's empire stretched almost 900 kilometres from the Adriatic to the Black Sea and over a thousand kilometres from the mouth of the Danube to the Peloponnese Peninsular and the Mediterranean coast.

Philip had plans to march into Asia Minor. However, the victory at Chaeronea was virtually the end of his conquests. It was also to mark a turning point in the relationship between him and Alexander. No matter how proud he was of his brilliant son, it seems that Philip had now decided to sire a fully Macedonian heir. In 337 BC, Philip took his seventh and last wife, Cleopatra, the daughter of a Macedonian noble (not to be confused with the famous queen of Egypt). Alexander's mother, Olympias, was a foreigner from Epirus, which meant that her son was only half-Macedonian. Philip's only other son, Arridaeus, was also the son of a foreigner, the Greek Philinna. However, any son that Cleopatra might bear the king would be fully Macedonian. Even if Philip himself decided that Alexander should remain his successor, there would certainly be other Macedonian aristocrats who would consider a son of Cleopatra to be a more legitimate king.[25]

Philip and Alexander both had violent tempers and during the banquet following Philip and Cleopatra's wedding, father and son almost came to blows. According to Plutarch, when Cleopatra's uncle, the general Attalus, made a remark about Philip now being able to father a legitimate heir of Macedonian blood, Alexander threatened the man and hurled his cup at him. Seeing the incident, the drunken Philip flew into a rage, drew his sword and charged at Alexander, only to trip and fall flat on his face. Standing over his father, Alexander is said to have shouted to the guests:

> Here is the man who was making ready to cross from Europe to Asia, and who cannot even cross from one table to another without losing his balance.[26]

Following the incident, Alexander and his mother left the capital and went to Epirus; to the court of Olympias' brother, also called Alexander. This man was now the chief of the Molossis tribe and the most powerful ruler in the region. Olympias was even more furious with her husband than Alexander was, and it seems that she hoped to persuade her brother to back her in a coup to remove Philip and make her son the king. To what extent Alexander was involved in (or even knew about) the idea is unknown. However, the plan never materialised, as Philip pre-empted his resourceful wife. He could have attacked Epirus and easily defeated any army the country could muster, but he was reluctant to involve himself in another war when much of his army was still away securing his position in Greece. Instead, Philip sent an envoy to Olympias' brother, offering him the hand in marriage of his daughter, another Cleopatra, if he returned Alexander to Pella. Cleopatra was Philip's daughter by Olympias, which meant that Alexander of Molossis was her uncle. Although the union would have been incestuous, it would place the Molossian chief in a position of high status in the new Macedonian Empire and he agreed. Somehow Alexander was fore-warned and he managed to flee across the border into Illyria. However, the Illyrians were afraid to offer him sanctuary and he had little choice but to return home. Olympias managed to remain in Epirus and her husband made no attempt to have her returned. Instead, he decided to divorce her. With Alexander back in the capital and under house arrest, it seems that Philip no longer considered Olympias to be any kind of threat.[27]

It is not known what happened to Antipater at this time, but his close personal friendship with Olympias and Alexander must have made Philip at least consider him to be a potential liability. Plutarch and Justinus refer to a new plan by Olympias to assassinate her husband and it is possible that Antipater was involved.[28] The three most important generals in Philip's army were Antipater, Parmenion and Attalus (Philip's new wife's uncle), but by mid-336 BC Parmenion and Attalus were away in the far southeast of Thrace preparing for the intended invasion of Asia Minor.[29] If Olympias was to stand any chance of making her son king, then she had to have Antipater's support, as he was in sole command of the home forces. Philip himself certainly suspected that his life was in danger from someone because he again consulted the Delphic Oracle, who warned him that someone close to him intended to take his life.

If there was such a plot to assassinate Philip, then his fate may have been sealed in the late summer when Cleopatra bore him a child. The historical sources are unclear as to whether this was a son or daughter, but Justinus refers to both, suggesting that Cleopatra may have had twins. He refers to Alexander killing a half-brother called Caranus when he became king.[30] Some historians have suggested that Caranus was Philip's son from a previous marriage, but this seems unlikely as he is not mentioned before this time. If this was Cleopatra's son, then it is likely that Philip really did intend to make him his heir as he had been given the same name as the founder of the Macedonian dynasty: perhaps as a sign that he was intended to be the first king born into a Macedonian Empire.

Whether or not it had anything to do with Olympias or Antipater, Philip was assassinated in October 336 BC during the celebrations following the marriage of Olympias' brother to her daughter. On the second day of the festivities, while entering a games arena, Philip was struck with a dagger and killed on the spot by one of his young nobles: a bodyguard named Pausanias. According to Justinus:

> Philip was going to view the games, unattended by his guards, walking between the two Alexanders, his son and son-in-law. Pausanias, a noble Macedonian youth, without being suspected by anyone, posting himself in a narrow passage, killed him as he was going through it.[31]

Diodorus provides more details.

> He [Pausanias] left horses ready at the city gates and came to the theatre carrying a Celtic dagger beneath his cloak. He then waited at the entrance and when Philip entered the theatre with the guards behind him, Pausanias saw his opportunity and rushed at him, stabbing him through his ribs and killing him stone dead. He then ran for the gates and the horses which he had already prepared for his flight. Immediately some of the bodyguards rushed to the body of the king while others raced in pursuit of the assassins . . . Having a good start, Pausanias would have mounted his horse and made his escape before they could reach him had he not caught his foot in a vine and tripped. As he was scrambling to his feet, Perdiccas [one of Philip's bodyguards] and others bodyguards reached him and he was killed with their javelins.[32]

According to Plutarch, many suspected Olympias and even her son Alexander of being behind the murder. Perdiccas, who was then one of Philip's bodyguards and who killed the assassin (thus preventing him from being questioned), was immediately promoted. The fact that after her return to Macedonia she had Philip's wife Cleopatra and a daughter killed did not improve her reputation. Whether or not the assassin really was part of a conspiracy or whether he acted alone is a mystery we shall examine in the next chapter. One thing that is certain, however, is that Philip's death left the country on the brink of civil war.

Although Philip had named the 21-year-old Alexander as successor, many Macedonian aristocrats were not prepared to accept him. There were those who considered Philip's eldest son Arridaeus to be the true king, and others who wanted to see Alexander's 23-year-old cousin Amyntas succeed to the throne (Amyntas had been the baby boy for whom Philip had originally acted as regent); there were also a number of nobles who claimed that Alexander had been behind his father's assassination, and they had intentions to seize power themselves. By far the most serious rival was Attalus. Apart from being one of the three most senior army officers, he was related to the royal family by marriage. However, he and one of the other three generals, Parmenion, were over 500 kilometres away from Pella in southern Thrace. Nevertheless, it would only take him a couple of weeks to return, and Alexander had to act quickly if he wanted to secure the throne. He knew that the fate of the country lay with one man – Antipater. Antipater was in command of the army in Pella and had assumed emergency powers and placed the capital under martial law the moment Philip had died. The troops under his control were fiercely loyal to their commander and whichever claimant Antipater decided to back would have the entire home army behind him. The day after the assassination, the Macedonian nobles met with Antipater and by the afternoon he had made his decision. Antipater presented Alexander to the army as their new king.[33]

Alexander's first act as king was to order the arrest of Attalus. However, to do this he also needed the support of Parmenion, the other commander of the eastern forces. This he secured, by making concessions. In the next few years many of Parmenion's relatives were placed in key positions of power: his son Philotas was made commander of the cavalry, his son Nicanor was appointed commander of the shield bearers and his son-in-law Coenus was put in command of a phalanx battalion. With Parmenion's support, Alexander relieved Attalus of his command and sent him into exile.[34]

According to Justinus, Alexander cleverly got rid of most of the nobles he distrusted in one go. He invited them to his father's funeral as honoured guests, and when they were all in one place accused them of complicity in Philip's murder and had them arrested. According to Alexander, the chief of these conspirators was his cousin Amyntas, who had intentions to regain the throne that was taken from him as a child. He, too, was arrested and quickly executed.[35]

Alexander's position was now secure and he was undisputed king. However, none of this would have been possible had it not been for Antipater's support. For this, Alexander rewarded him and, when the new king set off to conquer the Persian Empire in 334 BC, he left Antipater behind in Pella as Macedonian governor and as commander of all the Macedonian forces in Europe. As such, Antipater was second only to the king, and for the next eleven years he kept order at home, enabling Alexander to realise his ambitions of conquest. Alexander clearly trusted Antipater implicitly. That is, until the last few weeks of his life.

Throughout most of Alexander's campaigns, his mother Olympias had remained in Macedonia. Here, her friendship with Antipater continued. In fact, so close was their friendship that rumours even began to circulate, not only that they were lovers, but also that Antipater was Alexander's real father. Whatever the true nature of this relationship, by 323 BC it had gone sour and Olympias and her daughter tried to divide the civic council of Macedonia against Antipater. According to Plutarch: 'Even at home, Olympias and Cleopatra (her daughter) had raised a faction against Antipater, and divided his government between them.'[36]

Ultimately, Olympias began to write to her son accusing Antipater of conspiracy. At first Alexander ignored the accusations, assuming that they were due to petty personal squabbles, but as he became increasingly paranoid towards the end of his life the king began to take his mother seriously. According to Plutarch, when Alexander received a letter from Antipater protesting his innocence and accusing Olympias of jealousy and exceeding her authority in Macedonia, Alexander remarked: 'Antipater does not know that one tear of a mother effaces a thousand such letters as these.'[37] In the summer of 323 BC, when some of Olympias' friends arrived at Alexander's court in Babylon to support the queen mother's claims, the king summoned Antipater to answer the charges. Antipater, however, refused to go, claiming that he needed to remain in Europe as he feared a rebellion in Greece. Instead, he sent his son Cassander as an emissary to explain his absence and to refute Olympias' allegations.

When Cassander arrived, Alexander was furious to learn that Antipater had not come in person. According to Plutarch:

> Alexander took him [Cassander] by the hair with both hands and dashed his head against the wall. Another time, Cassander would have said something in defence of Antipater to those who accused him, but Alexander interrupting him, said, 'What is it you say? Do you think people, if they had received no injury, would come such a journey only to accuse your father?' To which then Cassander replied that their coming so far from the evidence was a great proof of the falseness of their charges.[38]

Alexander then dismissed Cassander, telling him that he would consider the matter, and that both he and his father would be severely punished if the allegations were found to be true. Neither of them, however, was ever to face punishment. Shortly after Cassander arrived in Babylon, Alexander was dead.

Of all the eight suspects in Alexander's murder, Antipater has to head the list. Nearly all the historical sources refer to contemporary rumours that he was behind the king's death. According to Arrian, for instance:

> I know that there has been much written concerning Alexander's death: for instance, that Antipater sent him some medicine which had been poisoned and that he took it and died . . . Antipater's son Cassander is said to have brought it, and some accounts say that it was contained in a hollowed mule's hoof, and that it was given

Alexander by Cassander's younger brother Iollas, who was his butler.[39]

Plutarch also refers to suspicions that Antipater had ordered Alexander poisoned,[40] and Justinus refers to the same rumours, saying that Antipater had sent Cassander with a contingency plan to assassinate Alexander if he failed to convince him of his father's innocence, and that his brother Iollas was ultimately instructed to poison the king.[41]

Could there be any truth in these rumours? The reason for Antipater's absence from Babylon seems genuine enough, as a major revolt did occur in Greece as he predicted, and there is no historical evidence to support Olympias' allegations, which were probably due to personal squabbles as Alexander originally believed. It is doubtful that the then 76-year-old governor of Macedonia had any designs on power or surely he would have acted much earlier. He could even have seized the throne himself when Philip had died. Nevertheless, it is possible that Antipater had given Cassander instructions to kill Alexander, as he had good reason to fear the king. Alexander had executed a number of his senior officers on the mere suspicion of disloyalty, including the old general Parmenion who, like Antipater, had always been loyal and helped secure him the throne. Even if the aging Antipater no longer feared for his own life, he may well have feared for his family. Also, there might have been another motive. Without Antipater, Alexander would never have become king; he would never have had the army that made him so successful and he would never have been free to conquer the Persian Empire. Alexander owed his old mentor everything, and Antipater may have considered his siding with Olympias to have been the ultimate act of betrayal.

If we assume that there was such a contingency plan to kill Alexander, then the question of Antipater's guilt revolves around whether or not his son managed to convince the king that his mother was wrong. If Alexander did ultimately believe Antipater, then there was no longer a reason to assassinate him. The problem is that the surviving historical sources do not reveal Alexander's decision on the matter. Alexander did meet privately with Cassander shortly before his death, but what transpired is unknown.

If Antipater had been behind Alexander's death, then it seems that Olympias was unwittingly to blame. It was she who had poisoned her son's mind against his lifelong friend. The reasons for her turning against Antipater are not mentioned by the historical sources, but they do portray her as a hard, cruel and manipulative woman who effectively neutralised anyone she regarded as a threat to her power. No better can this be seen than in the treatment of her own stepson, the next suspect in Alexander's murder – Arridaeus.

SUMMARY OF CHAPTER FOUR

Antipater had been accused of conspiracy, and there were rumours at the time that he had ordered his son Iollas, the royal butler, to poison Alexander on his behalf.

- In the early fourth century BC Macedonia rose to prominence as Europe's most powerful nation. Although ethnically distinct from the Greek realms to the south, Macedonia had absorbed much of Greek culture and even spoke its language. The Greek world had reached a zenith of civilisation over a hundred years before. However, by the time Alexander's father Philip II came to the Macedonian throne in 359 BC, Greece was a collection of declining city-states. Philip had ambitions to unite them into a single kingdom under Macedonian control and Antipater, above all others, was the general who helped him realise this goal.
- No one played a greater role in shaping Alexander's early life than Antipater. He was intimate with the royal family and had a close personal friendship with Philip's wife, Queen Olympias. When Alexander was born in 356 BC, some even suspected that Antipater was the true father. He certainly showed a keen interest in Alexander's education, helped shape his military genius and eventually secured him the throne.
- By 336 BC, Philip had gained control over much of Greece. However, in October that year he was murdered by his chief bodyguard. It was never proved whether or not the assassin acted alone but the murder left the country on the brink of civil war. It was Antipater who made sure Alexander became king by mustering the army behind the 21-year-old prince and seeing to the elimination of rival claimants. He was rewarded by being appointed supreme commander of all the Macedonian forces in Europe.
- In 334 BC, when Alexander began his twelve-year campaign to conquer the Persian Empire, Antipater remained behind as governor to secure the home front. During this time Olympias' relations with Antipater progressively deteriorated and she eventually began to write to her son accusing the governor of conspiracy. In the summer of 323 BC, Alexander summoned Antipater to court to answer the charges. Antipater refused to go, and sent his son Cassander to refute

Olympias' allegations. The historical sources nearly all refer to rumours some years later that Cassander was also sent with a contingency plan to assassinate Alexander if he failed to convince him of his father's innocence, and that his brother Iollas was ultimately instructed to poison the king.

- It is possible that Antipater had given Cassander instructions to kill Alexander as he had good reason to fear him. The king had executed a number of his senior officers on the mere suspicion of disloyalty. If we assume that there was such a contingency plan then the question of Antipater's guilt revolves around whether or not his son managed to convince Alexander that Olympias was wrong. The historical sources confirm that there was a meeting between Alexander and Cassander shortly before the king's death, but they fail to reveal the outcome.

5. ARRIDAEUS – THE EARLY DAYS

Arridaeus was the son of Philip's wife Philinna. Little is known of her background other than that she came from city of Larissa, the capital of Thessaly in northern Greece. She must have been of high status as Philip had married her as part of a non-aggression pact with the Thessalian leadership. The marriage took place around 359 BC and the following year Philinna gave birth to Arridaeus, Philip's first-born son and heir to the throne. Although Arridaeus' mother was not Macedonian, she was from Greek aristocracy and therefore considered a fitting queen in a country that both respected and had adopted Hellenic culture. Philinna may have been refined, educated and of noble birth, but she was to prove no match for the resourceful and ruthless Olympias.

Philip married Olympias shortly after Arridaeus was born to cement his alliance with the Molossians in Epirus. Unlike the aristocratic and pampered Philinna, Olympias was the daughter of a warrior chieftain from a rough, warlike tribe. The Greeks had a reputation for arrogance and tended to look down on those they considered uncivilised. Tribal society, such as existed in Epirus, was regarded as barbarian and Philinna must immediately have taken a dislike to Philip's new wife. The tribal peoples of Epirus, on the other hand, no doubt regarded the Greeks as pompous and mollycoddled, and the tough Molossian princess must have felt equally uncomfortable in Philinna's presence.

The Macedonians had adopted Greek culture and so Philinna would have felt relatively at home in the Macedonian court. Olympias, you would have thought, could not have been more out of place. In Hellenic culture – the culture of Greece – women had no rights under law and even a queen had no official say in politics. Instead, a resourceful wife needed to become an expert at intrigue. Surreptitiously influencing the men about her, raising hell when she failed to get her way, playing one courtier against another, and poisoning the occasional rival appears to have been the usual way in which a high-status woman could play the power game. In fact, it needed a hard-hearted and resilient woman to succeed and survive in this world of men, and Olympias had the ideal background to prepare her for such a role. Her people, the Molossians, were a Celtic tribe and in Celtic society women were often considered equal to men and even fought in battle.[1]

The Celts can be traced back to what is now Austria around 1200 BC, but by 700 BC they had migrated as far south as Epirus, and in the north

67

they occupied the British Isles. In fact, Olympias would have been more closely related to the modern Irish than she would to the Macedonians or Greeks. Celtic society was almost unique in the ancient world regarding its attitude to women. Women held legal rights; they could own property (which was not taken from them at marriage), choose their own husbands and even had the rights of redress in cases of sexual harassment. Furthermore, they could enter whatever profession they wished: they could govern, take prominent roles in political or religious life and, most astonishing of all, they could even be warriors. The ancient Greeks and Romans record that women often fought in battle, and there are a number of examples of Celtic warrior queens, such as the famous Boudicca who led a rebellion against Roman rule in Britain in the first century AD. As a Celtic princess, Olympias (or Myrtale, as she was then) would very likely have been trained for combat. In the TV series *Xena: Warrior Princess*, Xena is a Greek. In reality, Greek women were meant to sit pretty and keep quiet, whereas Celtic women were taught to fight and think for themselves. Any real warrior princesses at the time of ancient Greece would not have been Greek but Celtic women like Olympias. It is understandable that Philinna, no matter how cultured and educated she was, would stand little chance in the battle of wills and games of intrigue that she would eventually be drawn into with her new rival. Sadly, Arridaeus was to stand no chance of inheriting the throne.[2]

Olympias was strong willed and freely spoke her mind, something that ancient historians clearly regarded as unacceptable. As such, she is portrayed as wicked and divisive. Plutarch, for instance, blames Olympias solely for the problems that eventually beleaguered Philip's court.

> But the disorders of his [Philip's] family, chiefly caused by his new marriages and attachments (the troubles that began in the women's chambers spreading, so to say, to the whole kingdom), raised various complaints and differences between them, which the violence of Olympias, a woman of a jealous and implacable temper, made wider . . .[3]

Few women in history have been more reviled than Olympias. She was universally condemned as an evil, scheming, murderous witch. The only good words that were ever written about her were that she was beautiful. She was nineteen when Alexander was born in 356 BC and was evidently extremely attractive. Although the only surviving portrait of Olympias, a profile on a coin, reveals few of her features, we know that she must have been stunning; even the contemporaries who hated her were forced to comment on her beauty. Conversely, there are no surviving likenesses or descriptions of Philinna; even her age is uncertain.

Philip's other wives do not appear to have played any significant role in the life of the Macedonian court. Only Philinna was a threat to Olympias, as she had what seemed an ace card in her son Arridaeus. As he was heir to the throne, Philinna was Philip's chief wife and therefore the queen. Olympias clearly had no intention of remaining second best, and the birth of Alexander gave her a trump to play. If she could succeed in having him made heir, then she would be queen of Macedonia. She could have attempted to murder Arridaeus, but suspicion would no doubt immediately have fallen on her. Instead, Olympias cleverly decided to render Arridaeus unfit for the role as crown prince. She began by spreading rumours that in Thessaly Philinna had been a 'dancing girl'. This may have been true, as in Greece dancing was a respected theatrical art. In Macedonia, however, the only girls who danced were prostitutes, and this is clearly what Olympias intended everyone to believe. She presumably hoped that, if Philinna became perceived as a harlot in the popular imagination, Philip would be forced to divorce her and disinherit her son. Philinna's image was certainly tarnished, as even some of the later classical historians referred to her as a common woman. However, the rumours failed to influence Philip, who was rapidly growing so powerful that he was impervious to popular gossip. However, if Plutarch is right, Olympias devised another, more ingenious way of rendering Arridaeus unfit for the role of future king.

[Arridaeus] was deficient in intellect owing to bodily disease. This, however, did not come upon him in the course of nature or of its own accord, indeed, it is said that as a boy he displayed an exceedingly gifted and noble disposition: but after Olympias gave him drugs which injured his body and ruined his mind.[4]

Whether or not this was true is impossible to say, but even if Arridaeus' problem was of natural origin then Olympias would no doubt have used it to her advantage and constantly prompted questions regarding his suitability as successor. By the time Arridaeus was in his teens, Philip concluded that he was not fit to be king and named Alexander as his new heir.

69

Whatever Arridaeus' medical condition really was, it appears to have been intermittent. From various descriptions in the works of Diodorus and Arrian, it seems that the boy either had epileptic fits, psychotic episodes or periods where his mind would lose its grip on reality. However, for most of the time he appears to have been perfectly normal. There have been far more unstable rulers in history and, if it was not for Olympias' influence, Arridaeus might still have remained heir. What Philinna did, or had to say about any of this is a mystery, as she goes unmentioned again in the historical sources. She either died or slipped quietly into the background. Either way, Olympias had won. She was now the chief wife and Macedonian queen.

As a young man, Arridaeus had every reason to be jealous of his younger brother. Not only had Alexander taken his right of succession, but he was also a far stronger and more handsome youth. Arridaeus was weak and scrawny, whereas Alexander was athletic and handsome. Alexander surpassed his brother physically, and he had far more charisma and was particularly attractive to girls. It is said that he had an almost hypnotic gaze, made all the more mesmerising by the fact that his eyes were different colours: 'one eye dark as a night and one blue as the sky', as one description has it. Alexander also had a remarkable influence over men and he is said to have set the fashion for the clean-shaven look among the sons of Macedonian nobles. In fact, this was a fashion that continued throughout much of Europe well into Roman times. Nevertheless, it seems that intellectually Arridaeus was his brother's equal.[5]

In 343 BC, King Philip invited the famous Greek philosopher Aristotle to come to Macedonia and tutor the sons of Macedonian nobles. Philip wanted to make Macedonian court life more cultured, and by having the heirs of his aristocracy under his control he also hoped that he could keep their parents from interfering with his authority. Aristotle was to be well paid and accepted the position, and the star pupils in his new school were Alexander and Arridaeus, now thirteen and fifteen years of age. Aristotle taught them several important subjects, such as physics, mathematics, geography and theology, and the pair seemed to have done equally well. When Aristotle later wrote his work *On the Cosmos,* he dedicated it to the two boys whom he called 'the best of princes', which further suggests that Arridaeus was as quick to learn as Alexander.[6]

Olympias succeeded in getting virtually everything she wanted until around 340 BC, when relations between king and queen began to break down. Olympias had a tremendous influence over her son, which was apparently becoming increasingly annoying to Philip. It seems that

Philip and Alexander were growing further apart and Plutarch, for one, puts the blame firmly on Olympias. In 339 BC, Philip had plans to marry Arridaeus to the daughter of a Persian aristocrat, implying that the king was now considering reinstating his older son as successor. Even if he wasn't, Olympias convinced Alexander that this was his father's intention. According to Plutarch:

> Alexander's mother, and some who pretended to be his friends, presently filled his head with tales and slander, as if Philip, by such a marriage and important alliance, were preparing the way for settling the kingdom upon Arridaeus. In alarm at this, he [Alexander] despatched Thessalus, the tragic actor, into Caria [in the Persian Empire], to dispose Pixodorus [the father of the girl Arridaeus was intended to marry] to slight Arridaeus, both illegitimate and a fool, and rather to accept of himself for his son-in-law . . . But Philip, as soon as he heard of this, went to his son's apartment . . . and there reproved him severely, and reproached him bitterly, that he should be so corrupt, and unworthy of the power he was to leave him . . .[7]

After this, although the marriage failed to materialise and Alexander remained heir to the throne, relations between Philip and his younger son rapidly deteriorated. Just before the battle of Chaeronea in August 338 BC, when he was preparing to engage the Theban-led alliance and conquer southern Greek, Philip was injured by rioting soldiers. Alexander saved his father by fighting off the attackers, yet Philip never acknowledged that he owed his son his life. After the battle, Philip even appears to have become jealous of Alexander's success and he began to ridicule him in front of the troops, saying that his son's apparently high-pitched voice made him sound like a girl. By this time Alexander had lost all respect for his father and, according to Plutarch, he openly confessed that the only thing he owed Philip was his birth. In fact, he said that he had far more love for his teacher Aristotle: 'the one had given him life, but the other taught him how to live'.[8]

In 337 BC, Philip appears to have finally lost patience with Olympias and her son. His marriage to the Macedonian Cleopatra clearly implies that he intended to sire a new successor. The event at the wedding, when Philip tried to attack Alexander and Alexander openly mocked the king, was the last straw and Olympias and her son left Macedonia. Philip was unable to disinherit Alexander there and then, as there was no other heir that the majority of his nobles would accept. He could not risk creating divisions in his government at a time when much of his army was away from home. However, if Cleopatra bore him a son then all this would change. In fact, within a few months, even Arridaeus was considered more acceptable than he had been. It appears that, with Olympias no longer around, his health began to improve. The overbearing queen, or living in Alexander's shadow, may have been a psychological encumbrance to the young man. Alternatively, Plutarch may have been right about Olympias administering drugs to her stepson.[9]

For the time being, Alexander was still a threat and might well become a rallying flag for Philip's rivals. Besides which, the crown prince commanded much respect with the army. Within a few months Philip forced Alexander to return to Pella, where he had him placed under house arrest. The king now felt safe to divorce Olympias, effectively disinheriting Alexander. This may have been because his wife had given birth to the boy Caranus, mentioned by Justinus, or he may have been considering reinstating Arridaeus. One way or the other, if Alexander was to inherit the throne, or even survive, Philip would have to die – and soon. A few months later, in October 336 BC, Philip was indeed assassinated by the young nobleman, Pausanias. The question is – did he act alone?

According to Justinus, Pausanias killed the king because he refused to punish the general Attalus who had had him raped.

> Attalus had taken him to a banquet, made him drunk, and subjected him not only to his own carnal desires but, like a prostitute, to those of his fellow diners as well, so making the boy an object of universal ridicule among his peers. Outraged by this treatment, Pausanias had often made complaints to Philip, but being put off with various excuses, not unattended with ridicule, and seeing his adversary also honoured with a general's commission, he turned his rage against Philip himself.[10]

Diodorus also includes the rape incident in his account, but he also refers to another motive for the murder. According to him, Pausanias was Philip's homosexual lover, and his reason for the assassination, in part, was because the king had become infatuated by another man.

> Pausanias, one of the royal bodyguards, was much loved by the king because of his beauty. When he saw that Philip was becoming

infatuated by another Pausanias (a man who had the same name as himself), he shouted at him with abusive language and accused him of being a hermaphrodite and a man who encouraged the advances of anyone.[11]

In Plutarch's account, the new queen Cleopatra, Attalus' niece, was somehow also involved in Pausanias' rape. More importantly, Plutarch suggests that Olympias and Alexander may have encouraged the man to kill the king.

> Not long after this, Pausanias, having had an outrage done to him at the instance of Attalus and Cleopatra, when he found he could get no reparation for his disgrace at Philip's hands, watched his opportunity and murdered him. The guilt of which fact was laid for the most part upon Olympias, who was said to have encouraged and exasperated the enraged youth to revenge; and some sort of suspicion attached even to Alexander himself.[12]

Justinus too accuses Olympias of influencing Pausanias because Philip had divorced her. He also implicates Alexander on the grounds that his father had evidently named Arridaeus as successor.

> It is even believed that he [Pausanias] was instigated to the act by Olympias, Alexander's mother, and that Alexander himself was not ignorant that his father was to be killed; as Olympias had felt no less resentment at her divorce, and the preferment of Cleopatra to herself, than Pausanias had felt the insults which he had received. As for Alexander, it is said that he feared his brother [Arridaeus] by his stepmother as a rival for the throne.[13]

Whether Pausanias really was encouraged by Alexander or Olympias could not be proved, as the assassin was slain as he tried to escape. However, the fact that the chief bodyguard, Perdiccas, who had the assassin killed rather than taken alive for questioning, turned out to be one of Alexander's most dedicated supporters did little to allay suspicions at the time. Olympias had not been in Macedonia when Philip died, but she could secretly have communicated to Alexander the scheme to pressurise Pausanias. According to Justinus, Olympias' savage treatment of Philip's wife Cleopatra and her child, immediately on her return to Pella, convinced many that she had been behind the king's death.

73

> Next she [Olympias] forced Cleopatra, for whose sake she had been divorced from Philip, to hang herself, having first killed her daughter in her lap, and enjoyed the sight of her suffering this vengeance, to which she had hastened by procuring the death of her husband.[14]

In fact, if Justinus' account is accurate, Olympias virtually admitted that she had instigated her ex-husband's death.

> Last of all she consecrated the sword, with which the king had been killed, to Apollo, under the name of Myrtale, which was Olympias' own name when a child. And all these things were done so publicly, that she seems to have been afraid lest it should not be evident enough that the deed was promoted by her.[15]

Whatever the truth about Philip's death, Alexander did secure his throne. If Justinus is right and Arridaeus had been named successor, it means that his younger brother had now usurped him for a second time. However, whereas he eliminated his other rivals, Alexander not only spared Arridaeus' life, he did not even banish him as he did with Attalus. We can only assume that Alexander was fond of his brother. Unfortunately, Arridaeus' true feelings towards Alexander are not revealed by the historical sources. By this time, he certainly had much reason to resent him and had motive for Alexander's eventual murder – but it did not end there. At the beginning of Alexander's war with the Persian Empire, the unfortunate Arridaeus was again humiliated before the world.

At home, Alexander had quickly gained a firm grip on power. However, the foreign dominions saw his father's death as an opportunity to throw off the yoke of Macedonian rule. In the spring of 335 BC, Alexander was surprised by rebellions in both Thrace and Illyria and was immediately forced to suppress the revolts. Although Alexander's armies met fierce resistance, it was a swift and decisive war on both fronts and order was restored. Meanwhile, in Greece, rumours that Alexander had died during the campaign caused a revolt in many of the occupied cities. In Thebes, for instance, an entire Macedonian garrison was massacred. No sooner had he put down the rebellions in Thrace and Illyria than Alexander had to march south into Greece. Once again, Alexander proved his ability to act quickly and decisively. The city of Thebes was stormed almost immediately and the Theban army was crushed. It was here that Alexander first employed a strategy that he would use many times again. As an example, he severely punished the citizens of Thebes. The city was razed to the ground, and six thousand inhabitants were executed and thirty thousand sold as slaves. The other cities he promised to treat well so long as they surrendered without a fight. This they did and Alexander kept his word. The cities of the world now knew what to expect if they resisted Alexander and how they would be fairly dealt with if they capitulated. During his future campaigns, this strategy resulted in many cities being captured intact; it sped up invasions and preserved the lives of thousands of troops.[16]

The Macedonian dominion established by Philip had now been secured, but Alexander had his sights set on what his father had only dreamed about – the conquest of the mighty Persian Empire. Also known as the Achaemenid Empire, after Achaemenes, the family name of its rulers, the Persian Empire was started by King Cyrus the Great around 550 BC. Originally from Iran, the Persians held sway over a domain that also included all of what are now Iraq, Afghanistan, Syria, Lebanon, Jordan, Israel and Egypt and most of what is now Turkey. At the time Alexander came to the Macedonian throne, the Persian Empire was ruled by the 45-year-old Darius III, who reigned from his capital at Persepolis in southern Iran. According to Plutarch, Darius was unbelievably wealthy. Apparently, he lived in 'a marvellous palace with a surrounding wall flashing with gold, electrum and ivory; it had a succession of many gate towers, and the gateways were fortified with brazen doors and high walls . . .' Plutarch also describes the huge size of the empire and the remarkable way it was organised.

The whole empire of Asia, bounded by the Hellespont [Dardanelles] in the west and the Indus in the east, was divided into nations under generals and satraps [governors] and kings, slaves of the Great King, with couriers and scouts and messengers and signal-officers. And such was the orderly arrangement of this, and particularly of the system of signal-beacons which were ready to burn in succession from the uttermost limits of the empire that the king knew the same day all that was news in Asia.[17]

This was the biggest empire the world had yet known and Alexander intended to attack it. Many of his officers advised him that the whole thing was suicidal. However, Alexander believed that the Persian Empire was far more vulnerable than virtually anyone else seemed to realise. For almost three-quarters of a century Persia had been suffering from incompetent monarchs, while quarrels within the royal family, palace intrigues and assassinations had progressively weakened the empire. Moreover, the Persian aristocracy had grown soft and corrupt. Revenues that poured into Persia's royal treasury from tributes and taxes had been wasted on luxurious excesses rather than being spent on the empire's infrastructure and its armies, while the ruling classes had become accustomed to good living. Alexander was convinced that his army – the best the world had ever known – could take on this weakened empire.

Nevertheless, there were those in the Macedonian high command who were far from convinced. Alexander therefore intimated that his intentions were only to conquer a part of Asia Minor: a much more realistic objective. A century earlier the Greeks ruled most of what is now western Turkey, but by the beginning of the fourth century BC the area was firmly under the control of the Persians. By Alexander's time, thousands of Greeks still lived in this part of Asia Minor and their countrymen back home longed to see them free. If Alexander was going to take on the Persians, he needed the help of Greece to make up the numbers in his army. Accordingly, he promised to liberate the Greek cities of western Turkey and it seems that most Macedonian nobles ultimately assumed that this was to be the full scale of the campaign. Alexander finally got the backing he needed when he came up with an excuse for his crusade that he knew would appeal to the Macedonian populace. According to Arrian, Alexander decided to blame Darius for his father's death. Apparently, in a letter to the Persian king that amounted to a declaration of war, Alexander wrote: 'My father was murdered by your conspirators, whom you instructed.'

Darius probably had nothing to do with Philip's death, but Alexander had his justification to march. In May 334 BC, he assembled sixty boats and ferried his army from the Gallipoli Peninsula, across the Dardanelles and into Asia – never to return home.[18]

Alexander's army consisted of 4,500 cavalry, under the command of Parmenion, and just over 30,000 infantry, under the command of Parmenion's son Philotas. According to Diodorus, less than half of these men were actually Macedonian; the rest were from other countries in Alexander's empire, such as Greece, Thrace, Epirus and Illyria. There were even around 5,000 mercenaries. Alexander's total force of approximately 35,000 men was the largest army Macedonia had ever assembled. However, compared with the fighting forces of the Persian Empire, it was tiny. Darius had as many as half a million troops at his disposal. Nevertheless, they were spread out over a huge area and the Macedonian army was a far superior, professional force. Alexander was convinced that, in this war, strategy and tactics would count more than numbers. Many of his officers no doubt prayed that he was right.[19]

Alexander's army landed at Abydos, in what is now Canakkale in western Turkey. However, before engaging the enemy, Alexander decided to visit the ancient city of Troy, some 25 kilometres to the southwest. In Troy there was a shrine, said to mark the tomb of the mythical Greek hero Achilles, and the king wanted to worship there to ensure victory in the field. There was, however, another reason he wanted to visit Achilles' tomb. Alexander claimed to be his descendant and spiritual successor. According to some accounts, he even portrayed himself as Achilles reborn.[20]

When Alexander was being taught by Aristotle, he had been encouraged to read the works of Homer and so became fascinated by the legendary heroes of ancient Greece. Achilles was said to have been the mightiest of the Greeks who fought in the Trojan War, and was the hero of Homer's *Iliad*. According to Homer, at Troy, Achilles distinguished himself as an unbeatable warrior. After capturing 23 towns in Trojan territory, Achilles fell in love with a girl named Briseis. However, the Greek leader Agamemnon took the girl for himself, so angering Achilles that he refused to fight for Greece again. The war then went badly for the Greeks, who implored their greatest warrior to rejoin them. Achilles still refused to fight in person, but he agreed to allow his closest friend Patroclus to fight in his place. The next day Patroclus was killed by the Trojan hero Hector. Enraged, Achilles returned to the fighting and killed his friend's slayer. Eventually Achilles died in the war, but his death inspired the Greeks to finally defeat the Trojans.

Whether or not Alexander personally believed he was a reincarnated Achilles, he certainly used the idea to motivate his troops. Although his army was only partly Greek, it saw itself as a force to Hellenise the barbaric Persian world. In the story of the Trojan War, which many considered to be true, Achilles was an invulnerable hero who had made it possible for the Greeks to conquer Asia Minor. Who better for Alexander to associate himself with than Achilles? Even those who were not prepared to accept that he was Achilles personified had to admit that Alexander had a good case to claim the legendary hero as his ancestor. Alexander's mother Olympias was from Epirus and, according to the Athenian playwright Euripides (c. 480–406 BC), the royal house of Epirus were descended from Achilles through his son Neoptolemus.[21] In reality, the story of the Trojan War probably reflected a real war between the invading Greeks and the people of Troy over control of trade through the Dardanelles around 1200 BC.[22] However, if Achilles was based on an historical character and his son did settle in Epirus, then his dynasty had ended long before Alexander's time. Epirus was now occupied by Celtic tribes from the north and there was no longer a royal house of Epirus. And, even if there had been, it would not have been Greek. Nevertheless, as it was the common conception at the time that the Molossians were descended from Neoptolemus, Olympias could claim descent from Achilles and therefore so could Alexander.

As well as worshipping at Achilles' tomb, Alexander intended to hold grand festivities in Troy to play to the sentiments of the local Greeks. According to Homer, when Achilles' friend Patroclus died, athletic games were held to honour the hero at his funeral. Alexander intended to restage such games in Troy, with himself in the role of Achilles. This would be a sign to the Greeks of Asia Minor that a new Achilles had come to liberate them from Persian rule. However, if Alexander was to be the ancient hero returned, then someone had to play the part of a reborn Patroclus. As some ancient legends portrayed Patroclus as Achilles' brother as well as his best friend, Alexander at first decided on Arridaeus. Indeed, in honouring Arridaeus in this way, Alexander would also have been indulging those who still regarded his brother as the rightful heir. As Arridaeus had absolutely no military experience, this was probably the sole reason why Alexander had his brother accompany him on the campaign. All the same, in the end, Arridaeus never got to assume the role. He may have had some of the qualities of the legendary hero, in that he was educated and refined, but by no stretch of the imagination could he be considered, as Patroclus was, the bravest warrior of them all. In the end, Alexander was to opt for his childhood friend, Hephaestion. According to Arrian, Hephaestion was born in Pella around the same time as Alexander, where his father was a courtier to King Phillip. As the son of a Macedonian noble, he was educated at the school of Aristotle alongside Alexander and Arridaeus. Hephaestion appears to have become Alexander's closest friend, so he fitted the Patroclus role in this respect. Also, although he had not yet distinguished himself in battle, he was a cavalry officer and so had the potential to become a great and courageous warrior.[23]

Troy's inhabitants were mainly of Greek descent, and Alexander was made welcome in the city and the festivities were staged just as he hoped. First of all he visited the city's temple to the goddess Athena where a sacred relic hung above the altar – a magnificent shield that was said to have belonged to Achilles. With or without the priesthood's permission, Alexander took the shield and used it as a visible sign to all the Greeks of Asia Minor that he had assumed the role of his conquering, ancestral hero. During the celebrations that followed, Alexander sat in the seat of honour with Hephaestion at his side. The two men even took part in the games. Poor Arridaeus, however, had to take a back seat, and was forced to watch as his place was again taken by another man. Plutarch gives a brief description of the events.

> He [Alexander] went up to Troy, sacrificed to Athena and poured a libation to the heroes. At the tomb of Achilles, after anointing himself with oil and taking part in a race naked with his companions, as is the custom, he deposited crowns and remarked how fortunate Achilles was to have had a faithful friend while he was alive and a great herald of his fame after his death.[24]

Alexander was, of course, referring to Hephaestion. Alexander had once more, although perhaps not intentionally, humiliated Arridaeus before the world. As the war continued, Alexander went from strength to strength, while Arridaeus was totally eclipsed by his remarkable brother.

While the festivities had been taking place, the Persian governors of Phrygia, Lydia and Cilicia, and other smaller provinces in western Turkey, assembled a joint army that had dug in on the east bank of the River Granicus, the modern Biga Çay, ninety kilometres northeast of Troy. Alexander's army outnumbered the Persians, who had around 20,000 men, but the enemy forces appeared to be in a strong enough position to withstand any attack. In June 334 BC, Alexander's army arrived to find that the Persians had occupied solid, defensive positions on the opposite bank, which meant that the Macedonian army would have to cross the Granicus and be exposed to the arrows of the enemy archers. Alexander, however, knew that the Persians always held mass prayers to their gods at dawn, and used this opportunity to move his forces across the river. As it grew lighter, the Persians could see what was happening and launched a cavalry charge, hoping to outflank the Macedonians and attack their rear before they had chance to group. Alexander, though, quickly realised that the Persians had left themselves vulnerable by breaking their infantry lines to allow their cavalry through. On his famous horse Bucephalus and carrying Achilles' shield, Alexander personally led an immediate counterattack into the gap and scattered the Persian forces so that the Macedonian phalanx could make quick work of the enemy. According to Plutarch, nearly all the Persian forces were killed, while Alexander's losses were remarkably low.[25]

With the defeat of this army, western Turkey was opened up for the taking and further battles in the area were little more than skirmishes by Alexander's standards. By the end of the year, Alexander entered the Phrygian capital of Gordium, a few kilometres west of modern Ankara, and stayed there until the spring, waiting for reinforcements from home.

Alexander's perceived objective had been merely to free the Greek provinces of western Turkey. However, his true intentions had probably been far more ambitious all along. He had certainly decided on greater conquests by the time he took Gordium. Some of his officers, particularly the Greeks, were reluctant to become involved in further offensive action and Alexander needed some kind of sign, omen or portent to show that it was the army's destiny to go on to much bigger things. Luckily, he found just what he needed in the Phrygian capital – the legendary Gordian Knot.[26]

Gordium had been the seat of the fabled King Gordius, after whom the city was named. He appears to have been an historical figure who ruled Phrygia around 700 BC and a famous legend arose concerning his reign. According to Greek mythology, he was originally a poor wanderer at a time when Phrygia was in a state of turmoil and civil unrest. An ancient oracle had foretold that a common man would one day lead the country out of their problems and would be recognised because he would enter Gordium with nothing but a single wagon. Apparently, during a meeting of the city's high council to discuss the crisis, Gordius wandered into the town with his ox-cart. Believing him to be the prophesied saviour, the Phrygians made him their king. To thank the gods for his good fortune, Gordius erected a shrine to the god Zeus and had his wagon tied to a pillar in the centre of the temple, and there it remained as an important symbol of Phrygian unity. When Alexander arrived in Gordium, a cart, which was claimed to be the original, was still in the temple where it was tied to the pillar by a rope with a complex knot. According to a tradition that had grown up in the area, whoever could untie the knot would rule all of Asia. Evidently, the knot was made from hundreds of tightly interwoven thongs of cornel-bark, with no ends exposed. The Gordian Knot had become famous throughout the Greek world and many had tried to untie it. In fact, it appears to have become something of a tourist attraction, and local residents considered it the duty of every wanderer to visit their shrine and attempt to solve their puzzle. When Alexander came to the temple, he viewed the knot for a moment before drawing his sword and cutting it in two. 'So shall I deal with the kingdoms of Asia,' Alexander is reputed to have said. Alexander's men were impressed by his solution to the problem and took it as a sign that he would succeed in his ambition to conquer the Persian Empire.[27]

In the late summer of 333 BC, with much of Turkey under Macedonian control, Alexander moved south towards Syria. By now, Darius had amassed a huge army and was moving westwards. This time, the Persian king decided that he would face Alexander himself. Darius was an educated and intelligent man, but he lacked the energy and foresight of a good military commander. Nonetheless, he appreciated his opposition's capabilities and was leading a force twice as large as Alexander's. His 60,000 best troops included 20,000 Greek mercenaries, largely men who had fled from Greece when Philip had defeated their cities. These soldiers were familiar with Macedonian tactics and their infantry employed the Theban phalanx. It should have been a pushover for the Persian king, but things turned out very differently.[28]

In November 333 BC the two armies met at Issus on the Mediterranean coast just north of Syria. Alexander positioned himself with a good view of his opponent's line, and could see that Darius and the Greek mercenaries stood in the centre, with the wings occupied by the Persian infantry. Seizing the initiative, Alexander led his cavalry to the right, which Darius took to be an attempt to outflank him. In fact, his true objective soon became clear. When the Persian infantry on the right wing moved to face the Macedonian cavalry, they created a gap in the centre of their line that Alexander immediately wheeled towards, forcing a wedge that divided the enemy forces. At the same time, the Macedonian infantry made a frontal attack and the Persians and Greek mercenaries were routed. Even before the fighting was over, Darius left the battlefield and fled eastwards with his royal guard.[29]

After the battle of Issus, Alexander was so popular and had proved himself to be such a military genius that his legitimate right to rule was now academic. Whether or not Arridaeus should be the rightful king had become irrelevant. Alexander was not only better than any Macedonian leader who had gone before, he was also the greatest soldier Europe had ever seen. Arridaeus had been completely overshadowed by his younger brother and now seemed consigned to the sidelines of history. However, the poor prince was to suffer a further indignation when he and Alexander fell for the same women.

Immediately after the Persian defeat, an advance Macedonian force, under the command of Parmenion, was sent over 400 kilometres into Syria to take the city of Damascus and seize its treasury before it could be moved out. The Persian garrison was taken entirely by surprise by the swift action and completely overcome. Parmenion not only seized almost 55 tons of gold and great quantities of silver, but he also captured the Persian royal family and other courtiers whom Darius had left behind. Along with Darius' mother, his wife, his five-year-old son and his two little daughters, Parmenion returned to Alexander's camp with Barsine, the thirty-year-old daughter of Artabazus the governor of Phrygia.[30]

Barsine was already known to Alexander and Arridaeus, as she and her father had spent eleven years at the Macedonian court. Twenty-one years earlier, following a rebellion against the Persian king Artaxerxes III, Artabazus and his family were forced to flee to Macedonia where King Philip made them welcome. Here they stayed until Artabazus was eventually pardoned and allowed to return home at the end of 343 BC. Barsine had been brought up in Macedonia since she was nine years old and by the time she left she was obviously more of a Macedonian than a Persian woman. When she was twenty, Barsine spent a year being educated at Aristotle's school, where she and the fifteen-year-old Arridaeus struck up a close personal friendship. In fact, it seems that Barsine was the only real friend Arridaeus ever had. He was clearly infatuated by the older girl and when he met her again in 333 BC he fell in love. Her husband, the supreme commander of the Persian forces in Asia Minor, had been killed in battle and Barsine was now a widow. According to the *Historia*, Arridaeus intended to marry the woman but his brother intervened. Alexander wanted to legitimate his claim to be ruler of Asia Minor. To this end, he could have married the Persian king's eldest daughter Statira, but she was only about six years old. Instead, he decided that he would marry Barsine, as her father had been the ruler of the largest province in Asia Minor and her late husband had been the most senior Persian officer in the entire area. Arridaeus must have been devastated, as he immediately left Alexander's camp and returned home to Macedonia. Here he stayed, not seeing his brother again until shortly before Alexander's death in 323 BC.[31]

Arridaeus has more motives for murdering Alexander than any of the suspects on our list. Although it appears to have been nothing personal, Alexander twice usurped his right to succession, twice prevented him from marrying and eventually took the woman he loved. Although Alexander seems to have been fond of his older brother, he constantly humiliated him and totally surpassed, outshone and overshadowed him. While Alexander was off conquering the world, growing ever more powerful, Arridaeus was left behind in obscurity. It is quite reasonable to conclude that Arridaeus may have grown to resent his brother bitterly. In fact, Arridaeus had an additional motive to kill his brother. Alexander never named a successor and Arridaeus was perhaps the only king that the Macedonians would accept if he were to die. Alexander had not seen his brother for ten years until he arrived in Babylon as an envoy of Olympias in June 323 BC – and a couple of weeks later he was indeed dead. Had Arridaeus taken the first opportunity in years to finally get his revenge?

Back in 333 BC, however, Alexander was taking a path in his life that would ultimately give someone else a motive to kill him. As the broken-hearted Arridaeus returned home, Alexander also became besotted by Barsine. Although the planned marriage never went ahead, Alexander, according to Justinus, fell in love with her.

> Hence it was that he first began to indulge in luxurious and splendid banquets, and fell in love with his captive Barsine for her beauty.[32]

The feelings were evidently mutual as Barsine remained Alexander's devoted concubine for six long years. Sadly, during this time Alexander was to change and he began to treat the woman who had once been the love of his life shamefully. This behaviour may eventually have cost him his life, as Barsine is the next suspect in Alexander's murder.

SUMMARY OF CHAPTER FIVE

Arridaeus was Alexander's older brother who should have inherited the throne. It is possible that he bore a grudge against Alexander and eventually seized the opportunity to murder him and become king.

- Initially, Arridaeus seems an unlikely suspect as he is said to have been mentally incompetent. However, his problem – possibly schizophrenia – appears to have been sporadic. If he was sane for much of the time, then the events of his youth certainly provide him with a motive for Alexander's murder.
- Like Alexander, Arridaeus was the son of Philip II. He was born a couple of years before his brother, to Philip's first wife, a Thessalian woman named Philinna. Macedonian custom allowed for a man to have more than one wife and the year after Arridaeus' birth the king married Olympias, the daughter of a foreign king with whom he wished to cement an alliance. One year after her marriage Olympias gave birth to her own son, Alexander, and from the very start there can be little doubt that she intended to make him Philip's heir.
- All the historical sources agree that by the time he reached his late teens Arridaeus was widely considered mentally unfit to succeed his father. Displaying signs of military genius, Alexander was clearly a

more suitable successor and Philip had officially named him as heir. However, in 338 BC Philip divorced Olympias, and she and Alexander were forced to leave the court. Philip did not disinherit Alexander, but it may only have been a matter of time. It appears that Olympias' enemies argued that under supervision Arridaeus was still capable of becoming king. Diodorus accuses Olympias and Alexander of assuring Alexander's succession by orchestrating Philip's murder before he could proclaim Arridaeus his successor.

- Alexander must have been fond of his half-brother, as he did not have him killed as he did other potential claimants. Indeed, in 334 BC, when Alexander crossed the Dardanelles into what is now Turkey to begin the campaign against the Persian Empire, Arridaeus was invited to attend a special ceremony in the ancient city of Troy when Alexander and Hephaestion made sacrifices to the mythical heroes Achilles and Patroclus at the site of their shrines. What, however, were Arridaeus' feelings towards Alexander? Did he harbour a bitter resentment against his brother for depriving him of the throne and blocking his marriage plans? There are certainly reasonable grounds for suspicion.

- During Alexander's campaign Arridaeus remained behind in Macedonia and did not see his brother again for eleven years. When he finally did so it was when he arrived unexpectedly in Babylon and, just a few weeks later, Alexander fell ill and died.

6. BARSINE – THE GLORY YEARS

Alexander's relationship with Barsine must have been intense, as Arridaeus was not the only person to have been upset by it. Alexander's best friend Hephaestion found himself alienated by the affair and also left the king's side. He remains virtually unmentioned by all the historical sources for years, only reappearing at court after Alexander and Barsine eventually split up. There can be little doubt that Alexander had fallen madly in love. According to Plutarch, Barsine was the only woman he ever became romantically involved with outside of marriage.

> Alexander, esteeming it more kingly to govern himself than to conquer his enemies, sought no intimacy with any one of them [the women of Darius' court], nor indeed with any other women before marriage, except Barsine.[1]

Alexander appears to have had absolutely no interest in anyone else. In fact, Plutarch tells us, Alexander was not even tempted by the Persian queen who was supposedly 'the most beautiful princess then living'. When someone suggested that he should take Darius' wife, Alexander was not even curious to see her.

> He had not so much as seen or desired to see the wife of Darius, nor suffered anybody to speak of her beauty before him . . . Of the rest of the female captives, though remarkably handsome and well proportioned, he took no further notice . . .[2]

According to Plutarch, Alexander was so taken by Barsine that he had no interest in other sexual activities of *any* kind. Homosexual frivolities were considered acceptable diversions for Macedonian nobles, even married ones. However, when one of his officers seemed to think he might be interested in a couple of young slave-boys that were up for sale, Alexander was furious.

> When Philoxenus, his lieutenant on the sea coast, wrote to him to know if he would buy two young boys of great beauty, whom one Theodorus, a Tarentine, had to sell, he was greatly offended.[3]

Barsine appears to have been an outstanding woman. We know from Justinus' account that she was beautiful, and Plutarch praises her for being the ideal companion for Alexander.

> She had been instructed in the Greek learning, was of a gentle temper, and by her father, Artabazus, royally descended, with good qualities, added to the solicitations and encouragement of Parmenion, as Aristobulus tells us, made him the more willing to attach himself to so agreeable and illustrious a woman.[4]

How Alexander's overbearing and possessive mother felt about her son's relationship with Barsine goes unrecorded. She had known Barsine as a girl during her time at Philip's court, but now Olympias was at home in Macedonia and, as far as we know, the two women never met again. Nevertheless, we can make a fairly safe assumption that Olympias would have disapproved of her son's lover. To begin with, Barsine was seven years Alexander's senior and an older wife was considered improper in Macedonian tradition. Moreover, if Plutarch's description is anything to go by, Barsine had too much in common with Olympias' old rival Philinna for the two women ever to have got along. Although there is no direct evidence that Alexander's relationship with Barsine caused friction between him and his mother, he does seem to have fallen out with Olympias at exactly the time it began. Apparently, Alexander decided to give another woman the title of 'mother'. She was Ada, the queen of Caria in Asia Minor.

It was Alexander's policy to allow the native rulers of a conquered country to continue to govern, so long as they surrendered without a fight. This was a clever strategy as it meant that the local populace were likely to be more co-operative and consequently Alexander could avoid leaving behind large numbers of occupying troops. It also meant that future opponents would know that if they capitulated they would remain in power. If an enemy was unwilling to surrender, then Alexander would often seek an alliance with a native rival for their leadership and install them as ruler after his invasion. In the summer of 334 BC this is what happened in the Persian province of Caria, on the Mediterranean coast of Turkey. In 344 BC, Ada had become queen of Caria. (Although she was of Greek descent, her family had enjoyed semi-autonomous rule within the Persian Empire for some years.) However, in 340 BC the Persians had replaced her with her half-brother Pixodorus. When Alexander invaded Caria in 334 BC, Pixodorus refused to surrender and the siege of the capital of Halicarnassus claimed many

Macedonian lives. When Pixodorus was defeated, Alexander reinstated Ada as queen, although her army was placed under the command of a Macedonian general. While Alexander was in Caria, he and Ada became close friends and thereafter the pair continued to exchange letters. Moreover, shortly after the battle of Issus, Plutarch tells us, Alexander 'adopted her with the title of mother'.[5] The fact that Alexander made it known that he was now referring to the elderly queen of Caria as 'mother' can only be interpreted as a rejection of his real mother Olympias. Nothing else is recorded at this time that appears to have caused friction between Alexander and Olympias other than his relationship with Barsine.

There were also Macedonian nobles who disliked and distrusted Barsine and many of Alexander's officers considered her to be a dangerous enemy within their camp. Barsine's late husband Memnon had been the supreme commander of the Persian forces in Asia Minor; her father Artabazus was still one of Darius' generals and her brother Pharnabazus was in command of the Persian navy, which controlled the eastern Mediterranean. Pharnabazus' 300-ship fleet was the biggest problem Alexander's army faced, as it hindered the lines of supply from Greece. Its victories over the allied navies even incited a revolt by the Spartans that threatened to destabilise the entire Greek Peninsular. Alexander clearly had to consider such anti-Barsine sentiments, which is probably why he never married her. Nevertheless, nothing was going to persuade Alexander to give her up. As he continued southwards through Syria, Barsine remained close at his side.[6]

A few weeks after the battle of Issus, a messenger arrived at Alexander's camp with a letter from Darius, offering a huge ransom for his mother, wife and children. When Alexander refused to hand them over, the Persian king offered to give Alexander his entire empire west of the River Euphrates, which meant all of what are now Lebanon, Syria, Israel, Jordan, Egypt, and what remained of Turkey. Alexander again refused. His reply to Darius is still preserved in Arrian's account.

You tried to turn the Greeks against me and you sent aid to the Spartans . . . Your emissaries tried to corrupt my friends and end the peace which I made with the Greeks. I therefore fought against you as you started the quarrel and now I have defeated you on the battlefield . . . I now expect you to address me as king of Asia and when you write to me, do so not as an equal but as the ruler of all your lands. If you do not then I shall deal with you as an offender.

If you wish to be called king, then stand and fight me, or I will pursue you to wherever you may hide.[7]

Alexander's attitude may seem strange. Why did he not accept the offer and attack the rest of the Persian Empire at some later date? Alexander was probably playing safe. He not only needed the Greeks in his army, who would be more than a little concerned if Alexander made a deal with Darius, but he also needed the renegade troops from Asia Minor who had switched sides. Any deal with the Persian king might be seen as an act of betrayal. He needed replacements for his losses since his arrival in Asia, and he also needed to constantly leave men behind to keep control of the land he had already conquered. Alexander needed the Greeks and the collaborators, and an armistice with Darius, under any terms, would be sure to disaffect them.

Darius, for his part, may not have been as ineffectual as his offer makes him appear. He knew there was little to stop Alexander seizing all the possessions he offered him in any case. If his enemy did accept his deal, then the Persian king would have bought himself the time he needed to retrain his army along Macedonian lines. He had a few Greek mercenaries that employed the phalanx, but he would need the bulk of the infantry to adopt such formations if he was to stand a chance against Alexander. Training men for the phalanx took time, as Alexander's father had discovered, and Darius needed a couple of years of peace to get ready for a final confrontation. Alexander no doubt realised this too, which is another good reason for his rejecting the offer.

Another question debated by historians is why Alexander did not immediately pursue Darius into the heartland of his empire and completely defeat him before he had the chance to mobilise the few hundred thousand men he could still command. There were probably two main reasons for Alexander's decision to continue to systematically conquer the western Persian Empire. Firstly, he needed to neutralise the Persian fleet that hampered his supply lines. Secondly, if he attacked Darius in the east, with hostile Persian forces still intact in the west, he might find himself involved in a war on two fronts. Before doing anything else, Alexander would have to do something about Barsine's brother Pharnabazus and his navy.[8]

To the southeast of Syria lay Phoenicia, roughly what is now the Lebanon. For centuries the Phoenicians had been the world's greatest seafarers, and with their help the Persians had assembled a navy that was far superior to anything the Greeks or Macedonians could put to sea at the time. The men who built and sailed many of the Persian vessels were Phoenicians and the Phoenician port of Tyre was the home of the Persian Mediterranean fleet. If Alexander invaded Phoenicia and took the city of Tyre, then the Persian naval threat would be greatly reduced, if not eliminated. Most Phoenician towns surrendered as soon as Alexander approached. However, Tyre refused to come to terms and in January 332 BC the city was besieged. From the start, Alexander knew that it would be a difficult operation. Much of the city was built on an island, and it was surrounded by massive defensive walls. Furthermore, the Persians still controlled the sea and could continually bring new supplies. Tyre held out for almost six months, but in the end Phoenician ships from other coastal towns that had surrendered to Alexander changed sides and blockaded the city. In July, the walls were stormed and 6,000 defenders were cut down in street fighting. Only about 500 men on the Macedonian side lost their lives but, as was his usual policy when having to defeat an enemy by force, Alexander made an example of Tyre and 2,000 of its inhabitants were crucified on the beach.[9]

Much of Pharnabazus' fleet was still at sea and could have continued to be a thorn in Alexander's side. However, once they learned the fate of Tyre, Pharnabazus' Phoenician sailors and 200 of their ships deserted and returned home. What remained of the Persian Mediterranean fleet was defeated by the Macedonian navy and Pharnabazus was taken captive and sent on to Alexander in Phoenicia. What happened to him next is something of a mystery. Some of the historical sources say that he escaped by jumping ship when it stopped at the Greek island of Cos for supplies, while others say that Barsine persuaded Alexander to show her brother leniency when he arrived in Tyre.[10] The latter seems more likely as Pharnabazus is known to have switched sides: he is later recorded as serving as an officer in Alexander's army. If this is correct then it is yet another example of the tremendous influence Barsine had over her lover, who would usually have made an example of a Persian leader who had caused him so much trouble.

By the end of summer 323 BC the allied navy ruled the waves and it was easy to resupply the army, making it ready for its next objective, the city of Gaza, 300 kilometres south along the Mediterranean coast. Gaza was situated in an immensely important strategic location, controlling the narrow fertile strip of land that linked Asia to Africa. If Gaza fell to Alexander then Egypt would be his for the taking. The Persian king therefore sent orders that the city should hold out at all costs – something that it appeared to be in a position to do. Gaza stood on a hill eighty metres high and Alexander's engineers doubted that it could be taken; it was just too difficult to manoeuvre the siege engines into position. However, Aristobulus, Alexander's chief engineer, came up with a plan to dig tunnels under the walls and undermine the foundations. The ambitious plan took time but it eventually succeeded and, after a siege lasting almost four months, the walls were breached and the city was stormed. True to his usual policy, Alexander punished the resisting city, but this time the reprisals went much further than anything he had done before. Every adult male in the city was killed, and the Persian governor, Batis, was tortured to death in front of the survivors. According to the Roman historian Curtius:

> Batis was dragged before Alexander, who was ecstatic and filled with satisfaction but intended to severely punish his enemy, even though he usually admired the courage of an enemy. 'I will not grant you a noble death,' he said. 'Rather, you will suffer whatever torment I shall devise for you.' . . . While he still lived, Batis was tied to a chariot and dragged around the city while the king revelled in his pain.[11]

As Curtius points out, the severe and savage treatment of Gaza and its leader was untypical of Alexander at this time. Indeed, historians have criticised it as unnecessarily barbaric. However, Alexander may not have been as purely sadistic as Curtius suggests: he may have considered his actions expedient. He was certainly ruthless when the occasion called for it and this may have been such an occasion.

Alexander was about to march into Egypt, a country that was highly respected by the Greeks and Macedonians. Egypt's ancient culture was revered and Alexander wanted to take the country and its capital of Memphis intact. The Egyptians had suffered harsh Persian rule for eleven years and Alexander knew that there would be little local resistance if the Persian occupiers surrendered. The best way of assuring that the Persians would surrender without a fight was to make a spectacular example of a nearby town. The savage treatment of Batis may also have had additional propaganda value. In Homer's *Iliad* the Greek hero Achilles had defiled the body of his enemy Hector in a similar way. By emulating his legendary ancestor, Alexander may once again have been reinforcing for his troops the idea that he was a reborn and invincible Achilles.

Barsine had been with Alexander to watch the entire brutal spectacle. How it affected her is unknown, but she must have been appalled. Not only were many of the victims her own countrymen, but Batis also had been, like her own father, a provincial Persian governor. Nonetheless, her love for Alexander appears to have been unremitting as she happily accompanied him on what turned out to be a virtual six-month vacation.

In December 332 BC, as his army prepared to advance into Egypt, Alexander appears to have taken time off to visit the city of Jerusalem, eighty kilometres northeast of Gaza. Jerusalem was the capital of the Jewish kingdom of Judah, which had been under Persian rule for two centuries. Judah surrendered without a fight and Jewish mercenaries immediately joined Alexander's army to accompany him on the Egyptian campaign. There was no tactical reason for Alexander's detour to Jerusalem; he appears simply to have been intrigued to visit the famous city. In his work, *Jewish Antiquities*, the Jewish historian Josephus, who lived in the first century AD, wrote that Alexander was instantly captivated by Judaism.

> When Alexander had taken Gaza, he came to Jerusalem . . . And when Jaddus [the Jewish high priest] heard that Alexander was coming, he led a procession of priests and a multitude of citizens to greet him . . . When Alexander saw the procession and the high priest's golden breastplate on which the name of God was written, he approached by himself, saluted the high priest and adored that name . . . However, Parmenion alone went up to him [Alexander], and asked why he should adore the high priest of the Jews? 'I did not adore him,' replied Alexander, 'but the God whom the high priest served, for I know that that he watches over my army and will give me dominion over the Persians I believe that with this army under his divine conduct, I shall conquer Darius and destroy the power of Persia.' And when he arrived at the [Jerusalem] temple, he offered sacrifice to God, according to the high-priest's instructions.[12]

The single, universal God of the Jews was a theological concept that would have been completely alien to Macedonians, yet, if Josephus is right, Alexander was impressed by the Jewish religion, its splendid temple and its deity. In fact, Alexander believed that the God of Israel had personally chosen him to conquer the Persians. This is the first we hear of Alexander's religious motivations. Before this time he seems to have been a pragmatic, hard-nosed realist with little time for religious or mystical concepts of any kind. He pandered to the notions that he was a reincarnated Achilles, and may even have believed it himself, but he seems to have paid little more than lip service to gods. A profound change in Alexander's thinking seems to have occurred in Jerusalem: a new conviction that he had been divinely chosen for his role as world conqueror. It may have begun as a convenient political device, but before long Alexander clearly began to believe it himself. In fact, he soon began to claim that he was the son of the world's supreme deity. However, this was not the one God that the Jews believed in, Alexander decided, but the Greek god Zeus.

In December Alexander led his army into Egypt, where the Persian governor Mazaces surrendered without resistance. News of the fate of Gaza had struck terror into Persian hearts, and Mazaces knew that, with the Mediterranean and the Gaza Strip now under Macedonian control, there was no hope of reinforcements from Darius. On their own, the Persian forces in Egypt would stand little chance in a fight. By the end of the year Alexander had swung south to the Egyptian capital of Memphis, where he was not only welcomed as a liberator but also was proclaimed pharaoh by the grateful Egyptians. Immediately after he moved on north, past the pyramids of Giza.[13]

On his journey of conquest, Alexander had now visited three of what were to become known as the Seven Wonders of the World: the huge temple at Ephesus in Lydia, where omens of Alexander's future greatness were said to have occurred on the day he was born; the massive tomb of King Mausollos (from which we get the word mausoleum) in Caria, the province ruled by Queen Ada, Alexander's honorary mother; and now the great pyramids, monuments to the mighty pharaohs of Egypt, of which Alexander was now one. The wonders of the ancient world seemed to play a strange, fated role in Alexander's life. When he reached the coast at the western mouth of the Nile in January 321 BC, he decided to found the city of Alexandria, which he modestly named after himself.[14] Following Alexander's death, Ptolemy, his successor in Egypt, built a towering lighthouse in the city's harbour, which itself became one of the Seven Wonders. Of the three others, the Colossus of Rhodes (an immense bronze statute of the god Helios on the island of Rhodes) was not built for another sixty years, but the final two seemed to be almost linked to Alexander's life by destiny. The Hanging Gardens of Babylon was probably the splendid palace where Alexander eventually died, and the last of the wonders was of tremendous symbolic significance. This was a gigantic statue of the god Zeus that stood in a temple in the Greek town of Olympia. Not only was Alexander's real mother, Olympias, named after the town, but also he was to adopt the mythical Zeus as his heavenly father.

If Josephus is right, then Alexander had already begun to think that he had been divinely chosen for conquest when he visited Jerusalem.

Here, for the first time, he directly encountered a religion that taught that there was only one god. For a man who had designs on world conquest, the notion of a single, universal deity would have had appeal. Until this time, Alexander had been invading regions that had ties to the Greek world and many of the inhabitants had Greek ancestry and were also familiar with Greek mythology. Alexander's claim – that he was the new Achilles on a campaign of liberation – appealed to these people who had long lived under Persian rule.

However, once he had moved on from Syria, Alexander was in areas where Greek mythology had no significance. Alexander had previously enjoyed the support of large sections of the local population who were happy to become a part of his empire. From now on, Alexander realised that he would not only have to win wars, but he would also have to win the peace. If he wanted to go on to further conquests, with his relatively small army, he could not afford to tie up thousands of troops to keep control of the ground he had already seized. New provinces of the Persian Empire might indeed welcome him as a liberator from a harsh regime, but it would not be long before the Greeks and Macedonians were themselves considered the enemy occupiers – just as the Americans discovered in modern Iraq. One way in which Alexander could avoid unnecessary conflict was by a policy of religious and cultural tolerance; even more so if he could portray himself as a divinely chosen liberator. The problem was that only the Jews believed in a single, universal god. If the entire world had been monotheistic, then he could have continued with the notion that he was chosen by this one god. However, in Egypt, Alexander conceived a clever variation of this theme; that the supreme deity of every religion was the same god under another name, and he, Alexander, was not only chosen by, but was also the son of that god.

The Greeks already considered that many gods of foreign cultures were actually their own deities under different names. As such, the supreme Egyptian god Amun-Ra, which the Greeks called Ammon, was thought to be one and the same as their own father of the gods, Zeus. It was when the Egyptians proclaimed Alexander their pharaoh that the idea that he was the earthly son of Zeus appears to have first occurred to him. In Egyptian belief, the pharaoh was the incarnation of Horus, the divine son of Amun-Ra.

Greek mythology had an equivalent in the mythical hero Heracles. Hercules, as he is better known, had an earthly mother but his father was Zeus. If the Egyptians were happy to believe that Alexander was the personification of Horus, then perhaps the Greeks would accept that he was a reincarnated Hercules. Indeed, if Plutarch is right, then Olympias had already claimed that Alexander was a spiritual son of Zeus because of the dream she had at the time he was conceived. Alexander was as quick to recognise the importance of cultural propaganda as he was to seize a military initiative, and began to take this idea much further. If he was to continue his war against the Persian Empire, then he would soon be fighting in the Persian homeland where the supreme god was Oromasdes. This god also had an equivalent of Horus and Hercules: the divine Mithra, the son of Oromasdes who, in Persian mythology, aided his father in the struggle against the forces of darkness on earth. If Alexander could portray himself in a multicultural way, as the son of the supreme god of the region in whatever country he invaded, then his mission of conquest could be depicted as something of a holy crusade that might appeal to many oppressed peoples.

It is not known quite how the idea crystallised or, for that matter, if he actually believed it himself at this point, but it may have come in part from Barsine. Having been raised and educated in Macedonia, she was as familiar with Greek civilisation as she was with her own native Persian culture. She was not only Alexander's concubine, but also appears to have become his interpreter and adviser on Persian affairs. According to the *Historia*, when the army was in Alexandria in January 331 BC, Alexander became involved in an argument with his senior officers over what he planned to do next.

He disputed with his generals, even losing his temper with Parmenion when he questioned him concerning the wisdom of putting such store in the words of his foreign mistress.

This 'foreign mistress' is not named, but there is no one recorded at this time that it could have been other than Barsine. If Plutarch is right, then Alexander had no interest in any of the other foreign women who could be referred to as a mistress.[15]

The matter in dispute was Alexander's decision to spend the winter on an expedition far into the desert of what is now Libya, to visit the shrine of the chief oracle of the Egyptian god Ammon. According to Arrian:

At this point Alexander held a desire to visit the temple of Ammon; his wish was to consult the god, as the oracle was said to tell the truth and it was believed that Heracles had once consulted the oracle in his time.[16]

The shrine was far out in the desert, some kilometres west of Memphis in an oasis now called Siwa. If the *Historia* is right then it seems that Barsine had advised him to go there and consult the oracle, and Justinus explains why.

> He then went to the temple of Ammon, to consult the oracle about the event of his future proceedings, and his own parentage.[17]

According to Justinus, there existed a rumour that Alexander was not the true son of Philip. In fact, he was said to be the son of a demon.

> For his mother Olympias had confessed to her husband Philip, that she had conceived Alexander, not by him, but by a serpent of extraordinary size. Philip, too, towards the end of his life, had publicly declared that Alexander was not his son; and he accordingly divorced Olympias, as having been guilty of adultery.[18]

This seems to have been gossip put around by Philip in 337 BC, as both an excuse to divorce his meddling wife and as a reason to disinherit Alexander. However, Alexander now cleverly manipulated this same rumour to his own advantage. Evil spirits were often believed to appear as serpents but, according to Greek mythology, the god Zeus also assumed the guise of a snake to have intercourse with the goddess Persephone. Alexander was now so powerful that it no longer mattered whether he was Philip's son or not. Nonetheless, he could use this same familiar rumour to signify that he was, like Hercules, the incarnate son of Zeus.

The Greeks were already familiar with the oracle of Ammon and considered the priest to speak with the voice of Zeus. They were also well aware of the tradition that Hercules had consulted this oracle (or, at least, one of his predecessors). A visit to the oracle was an opportunity Alexander could not resist. As he was now Egypt's pharaoh, he could have been fairly sure that the oracle would endorse him as the incarnate Horus. Accordingly, in Greek eyes, he would be officially recognised as their equivalent, Hercules. If this was Barsine's idea, then it would certainly validate Plutarch's opinion that she was a bright and clever woman. With two separate cultures having sanctioned him as the son of a supreme god, it would set a precedent for his forthcoming campaign into the Persian homeland. Those who wished to see the Persian king Darius deposed would have a ready-made pretext in accepting Alexander as a personified Mithra.

The month-long journey across the Sahara to Siwa was arduous, but well worth it. According to Justinus, everything worked out just as Alexander hoped:

The priests, as soon as he entered the temple, saluted him as the son of Ammon. Alexander, pleased with the god's adoption of him, directed that he should be regarded as his son ... On putting a third question, he was told that success in all his wars, and dominion over the world, was granted him. A response was also given by the oracle to his attendants, that they should reverence Alexander as a god, and not as a king.[19]

From all accounts, the Greeks and Macedonians in Alexander's army both accepted that he was Hercules reborn. The new line was that Alexander was the descendant of Achilles, and endowed with his valour, but was in actuality Hercules himself. However, not everyone was happy with Alexander's new role as the son of a god. Once he returned to the Egyptian capital of Memphis in March 331 BC, he learned that the Jews in the city of Samaria had denounced him as a pagan idolater and had revolted. His six-month vacation was over.

The rebellion in Samaria was quickly suppressed in May 331 BC, and Alexander returned to the city of Tyre in Phoenicia. However, here he received disturbing news: Darius was assembling a massive new army, 750 kilometres to the northeast, at Arbela in what is now northern Iraq. His intelligence reliably informed him that Darius intended to retake his western empire with a force of almost 200,000 men. The Macedonian-led army may have been the best and most highly trained in the world, but there was no way that it could hope to survive such an onslaught. As far as many of Alexander's officers were concerned, their only hope was to return home. However, Alexander had other plans. He waited until the middle of the summer while a contingent of 15,000 new troops arrived as reinforcement from Macedonia, and by the end of July he had an army consisting of some 40,000 infantry, 7,000 cavalry and around 2,000 supply wagons. Nevertheless, Darius still had around four times this number, and was preparing to advance west from Arbela. Any other commander would either have retreated or, at the very least, dug in around Tyre and assumed a strong, defensive position. Alexander, however, decided to attack.[20]

Alexander knew that the Persian army was not yet fully prepared and would also be taken by surprise. Nevertheless, most of his generals regarded the entire enterprise as suicide. It was not only that Alexander intended to take on a vastly superior force; he would also be fighting in unfamiliar territory. Until then, the Greeks and Macedonians had been fighting in the Mediterranean world that they knew well. Also, the war in Asia Minor, Phoenicia and Syria had been considered a defensive war, meant to put an end to Persian occupation of the area and eliminate the dominance of the Persian navy, both of which were real threats to Alexander's empire in Europe. Once his army moved east and crossed the River Euphrates in August 331 BC, however, it was very much in unknown territory: moreover, it was on the offensive into the Persian homeland. It was now that Barsine may have become invaluable to Alexander as his adviser on Persian affairs and, perhaps, even as the instigator of a line of intelligence that led to her lover's greatest victory.

When he took on Darius' huge army, Alexander knew precisely what he faced. He not only knew troop positions, but was also aware of the strategic strengths and weaknesses of the entire force. Diodorus informs us that he had intelligence from the Persian camp, but the names of those involved in this spy network are not revealed. However, the information must have been supplied by someone very high up in the enemy command, and the most likely source was Barsine's father Artabazus. He was one of Darius' most senior generals and privy to all the Persian plans. Artabazus had to have been of help to the Macedonians, for when Darius was eventually defeated Alexander not only spared his life, but also appointed him as supreme commander of his entire rearguard. Artabazus had to have done something impressive for Alexander to have trusted him in this way. The only conclusion that can reasonably be reached is that he had been the high-level informer that gave Alexander the vital edge to overcome seemingly impossible odds.

If Artabazus was Alexander's superspy, then someone had to have been the go-between, and the most likely person to have played that role was his son, Barsine's brother Pharnabazus. It is something of a mystery why there are two separate accounts of Pharnabazus' fate after the defeat of his Mediterranean fleet. The fact that one story tells that he escaped and the other that he was shown clemency by Alexander could be explained by the fact that both were accurate renderings of contemporary accounts. We know for certain that after the defeat of the Persians Pharnabazus also fought for Alexander and was placed in charge of a cavalry division. Like his father, he must have been of use to Alexander during the earlier campaign. It is therefore possible that, following his navy's defeat, he was taken to Alexander at Tyre as some sources contend, but switched sides. The story that he escaped in Cos may have been falsely circulated so that he could be safely returned to the Persian side. If this scenario is correct, then Alexander had Barsine to thank. It was she who had persuaded Alexander to let her brother live. She would have needed to give Alexander a pretty convincing reason to spare his life: what better reason than turning him as a spy to infiltrate the enemy command.

On 1 October the two armies finally met at Arbela. It had been reported to Darius that Alexander was approaching and the Persian king could not believe his luck. The Macedonians and their allies were not only marching right into the clutches of his huge army but also on to his chosen battleground. It seemed that he would not have to fight a war to regain his western empire after all: he could simply stand his ground and cut down Alexander's army where he was.

However, Darius had not taken into account Alexander's extraordinary ability to outthink his opponent. Judging by Diodorus' graphic account of the battle, Alexander seems to have lulled Darius into a false sense of security by seeming to be following precisely the same plan he had used at Issus.[21] At Issus, Alexander led his cavalry to one wing of the Persian army and Darius had been fooled into thinking he was being outflanked. When the Persian infantry moved to face the Macedonian cavalry, a gap was created in their lines which Alexander immediately moved towards, forcing a wedge that divided the enemy forces. Simultaneously, the Macedonian infantry made a frontal and devastating attack on the Persian centre.[22] Darius was not going to fall for the same trick twice. This time, when Alexander made his move, Darius stood firm and deployed a mass chariot attack on the Macedonian infantry. These huge chariots with scythes attached to the wheels were the tanks of their day and on flat ground, such as Darius had chosen, they could plough through an enemy's ranks and tear them to shreds. These were followed close behind by the Persian cavalry, which was intended to ride through into the broken lines of the phalanx and wreak havoc. According to Diodorus, this was exactly what Alexander expected him to do and he had prepared an ingenious countermeasure.

> The chariots attacked at full gallop causing great terror in the Macedonian ranks . . . However, as the king [Alexander] commanded, the phalanx beat upon their shields with their spears making such a great noise that it frightened the enemy horses which turned about and charged back into their own ranks . . . Such was the terrible injuries of the scythes as they cut the Persians to pieces, sending men to the ground and their severed heads tumbling with their eyes still open and their faces frozen in fear.[23]

The Persian cavalry were thus thrown into turmoil and those riders that reached the Macedonian lines found themselves impaled on the long spears of the enemy phalanx. With the centre of the Persian infantry forced to divide by their stampeding chariots and retreating cavalry, Alexander's own cavalry charged into the breach and his phalanx advanced. Once again, the Macedonian infantry were able to repeat the mass slaughter it had inflicted at Issus. Although heavy, bloody fighting continued throughout the day, Alexander had gained complete control of events and the Persians were utterly defeated. The 200,000-strong enemy force was decimated and the survivors fled in disarray. Remarkably, Alexander lost less than 5,000 men. The battle of Arbela was not only Alexander's greatest battle; it is also considered to be one of the most decisive battles in the history of warfare.

Once again, Darius fled the battlefield and escaped with his life but, for all intents and purposes, the huge Persian army was completely defeated and the heart of the Persian Empire was exposed. After looting the Persian camp and plundering the town of Arbela, the Macedonian army moved on into Babylonia where, just three weeks later, the provincial capital of Babylon, almost 500 kilometres to the south, surrendered without a fight. True to his renowned policy, Alexander spared the city and allowed the Persian commander Mazaeus to remain as governor.[24] Two months after that, the first of the cities in Persia itself was in Alexander's hands. This was Susa (modern Shush), some 250 kilometres east of Babylon. It too was taken unopposed and its commander, Abulites, was permitted to remain in power.[25]

It was in the city of Susa that Alexander eventually decided that he would leave behind the members of the Persian royal family he had captured after the battle of Issus. Darius' queen had died in childbirth some months before and his young son also died around the same time. Diodorus tells us that Darius' mother and his two young daughters, Statira and Drypetis, remained in Susa to be brought up with a Greek education as Macedonian-style princesses.[26] Almost immediately, Alexander moved on to Persepolis, the capital of the entire Persian Empire, 600 kilometres to the southeast. Alexander's march from Arbela into the heart of the Persian Empire had been virtually unopposed, but at Persepolis he encountered his first serious resistance. The Persian defenders managed to hold a line to the north of the city for ten days, but on 30 January 330 BC Alexander captured the city, ordered it sacked as a reprisal and stood in the palace of Darius' capital. Darius, however, was nowhere to be seen. He was 700 kilometres to the northwest in the Persian city of Ecbatana, attempting to assemble a new army.[27]

Alexander stayed in Persepolis for four months, from where he invited the Persian nobles still loyal to Darius to capitulate. Some did, but the majority refused. Even though the war was far from over, Alexander proclaimed himself the king of Persia. By June, Alexander reached Ecbatana, modern Hamadan in northern Iran, hoping for a final showdown with the true Persian king. However, when he arrived he discovered that Darius and his new army had moved east into the huge province of Bactria. However, in mid-July Alexander received the news that Darius had been killed by his own men, and his second-in-command, Bessus, had proclaimed himself king and decided to continue the war.

According to Arrian, with Darius dead, Barsine's father and her brothers immediately came over to Alexander's side:

> Bessus gained the support of the Bactrian cavalry and all the Persians who had been with Darius accepted him as their king, except Artabazus and his sons . . . They were unable to prevent what had occurred but refused to take part. Instead, they made their way across country and offered themselves and their men to Alexander.[28]

This passage reinforces the theory that Artabazus had been Alexander's chief informer in Darius' camp. Not only did Alexander so trust him that he made him commander of his rearguard, but also Artabazus immediately defected to the Macedonian side once Darius was dead, rather than fight on with Bessus. Furthermore, it shows that Barsine's brother Pharnabazus was with him to have acted as the go-between, as he is later identified as one of the sons mentioned by Arrian.

The war with Bessus dragged on for two more years, in the hostile desert and mountainous territory of Afghanistan. None of the historical sources refers to Barsine again until the end of the campaign, but she and Alexander must have continued as lovers as in the summer of 327 BC, in hill country to the north of Afghanistan, she gave birth to Alexander's son whom he named Heracles. However, within a few weeks of the birth, Alexander met and fell madly in love with the sixteen-year-old Roxanne. For Barsine, now 36, it was bad enough that her lover had fallen for a girl twenty years her junior, but what he did next was to add intolerable insult to injury. Alexander immediately married Roxanne and made her his queen. For six long years, Barsine had been at Alexander's side. She had loved him, been his invaluable aid and had given him a son. Now that his war with Persia was over and its empire was his, Barsine might have expected that he would finally marry her and make her queen. Instead, he married a girl who was virtually a child after just a few weeks of knowing her.

Completely besotted by Roxanne, Alexander seems to have totally ignored Barsine and her child. Whether Alexander forced her to go is unrecorded, but a few days after the marriage Barsine left with her son and returned home to Pergamum in Asia Minor, where she remained for the next four years. She did not see Alexander again until the early summer of 323 BC, when he summoned her to Babylon so that he could see his child. Barsine arrived at court in late June, and just a few days later she was present at Alexander's last feast.[29] If it was Barsine who poisoned Alexander, then she had a double motive for the murder. Not only had she been humiliated before the world by being jilted for a slip of a girl, but also her son was still Alexander's only male child and so the nearest thing to an heir should he die.

Barsine and her child left the court to return home and did not see Alexander again until a few weeks before he died. His campaign over, he had summoned her to Babylon so that he could see his four-year-old son for the first time in years. As his only son, Heracles was still the closest thing he had to an heir. However, Alexander now had two official wives and either of them could bear the king a more legitimate successor at any time. As it might prove to be years before Barsine would be so close to Alexander again, had she seized the opportunity to take both revenge on her former lover and secure the throne for her child?

Considering that he continually faced the prospect of death, it may seem strange that Alexander had still not named any kind of successor. He was probably playing safe: once he named an heir then this person or his supporters might be inclined to kill him. Paradoxically, if Barsine murdered Alexander in the hope that her son could fill the gap, then his caution backfired. In fact, the open question of succession also gave Alexander's most powerful officer, Seleucus, his motive to assassinate the king. Seleucus was of humble origins, so would stand no chance of being chosen as Alexander's successor. However, in June 323 BC, he was better placed than anyone else in the entire empire to seize control if Alexander were to die. The feared Seleucus, commander of the elite shield bearers, is the next suspect on our list.

SUMMARY OF CHAPTER SIX
Barsine was Alexander's lover for six years and bore him his first child. By June 323 BC, however, she was a neglected woman with every reason to despise Alexander for jilting her for a girl less than half her age.

- In November 333 BC, the 24-year-old Alexander had already conquered much of what is now Turkey. With an army of 30,000 men, at the battle of Issus, he defeated a Persian force twice that size. The Persian king Darius III had fled but his family were captured, as also was Barsine, the daughter of the governor of Asia Minor.

- Although she was a widow, eight years his senior, with a daughter ten years old, Alexander seems to have fallen immediately in love with Barsine, and for the next few years she remained his concubine. The relationship must have been intense because it seems to have alienated Alexander's best friend Hephaestion. Almost immediately, he left his king's side and remains virtually unmentioned by all the historical sources for years.

- In 332 BC, Alexander's army pushed on south through Syria and Gaza and by the end of the year they entered Egypt where the Persian governor surrendered without a fight. The Egyptians had suffered harsh Persian rule for eleven years and not only welcomed Alexander as a liberator, but also proclaimed him pharaoh. Barsine spent the winter in Egypt, accompanying Alexander on an expedition to Siwa, in the Libyan desert, to visit the shrine of the god Ammon. Here the king consulted an oracle who told him that he was the son of the god and that he would conquer the world.

- Barsine would remain Alexander's concubine for four more years, but the indications are that her lover's obsession with warfare and conquest was to drive them apart. By the summer of 330 BC, Alexander had defeated what remained of Darius' army and the Persian king was dead. However, he decided to move on and conquer the huge eastern province of Bactria.

- Barsine must have rekindled the relationship with Alexander as in 327 BC she bore him a child. However, no sooner was the boy Heracles born than Alexander met the much younger Roxanne. The king paid Roxanne the honour he had always denied Barsine by marrying her and making her his queen.

7. SELEUCUS – THE HARSH CAMPAIGN

By the summer of 330 BC, Alexander had conquered the entire western half of the Persian Empire and also its heartland. He held all of what are now Syria, the Lebanon, Israel, Palestine, Egypt, Iraq, most of Turkey and western Iran; yet the eastern Persian Empire that still remained was as large as all these countries put together. Known as Bactria, this huge area included modern Afghanistan, Turkmenistan, southern Tajikistan, and even part of what is now Pakistan. Alexander had desperately hoped that the governors – or satraps as they were known – of the Bactrian provinces would lay down their arms once Darius was dead. Bactria was a huge region to conquer, and Alexander realised that taking it by force would involve a campaign in unfamiliar desert and mountainous terrain. In fact, he would end up having to fight a protracted guerrilla war.

The satrap of Bactria was the most important man in the Persian Empire after the king. Usually he would be the next in line to the throne: the king's eldest son if he were old enough. Darius' only son, however, had been still a child, but by the summer of 330 BC he was dead. Bessus, the man who ruled in Bactria at the time Darius fled into the area, was therefore the king's chosen successor. Darius was to bitterly regret his choice of heir, as Bessus immediately had him arrested.[1]

Bessus did not intend to kill Darius himself – he wanted Alexander to do that for him. He no doubt had a variety of reasons for deposing the king; not least the fact that he would assume control of what remained of the empire. However, he also thought that, if he delivered the king into Alexander's hands, it would mean the end of the war. It seemed unlikely to Bessus that the Macedonians would be interested in the remote provinces of Bactria, in which they would be forced to fight a war of a completely unfamiliar type. Bessus had seized what he considered to be an ideal opportunity to become supreme Bactrian ruler. Few Persians still had faith in Darius. He had not only lost two crucial battles he should seemingly have won, but also he had twice fled like a coward from the battlefield. When Darius arrived in the province of Parthia, in the far north of Iran, to find himself under arrest, what remained of his army had no hesitation offering their allegiance to Bessus.[2]

When Alexander reached Ecbatana to discover that Darius and his army had moved east, he immediately followed with his cavalry. Once he was inside Parthia, however, he was met by a delegation from Bessus who told him that Darius was under arrest and would be handed over if Alexander would negotiate peace.[3] This presented Alexander with an awkward dilemma. If he accepted Bessus' offer, he would not only be accepting the independence of the eastern half of the empire, but also he would have to decide on Darius' fate. If Alexander wanted to securely rule the empire he had already seized, there was no way he could allow Bactria to remain independent. Not only would the area be a constant threat to stability in the west, but also it could offer support and a safe haven for Persian resistance. If he accepted the deal and then went back on it, he would lose his reputation for always keeping his word, something that had been an immensely effective propaganda tool in winning the peace in the regions he had already conquered. As for the fate of Darius, if Alexander had him executed then he would be guilty of regicide and the Persian aristocracy would never accept him as their king. Alternatively, if he let him live, then Darius would always be a rallying flag for opposition. It would be far better if the Persian king were killed in battle. On the other hand, if he refused the offer, then he knew that Bessus would no doubt kill Darius himself, take control and continue the war – a war in the kind of hostile terrain that even the twentieth-century army of the mighty Soviet Union found impossible to triumph in. It would be better that a Persian killed Darius than a Macedonian.

In the end, Alexander decided not to negotiate. If Bessus killed Darius, then Alexander could muster support from the Persians in his own territories in a crusade against the murderer of their king. What he most desired, however, was that forces loyal to Darius in the east would refuse to follow Bessus and further war could be avoided. Unfortunately, this was too much to hope for. Alexander relished the kind of campaign he had fought so far, but from now on it would be a different kind of warfare, about which he had little experience. The invincible Macedonian phalanx and his mass cavalry formations would be useless in the mountains of the east. Alexander had to act quickly if he was going to catch the Persian forces in the open. Accordingly, he did not give Bessus a chance to even start negotiating; he immediately deployed a force of light infantry to engage the Persians, going on ahead himself with a cavalry division.[4]

Bactria's main army was far to the east, but Bessus and a contingent of his cavalry were leading the remnants of Darius' army on a hasty retreat into the mountains, with the Persian king tied up in a wagon. Arrian describes what happened next, somewhere in the region of what is now Dâmghân.

Alexander came upon the Persians at daybreak. Their numbers were small and many fled the moment they saw that it was the king himself who led the pursuers. Some attempted to fight but ran away after losing only a few men. Bessus and his escort of six hundred horsemen tried to get Darius away in the wagon in which he was held, but when Alexander's soldiers were close Nabarzanes and Barsaentes [two of Bessus' officers] struck him down and escaped. The wounds which Darius received were fatal blows and he died before Alexander could see him.[5]

With Bessus' escape, Alexander knew that there was no choice now but to fight what would be a long and harsh campaign.

Bessus may not have had an army that could hope to take on Alexander's forces in open country, in a conventional battle, but his power was based on swift mounted archers who could strike anywhere and at any time. As the United States was to discover in Vietnam, guerrilla warfare has no front lines. Alexander's forces could be continually whittled down and supply lines disrupted by small bands of warriors who could strike, wreak havoc and disappear into the mountains. The army that followed Alexander further into Bactria would have to get used to hard living, continual harassment and extreme climatic conditions: all the circumstances in which mutinies occur. To make matters more unpredictable, large parts of Alexander's 40,000-strong army were no longer just Greeks and Macedonians. Among the increasingly multinational army, he had Egyptians, Syrians and Babylonians fighting with him. Many of these foreign troops had fought to destroy Darius' empire and, with Darius dead and their prime objective achieved, it was going to be difficult to stop them deserting in the gruelling months ahead. Moreover, Alexander even had around 6,000 Persians who had joined him when Barsine's father Artabazus had switched sides. After he had taken Persepolis, assuming that the war was over, Alexander had sent home about the same number of battle-weary Macedonian troops. He now needed every man he could get, and he needed something to make sure that they remained firmly under his control. This was to be his elite shield bearers, of which Seleucus was second-in-command.[6]

The shield bearers – or Hypaspistes as they were called – were a small but highly trained contingent of heavily armed infantry who had once been the Macedonian royal guard, deployed to protect the king in battle. Unlike most infantry who were mainly spearmen, they were expert swordsmen and even archers. During the reign of Alexander's father

Philip, they had been given the additional role of maintaining discipline in the ranks and became the world's first military police force. Now, however, Alexander decided that he would greatly extend their powers. He doubled their number to around 6,000 men and used them to instil terror into both the enemy and his own troops. The Hypaspistes traditionally only admitted Greeks and Macedonians into their ranks, and this was to remain unchanged. If they were required to suppress revolt in a foreign contingent, then Alexander needed to know that their loyalties lay with Europe. Their officers had always enjoyed a privileged position in the Macedonian army, but now Alexander gave them complete autonomy. Even a general in the regular forces would have to think twice before giving orders to a junior officer of the Hypaspistes. The Hypaspistes were now not only the best trained, the best supplied and most loyal of Alexander's troops, but they were also the most feared. They were an army within an army; the nearest equivalent in modern times would be the Nazi SS. Like the SS, the Hypaspistes were divided into crack terror troops, an elite guard and a political police unit. The Hypaspistes secret police, not dissimilar to the Gestapo, organised a network of informers and spies that worked inside the regular army to alert Alexander to the merest whisper of dissatisfaction. In fact, it is no coincidence that the Hypaspistes were so similar to the SS; Hitler himself admitted that he got the idea from Alexander the Great.[7]

In the later summer of 330 BC, when the Hypaspistes were reorganised, their commander was the general Parmenion's son Nicanor; Seleucus was his deputy. Nothing is known of Seleucus before this time other than he was a Greek, about the same age as Alexander, who had risen through the ranks from the position of common soldier. Officers in Alexander's army were usually from rich, aristocratic families and field promotions from the ranks were rare. For Seleucus to have gained a commission in the Hypaspistes means that he must have been an exceptional warrior. He was certainly ambitious and ruthlessly cunning, as Nicanor was soon to find out.[8]

Before advancing east into the heart of Bactria, Alexander first needed to ensure that his rear was safe. It was essential to keep open the lines of supply, as the army would be entering terrain where it would be difficult to live off the land. To ensure this, in August, Alexander sent two battalions into the mountains of Hyrcania, in what is now Turkmenistan, to the north of Iran, to occupy the area and prevent it being used as a base for tribal raiding parties loyal to Bessus. Once the region was secure, Alexander left Parmenion behind in Ecbatana to control the road from the Mediterranean to the East and led his main army southeast into Afghanistan, to a city the Macedonians called Prophthasia (modern Farâh).[9] It was here, in December, that Seleucus first made his name.

The Bactrian capital of Bactra (Balkh, near modern Mazâr-e Sharîf) lay almost 700 kilometres to the northwest of Prophthasia, and it was here that Bessus and his main force were preparing for Alexander's attack. The only logical way that Alexander's army could advance towards Bactra was the direct and easiest route via the Farâh Rud valley. Alexander, though, had another, far more ambitious plan. Bactra was famously well defended by huge, ancient walls. Also, it lay at the end of a canyon where Alexander's forces could be repeatedly ambushed and cut down by enemy archers as they advanced. The only hope of taking the city was by a surprise attack. The Hindu Kush Mountains ran southwest through central Afghanistan and Bactra was situated on the northern side. Directly across the mountains, some 250 kilometres to the southeast, was the town of Charika, near what is now Kabul. Alexander decided that he would lead his army here and make what appeared to be an impossible crossing of the mountains to Bactra and launch a sneak attack. The plan was ambitious, but it had two potentially fatal liabilities. Firstly, crossing the frozen and perilous Hindu Kush Mountains would subject his troops to the most gruelling conditions imaginable. Such a manoeuvre had never been attempted before and Alexander's men would need to be extraordinarily motivated and well disciplined if it were to have the slightest hope of success. Secondly, the plan relied upon complete surprise: if Bessus got one word of what was being planned, the army would be sitting ducks if and when they arrived. Alexander intended to make sure that no defeatist talk started among his troops and he needed to make absolutely certain that there were no spies anywhere in his camp. Nicanor assured Alexander that his Hypaspistes would guarantee that nothing went wrong: his men would arrest anyone suspected of defeatist talk and all potential spies would be weeded out. A number of officers were soon to find themselves victims of the Hypaspistes – including Nicanor himself.[10]

Alexander's most senior general, apart from Antipater (who was back in Macedonia) was Parmenion. His son Nicanor was in charge of the Hypaspistes and another son, Philotas, was commander of the cavalry that accompanied Alexander into Bactria. Shortly after their investigation began, Nicanor's agents discovered that one of Philotas' officers had been openly criticising Alexander's plans. When the man was questioned, Nicanor learned that his brother Philotas had known of the officer's transgressions but had kept quiet in order to protect him. As the man had been a good cavalry officer and Philotas had decided there was no serious threat in what the man had been saying, Nicanor disciplined the officer but saw no reason to name his brother in his report to Alexander. This was a mistake that the ambitious Seleucus quickly exploited to his own advantage. He went directly to Alexander and informed him that not only Philotas had failed to report defeatist talk among his men, but also that Nicanor had covered for his brother. Seleucus may simply have been doing his duty, but he also knew that, if his superior's loyalty came under suspicion and he was dismissed, then he would be the logical choice for the new head of the Hypaspistes.[11]

At first, Alexander decided to ignore the matter and merely reprimanded Philotas and Nicanor for negligence. After all, their father Parmenion was his second-in-command and their family had been loyal to Alexander since the start of his reign. Nicanor would certainly have been angry with Seleucus for going behind his back, but there was nothing he could do about it. Seleucus, on the other hand, had recognised a weakness he could continue to utilise against his commander. He realised that, if he could find – or even fabricate – evidence to show that Philotas had personally criticised Alexander, rather than simply turning a blind eye to the offence in others, then Nicanor would be guilty of something far more serious than negligence: he would appear to have been an accessory. It was not long before Seleucus' agents found someone who claimed, or was coerced into claiming, that Philotas had openly denounced Alexander on a number of occasions. She was a Persian captive named Antigone, who had been sleeping with Philotas for some time.[12] However, Seleucus knew that if he were to directly confront Alexander with allegations against Philotas for a second time, with no more than the word of a slave-girl to go on, then it might well appear that he was personally defaming the cavalry commander for reasons of his own. He therefore came up with a clever scheme. Rather than tell Alexander about the girl's accusations himself, he persuaded one of Alexander's most trusted officers to inform him. This was Craterus, the cavalry's second-in-command. Craterus would presumably have taken little persuading, as he stood to gain as much by discrediting Philotas as Seleucus did himself. With Philotas gone, he would be his replacement. According to Plutarch, when Antigone was brought before Alexander, she swore that her lover had boasted that all the Macedonian victories were down to him and his family.

> He declared to his mistress, that all the great actions were performed by him and his father, the glory and benefit of which, he said, together with the title of king, Alexander reaped and enjoyed by their means.[13]

If Antigone was to be believed, Philotas was spreading talk that it was due to him and his father that Alexander had become king at all. In fact, this was partially true. If Parmenion had not joined with Antipater and supported Alexander's claim to the throne, then he may never have succeeded Philip in 336 BC. This made Antigone's accusations all the more poignant: if the girl had been bribed or intimidated into lying by Seleucus, then she had been fed a clever line. Alexander realised that there was a kernel of truth in what Philotas supposedly said, and just the idea of such gossip would have infuriated him. Nevertheless, Alexander had trusted Parmenion and his family implicitly; besides which, he would need more than the word of a Persian slave-girl to act against Parmenion's son. Although he remained sceptical, the idea that Parmenion's family might conspire against him had been firmly seeded in his mind.[14]

Seleucus no doubt realised that it would only take another such accusation for Alexander to seriously question Philotas' loyalty. A few days later, his agents came across a Macedonian soldier called Limnus who had openly gone around claiming that he intended to kill Alexander. His motives are unknown, but the man was clearly deranged. Nevertheless, he was picked up and interrogated. Apparently, under torture, he implicated Philotas in the plot, saying that he had offered to get him an audience with the king so that he could assassinate him. Unfortunately, the soldier was about as credible as someone claiming to be the Queen of Sheba. However, when Alexander demanded to see the witness himself, Limnus was conveniently killed – supposedly while trying to escape – before the king had a chance to question him.[15]

By now, Philotas' name had come up three times and each allegation had been more serious than the last. Alexander had to do something and ordered Philotas to be detained. Plutarch tells us that, the moment it was known that Philotas had been arrested, many of his rivals began to testify against him.

> As soon as his [Alexander's] displeasure against Philotas began to appear, presently all his [Philotas'] old enemies showed themselves, and said openly, the king was too easily imposed on, to imagine that one so inconsiderable as Limnus should of his own head

undertake such an enterprise . . . When they had once gained the king's ear for insinuations of this sort, they went on to show a thousand grounds of suspicion against Philotas, till at last they prevailed to have him seized and put to the torture, which was done in the presence of the principal officers, Alexander himself being placed behind some tapestry to understand what passed.[16]

Neither Plutarch nor any other source describes the details of these proceedings, but they were blatantly unfair. The main witnesses were all friends of Craterus, who had every reason in the world to fabricate evidence. Seleucus had cunningly drawn Craterus into his plan; after having informed on his commander, Craterus was tied irreversibly to the scheme. If Philotas was exonerated, then Craterus would stand little chance of remaining as the cavalry's second officer. If Philotas was found guilty, however, Craterus would almost certainly be given overall command. But, however unjust it was, Alexander's paranoia had been awakened and he decided to have Philotas executed.

By this time things had gone so far that the farcical trial gave way to a virtual witch-hunt. Alexander ordered that all of Philotas' family be put to death. According to Plutarch:

After his [Philotas'] death, he presently sent into Media, and put also Parmenion, his father, to death, who had done brave service under Philip, and was the only man of his older friends and counsellors who had encouraged Alexander to invade Asia. Of three sons whom he had had in the army, he had already lost two, and now was himself put to death with the third.[17]

This third son was Nicanor. As Nicanor's deputy, and for services rendered, Alexander appointed Seleucus the new chief of the feared Hypaspistes.

Few of the troops would have shed a tear at the death of Nicanor, but Philotas had been a popular officer and there were murmurings in the ranks. Most of all, however, Alexander had killed Parmenion on what appeared to have been no evidence at all. If Parmenion could be executed on a whim, then who would be safe from Alexander's paranoia? According to Justinus:

At this instance of cruelty, all the soldiers, throughout the camp, began to express their displeasure, being concerned for the fate of the innocent old general and his son, and saying, at times, that they must expect nothing better for themselves.[18]

Seleucus' first job as commander of the Hypaspistes was to do something about the subversive gossip and restore discipline. To this end, he presented Alexander with an ingenious proposal to ferret out all those who may have been inclined to mutiny. Justinus continues by explaining what he did.

> These murmurs coming to the knowledge of Alexander, he, fearing that such reports would be carried to Macedonia, and that the glory of his victories would be sullied by the stain of cruelty, pretended that he was going to send home some of his friends to give an account of his successes. He exhorted his soldiers to write to their relatives, as they would now have fewer opportunities on account of the scene of warfare being further from home. The packets of letters, as they were given in, he commanded to be privately brought to him, and having learned from them what everyone thought of him, he put all those, who had given unfavourable opinions of his conduct, into one regiment, with an intention either to destroy them, or to distribute them in colonies in the most distant parts of the earth.[19]

Seleucus, it seems, had invented the concept of the convict death battalion, which would one day be made famous by Soviet dictator Joseph Stalin in the Second World War. In one swoop, those foolish enough to put their opinions in writing were rounded up, and the punishment for sedition was made patently clear. From now on, Seleucus became the most feared man in the Macedonian army.

In January 329 BC, Alexander began his 600-kilometre march north-east to Charikar, stopping at Kapista (modern Kandahar), the provincial capital of Arachosia, about halfway along the route. Here he rendez-voused with fresh troops brought by one of his closest friends, Clitus, who he placed in command of the cavalry over Craterus. The 40,000-strong army continued on along difficult roads that soon became mountain tracks. Supplies could no longer be carried by wagon, which meant that pack animals had to be used, making progress along the snow-covered foothills of the Hindu Kush Mountains slow and laborious work. To make matters worse, a messenger arrived with news that a revolt had occurred in the Bactrian province of Aria, which Alexander had conquered the previous summer. This was a serious threat to Alexander's rear, and he was forced to send back 6,000 men under the command of Artabazus to restore order. Finally, in March, the army arrived in Charikar and Alexander prepared for the most ambitious and dangerous endeavour of his life.[20]

Immediately, Alexander made a base camp at Charikar and set off with about 30,000 men to cross the mountains. Ideally, he needed to wait for the thaw, but he had to move fast. Once warmer weather set in, the snows would melt and Bessus would not only be able to send scouts into the mountains, but he could also deploy troops to block the passes. Alexander's army had to cross the mountains in the most treacherous conditions. For days they trudged along slippery, narrow tracks, set high up into stark and frozen cliffs. The bitter wind howled relentlessly, and continually men and horses lost their footing to fall to their deaths on jagged rocks, hundreds of metres below. Incredibly, Alexander's army succeeded with relatively few casualties (around 2,000) and they made the 250-kilometre crossing in less than a month.[21]

The operation was a resounding success. In May, Alexander's army took the mountain tribes on the northern side of the mountains completely by surprise and captured the town of Khawak in the foothills. When news of Alexander's arrival reached Bactra, there was panic. The entire garrison was only about 8,000 men to Alexander's 30,000. Alexander may not have been in the kind of terrain where he could effectively deploy his troops for the conventional sort of battle he liked, but sheer numbers meant that the Persians wouldn't stand a chance. Many of the Persian defenders fled to the hills, leaving Bessus with a couple of thousand loyal troops in his doomed capital. Having no alternative, Bessus fled north and crossed the River Oxus into the last free province of the Persian Empire – Sogdiana, in the far north of Afghanistan and what is now Tajikistan and part of Turkmenistan. Bactra was taken without resistance and here Alexander rendezvoused with Artabazus and his force, which had put down the revolt in the west and had come to Bactra the direct and easy way. However, Alexander could not afford to rest his exhausted army. He had to pursue Bessus and his men before they could escape and set up a guerrilla base in the mountains of Sogdiana. The allied army had already faced the most dreadful conditions, crossing kilometres of ice-covered rock and even glaciers. According to Curtius' account, the men had run out of provisions and had resorted to eating their pack animals. Now they were immediately faced with the extreme opposite – a 75-kilometre march through a hot, parched and arid desert.[22]

Provinces and cities of the eastern Persian Empire.

Leaving Bactria in Artabazus' command, Alexander left most of his baggage behind and moved north into the desert with a lightly armed force. It was now June and the summer sun beat down mercilessly. Curtius describes the crossing:

The searing heat scorched the sands and all around them was baked hard as if by infernal fire. Even the daylight was obscured by the vapours of the burning heat and the vast wasteland seemed like a mighty ocean of sand. Only by travelling at night could the men march; as each morning the arid air would become devoid of all moisture, burning their mouths and throats.[23]

What made matters worse, Curtius explains, was that, when the water ran out, the men began to consume their rations of wine, and even their oil, which resulted in even greater thirst. In fact, for a day or so, half the army staggered through the desert in a drunken stupor. Alexander was determined to set an example. On one occasion, when he was offered water by one of his aides, he refused, saying that he would suffer like his men. When they finally reached the Oxus, however, more men died than had perished in the desert crossing as they greedily gulped down water that ruptured their parched stomachs.[24]

Bessus had hoped to prevent Alexander's army crossing the river by burning all the boats he could find. Once again Alexander came up with an ingenious solution, making rafts by stuffing the army's animal-skin tents with hay. It took five days, but the army was eventually ferried across to the northern bank. Realising that they were beaten, the last Persian army laid down their arms and Bessus' deputy, the Sogdian leader Spitamenes, took control, arrested his leader and handed him over to the enemy. Bessus was to be accorded an even grislier end than Batis, the governor of Gaza, three years earlier. He was savagely mutilated by having his nose and ears cut off and then crucified.[25]

A few weeks later Alexander was in the Sogdian capital of Cyreschata, where he formally accepted the surrender of Spitamenes and his troops. Alexander the Great was now undisputed ruler of the entire Persian Empire.

Seleucus and his Hypaspistes played an essential role in maintaining order in the allied army during the unforgiving three months of marching; first across the frozen mountains and then across the searing desert. From a purely military perspective, Alexander had made a wise decision to restructure the Hypaspistes into a ruthless and autonomous force. Most of Alexander's army would have had no idea why they should be pitting themselves against such harsh conditions in some out-of-the-way place they had never heard of. They had absolutely nothing to gain from it all: but the Hypaspistes made certain that they had everything to lose if they tried to desert. With the war won, however, the Hypaspistes soon became a liability – although Alexander appears to have been blissfully unaware of it.

Like the SS of the Second World War, the Hypaspistes immediately went on a murderous rampage of terror once Sogdiana had surrendered. In late July, Alexander sent a contingent of Hypaspistes into a small Sogdian town to arrest a number of suspected partisans. Rather than maintain a low profile, the crack troops stormed the town and massacred its unarmed inhabitants. Alexander would previously have deplored such an unnecessary atrocity: not simply because there was absolutely no military justification for it, but because it would be sure to incense an already pacified population. However, five years of almost continuous warfare had changed him. He not only failed to discipline the men responsible, but he also made no attempt to apologise to the Sogdian leader Spitamenes. This was a foolishly cynical attitude to take. If the local population were to rise in rebellion, then the Macedonian-led army would find itself faced with a protracted guerrilla campaign in the Sogdian mountains, just as the Soviet Union did in the twentieth century. No one wanted or would benefit by such a war, but the Hypaspistes seemed determined to start one. Over a brief month of peace, when diplomacy was called for during insignificant local disputes, the terror troops would respond by murdering defenceless civilians.[26]

Only one of Alexander's generals questioned him on the wisdom of allowing Seleucus and his men to continue to behave in such a manner. This was Clitus, the supreme cavalry commander. He had known the Alexander of old: the warrior who recognised the value of his officers' opinions, openly encouraged their questions and regularly sought their advice. However, Clitus had been back in western Persia when Alexander had reorganised the Hypaspistes and the Philotas trial and the army purges had occurred. He obviously knew about them, but had wrongly assumed that Alexander was still the same man at heart. When he advised Alexander that it was time to disband the Hypaspistes, or at the very least curtail their power, Alexander flew into a rage and accused his lifelong friend of treason. He was lucky that he was not demoted, or even arrested for daring to question the existence of Alexander's elite guard. No one in a position of power would risk rising to Clitus' defence. The other most senior general, the infantry commander

Coenus, was the late Philotas' brother-in-law and had only narrowly escaped being tarred with the brush of treason, while Craterus, Clitus' deputy, would have been as happy to see his new commander removed as he had been when Philotas was executed. And it goes without saying that he would get no support from Seleucus.[27]

Alexander should have taken his friend's advice, because a few days later the Hypaspistes committed one atrocity too many. One of Alexander's officers married a daughter of Spitamenes, the Sogdian leader, but continued a homosexual affair with his servant. Although this was acceptable in Greek culture, the Sogdians considered it to be a massive insult. According to their beliefs, there would have been no problem if the man had had an affair with another women, but her husband having a homosexual relationship meant that the girl was an inadequate wife. Even though she was a tribal princess, she was shunned by the entire community. The officer was seized by a mob and hanged. Alexander ordered the perpetrators to be executed, and that should have been the end of the matter. However, once again, the Hypaspistes went on a murderous rampage, punishing innocent Sogdians. The incident led to a full-scale rebellion led by Spitamenes himself. Even if Alexander had considered standing down the Hypaspistes, it was now too late. He needed them more than ever. This new and avoidable conflict played right into Seleucus' hands. If the war had been over, then there would no longer be a need for his elite special force. The barbaric war crimes committed by the Hypaspistes had worked to his advantage, and may even have been instigated by Seleucus for this very purpose.

Once again, Alexander was faced with a new and unfamiliar type of warfare. The opening months of the Sogdian campaign were fought in a sandy steppe region unsuited for the deployment of the phalanx. Furthermore, the Sogdians had exceptional mounted archers that could run rings round the Macedonian cavalry in such country. Alexander was to face his first military setback since he had set out from Macedonia. Although he succeeded in capturing seven Sogdian forts by the end of the year, he was forced to retreat to Bactra for the winter and a Greek rearguard of some 3,000 men was completely annihilated.[28]

By the last weeks of 329 BC, Alexander's army north of the Hindu Kush Mountains was down to almost 25,000 men. Although it still outnumbered the Sogdians, the enemy was fighting a hit-and-run campaign and their numbers were being increased all the time by rebel Persians who were continually joining them from the south: particularly since they received news of Alexander's retreat. Clitus urged Alexander to forget about Sogdiana: it was a small and insignificant area of no strategic or economic significance. If Persian rebels wanted to flee there, then let them. The River Oxus would be easy to defend and no Sogdian army would be equipped to make an effective crossing. However, Alexander's reputation was at stake. If he could not deal with a tiny and backward province like Sogdiana, then dissidents throughout his entire empire might be inclined to revolt.[29]

Alexander immediately sent word for around 10,000 Greek reinforcements from Europe and Asia Minor, which were brought to him by the Macedonian admiral Nearchus, who was no longer needed at sea. He then set about a complete restructuring of his army. Knowing that horsemen were by far the most important troops in Sogdian territory, Alexander left two-thirds of his infantry behind to hold Bactria, under Nearchus' control, while the remainder, under the command of Coenus, were to occupy the Sogdian plains and set up fortified base camps. The cavalry, under Alexander's direct control, would then operate in the Sogdian Mountains, seeking out and destroying the guerrillas in their strongholds. Seleucus and a division of his crack mounted troops were to accompany him.[30]

The new strategy worked and over a period of a year Sogdian resistance was gradually worn down. The campaign was arduous and dirty and the Hypaspistes' terror tactics were mercilessly deployed, sacking the mountain villages that were thought to have harboured rebel troops. It is not known how many innocent men, women and children were murdered, or how many settlements were burned to the ground in this war of attrition, but by the end of 328 BC, the Sogdians were all but beaten. In December Spitamenes was finally killed by Coenus' troops and his head was sent to Alexander.[31]

By the end of the Sogdian campaign, the Hypaspistes' reputation for brutality was known throughout the empire. There was a time when Alexander would have been horrified by their tactics, but those days were well and truly behind him. Alexander may always have been ruthless when he considered the occasion demanded it, but he had lived by what was then considered an honourable warrior's code. Now, however, he could no longer be considered to be anything but a butcher. In fact, he seems to have been driven so wild with slaughter that he even murdered one of his closest friends in cold blood. Shortly before the death of Spitamenes, Alexander's old friend and cavalry commander Clitus once again dared to criticise Alexander at a banquet he was holding to celebrate a victory over the Sogdians. According to Justinus, Clitus was drunk and began to condemn Alexander for darkening the name of his father, Philip, who would never have resorted to such barbaric tactics.

> Clitus, one of the older guests, trusting to his hold on the king's friendship, in which he held the principal place, defended the memory of Philip, and praised his acts. He so provoked Alexander that he snatched a weapon from one of the guards, and slew him with it in the midst of the guests. Exulting at the murder, too, he scoffed at the dead man for his defence of Philip, and his commendation of his mode of warfare.[32]

Plutarch records the same incident, elaborating that the weapon used was a spear.[33]

Everyone knew that it was dangerous to question Alexander, but it is doubtful that anyone expected him to kill his senior general – and someone who had been a close friend since childhood – with his own hands for simply speaking his mind. Philotas and his family may have been executed by the paranoid Alexander, but at least there had been some kind of trial. Clitus was murdered by Alexander in a violent rage in front of the entire court. Military justice, such as it existed, no longer applied to the king. He was now above the law. With the death of Clitus, one of the last voices of reason seems to have been silenced in the Macedonian high command. Most of Alexander's senior officers were now as cold-blooded as he – and the worst of them was Seleucus.

From now on, Seleucus was answerable to no one but the king. He had his own army within an army and his powers were virtually unlimited. However, placing so much power in the hands of one man may have been a mistake that Alexander eventually paid for with his life. In Babylon in June 323 BC, the one person best placed to seize control in the event of Alexander's death was Seleucus. The cavalry and infantry were camped outside the city, but the Hypaspistes were garrisoned inside where they were exclusively in control. These hand-picked troops were fiercely loyal to Alexander – but was their commander, Seleucus? Was this an opportunity too good for an ambitious man to resist? The Macedonian and Persian empires were now united under one all-powerful leader, but a leader who may throw the whole thing away in a mad scheme to conquer the entire world. The foray into India had almost proved Alexander's undoing, as we shall see in the next chapter; if he went ahead with his plan to invade Arabia, Carthage and Italy, who could tell what trouble might result. If Seleucus had designs on absolute power, then this was the time to seize the empire intact. Seleucus' record speaks for itself: he was ruthless and he was cunning. If he usurped Alexander in an overt coup, then his own men would consider him a traitor to their beloved leader. However, if Alexander were to die from an apparent disease, or by the hand of an unknown assailant, then Seleucus, with his feared Hypaspistes, would be ready to seize power and maintain control. Indeed, when Alexander died, Seleucus was the most successful general in the civil war that ensued, and gained command of much of what had been the Persian Empire. His dominion became the Seleucid Empire, named after him, and lasted for almost two and a half centuries until it was conquered by the Romans. Did he gain this empire because he had assassinated Alexander, or did someone else unwittingly do it for him?

Back in the winter of 327 BC, though, the ruthless Seleucus performed an uncharacteristic act of compassion. He saved the life of one of Spitamenes' daughters when she was about to be raped by his troops. Moreover, Seleucus fell in love with her, and after Alexander's death he married the woman and she became the first Seleucid queen. However, Seleucus was not the only one that year to fall in love with the daughter of a Sogdian leader and make her a queen. In the spring, Alexander met the daughter of the last Sogdian chief, and he too fell in love. She was Roxanne, a young girl who eventually had her own motives to slip poison into Alexander's wine.

SUMMARY OF CHAPTER SEVEN

About the same age as Alexander, Seleucus was a common soldier who rose through the ranks to become one of the most senior Macedonian officers. Had this ambitious professional officer assassinated Alexander to seize his empire for himself?

- By the late summer of 330 BC all that remained of the Persian Empire was its eastern province of Bactria – roughly what is now Afghanistan. Its governor, Bessus, refused to surrender and Alexander was forced into a protracted campaign in unfamiliar desert and mountainous terrain. The Bactrian capital was at Bactra, near modern Mazâr-e Sharîf, and Alexander decided to lead his army, now 40,000-strong, into the region of Gandara near modern Kabul. From here he mounted a gruelling, unprecedented 250-kilometre march over the frozen and perilous Hindu Kush Mountains to launch a surprise attack on the city.
- In April 329 BC, Bactra was taken but Bessus fled, only to be arrested by his second-in-command, Spitamenes, and handed over to Alexan-

der for execution. Unfortunately, this was by no means the end of the war. One of Alexander's officers married Spitamenes' daughter and humiliated her by continuing a gay affair with his servant. Although this was acceptable in Greek culture, the Bactrians considered it a massive insult and the man was killed. When the perpetrators were executed, it led to rebellion and for two more years Alexander was forced into a guerrilla war in the mountains of Sogdiana in the Bactrian north.

- It was during the Bactrian campaign that Seleucus proved himself to be one of Alexander's most able officers. He was promoted to commander of the Hypaspistes (meaning 'shield bearers'), an elite unit of heavy infantry whose purpose it was to protect the king. They were, in effect, the royal guard, such as the praetorians were to the later Roman emperors. They were also a kind of police force used to maintain both civil and military order and were the most feared and highly trained troops in Alexander's army.

- Although junior to the commanders of the infantry and cavalry, the commander of the Hypaspistes now had direct control of discipline throughout the entire Macedonian and allied army. Placing so much power in the hands of one man may have been a mistake that Alexander eventually paid for with his life. In Babylon in June 323 BC, the one person best placed to seize control in a military coup was Seleucus – which is exactly what he may have decided to do.

- Fearing that they had gained too much influence, Alexander had a habit of replacing senior officers between campaigns. The conquest of the Persian Empire was over and Alexander was already planning an invasion of Arabia: a reshuffle in the high command was almost inevitable. In June 323 BC, if Seleucus had his eyes on Alexander's crown, it may have been a case of now or never.

8. ROXANNE – LAND OF MYSTERY

In the spring of 327 BC Alexander led a final mopping-up operation against what remained of the Sogdian resistance. The last Sogdian chief, Oxyartes, who had taken over after Spitamenes' death at the end of the previous year, was holding out in a mountain fortress known as the Sogdian Rock. Arrian describes what occurred:

> News arrived that the last of the rebel natives had sought refuge on the Sogdian Rock, and with them was Oxyartes and his wife and daughters. He had refused to submit and believed that the rock was invulnerable to attack. This was the last stronghold of the rebels and, should it fall, then it would be the end of all resistance. Alexander found that it had sheer cliffs on every side and it seemed that assault was impossible. Those in the fortress on its summit were well supplied for a long siege, but Alexander was determined to take it quickly ... He assembled three hundred men who were his best rock-climbers and gave them tent pegs which they used to drive into the snow and ice of the cliffs and to these they attached lines of rope so that they could climb to the top. Under cover of darkness, they made their way upwards but, though thirty of them fell to their deaths, they reached the summit ... The surprise of seeing Macedonians in their camp, so alarmed the natives that they imagined that they were a part of some much larger force and they surrendered ... There were many women and children among the prisoners that were taken that day and with them were the wife and the daughters of Oxyartes.[1]

One of these daughters was Roxanne, whom, according to Arrian, Alexander fell immediately in love with.

> She was a young girl of marriageable age, and the Macedonians said that she was the most beautiful woman they had seen in Asia ... Alexander straight away fell in love with her and even though she was a prisoner he took her as his wife.[2]

From other references in Arrian's work, we can deduce that Roxanne was only sixteen years of age. None of the historical sources gives an account of the marriage ceremony but a painting of it was made by a contemporary artist named Aetion. It no longer exists, but is described by the second-century Greek author Lucian of Samosat.

> The picture shows a bedroom scene with a matrimonial bed upon which Roxanne is sitting. She is the most beautiful girl with dark complexion and long, flowing hair. She sits looking down in modesty as Alexander stands beside her and offers her a garland of flowers . . . Beside Alexander stands Hephaestion, his best man, who holds a blazing torch and leans against a young boy at his side.[3]

If Lucian is right, then it seems that Hephaestion was once again Alexander's best friend. They had apparently been estranged from one another after Alexander began his affair with Barsine six years before. Although Hephaestion had accompanied Alexander into Persia and Bactria, and had taken part in a number of military engagements, the historical sources only mention him briefly during this time. From now on, however, he is firmly back in Alexander's entourage. There is no specific mention of Barsine having caused friction between the two men, but the fact that their friendship appears to have cooled the moment she came on the scene and resumed once Barsine had been driven away suggests that she must have been involved.

Alexander had fallen in love with Barsine at a time when he did not want to antagonise his troops by marrying a woman whose father and brother were two of the enemy's most important officers. By the time Artabazus and Pharnabazus had changed sides, his affections had probably waned. In Roxanne's case, however, there was no such problem. The war with the Persian Empire was finally over. Besides which, Alexander no longer seemed to care what anyone thought. There was no political reason for Alexander to marry Roxanne, as her father was a minor figure of no real importance. In fact, Alexander considered him of such little relevance that he allowed him to live. As Arrian says, Alexander must simply have fallen in love.

The historical sources describe Roxanne's stunning beauty, and her lively and vivacious personality. Moreover, she seems to have been highly intelligent. She may not have had the benefit of a Greek and Persian education like Barsine, but she appears to have had a remarkable memory and an enquiring mind. For example, the *Historia* records that she was able to learn a new language fluently within a few months.[4] This was something that would make her extremely useful to Alexander over the next two years, as he embarked on yet another campaign – this time into the mysterious land of India.

By the end of 327 BC, Alexander's army really thought it was going home. Many of the Greeks and Macedonians had been fighting almost continually in Asia for seven years. Alexander's empire was the largest the world had ever known and it encompassed what had once been the entire Persian Empire and most of southeast Europe. Surely this was enough for any man to rule? However, Alexander seems to have acquired such a taste for military conquest that he was unable to stop. To the east of Bactria lay the virtually unknown subcontinent of India. Even the Persians knew little about it and no European is known to have set foot in the region before. In fact, so little did the Europeans know that their best accounts (Heroditus) described it as a land inhabited by giant ants. Nevertheless, Alexander was determined to conquer it. According to the *Historia*, 'Alexander was resolute that he would continue east until he reached the sea at the end of the world'.[5]

India had been divided from the Persian Empire by the River Indus and, from what the Persians understood, the immediate eastern side of the river was divided into three kingdoms: Gandara in the north, Pauravas along the central course and Sindhu in the south. (These kingdoms were merely what are now Eastern Pakistan and the eastern Punjab: Alexander had no idea how big India really was.) The kingdom of Gandara stretched north to the Hindu Kush Mountains and had been partially conquered by the Persians. In fact, Alexander had already seized the Persian region of Gandara when he had set up a base to the south of the mountains at Charikar, three years before. It was to Charikar, therefore, that Alexander led his army in February 326 BC, and it was from there that he intended to begin his expedition across the Indus and into India proper.

His army was around 110,000 men, of which less than half were Europeans. There were around 30,000 Persians, 20,000 Egyptians, Babylonians and Assyrians, and about 10,000 Bactrians, including around 3,000 Sogdians under the command of Roxanne's father Oxyartes. This army was divided into two, half of which was a vanguard under the command of Hephaestion that went ahead to the Indus to build a bridge over the river. The rest, including the main infantry and cavalry divisions under Coenus and Craterus, remained behind with Alexander until the bridge was completed and they could advance into India in force. It was the depths of winter and Charikar was a harsh place to be at that time of the year. Diodorus describes the terrible conditions which the soldiers, most of whom came from countries with hot climates, had to endure.

> The area was covered by snow and was often inaccessible because of the extreme cold. There were no trees in this barren land, yet it still supported many villages which had strange houses with tiled roofs which were drawn up into a point. At the pinnacle of this roof there was a hole through which smoke from fires escaped, and only by this smoke was the whereabouts of many settlements known. Nowhere in this landscape was there any sign of cultivation, as everything is white and blinding because of the ice and snow. No bird or animal could be seen as there was nothing anywhere for them to eat. Nevertheless, Alexander ordered that his army overcome the harshness of the region and continue to exercise and train. Many of these soldiers became blind with the harsh brilliance of the sun upon the snow, while others fell exhausted and were left behind or became lost.[6]

In March, while Hephaestion's men were building their bridge, Alexander led a short excursion into the foothills of the Himalayas, in Upper Gandara, the far north of modern Pakistan. His intention was to secure the region so that his supply road from Charikar was secure. However, what occurred was nothing less than a campaign of genocide. Firstly, when Alexander received little more than a flesh wound during the siege of a Gandarian hill fort, he ordered all those inside to be massacred. Alexander had become a bloodthirsty tyrant, and he now lost the last vestige of his own warrior's code and completely abandoned his former policy of sparing the lives of those who surrendered without resistance. When he arrived at the town of Massaga (modern Chakdarra), he offered the defenders a place in his own army if they gave up without a fight. They agreed, but when they emerged from their defences Alexander had them cut down in a shower of arrows. His once-valued reputation for always keeping his word was now worthless.[7]

Nevertheless, although Alexander appeared to have acquired the soul of a butcher, he still retained the eyes of a tourist. Winter was over and Alexander's army finally moved southeast towards the bridge over the Indus that Hephaestion was building. The snows thawed and they descended into warm, fertile countryside. On the way, the army passed through a town called Nysa where, for the first time, they encountered the temple of an Indian god. Alexander's admiral Nearchus, who was accompanying the army in case they needed to build boats at some point, later wrote that he was greatly disturbed that his king would desecrate the shrine. He feared that it would unnecessarily antagonise the local population and lead to bitter resistance as they proceeded further into a completely unknown land. However, as it turned out, he had nothing to worry about. Alexander was fascinated by the place and decided to stay for a few days so that he could get to know the Indian customs. Arrian describes how Alexander was received by the locals and how they apparently delighted him by accepting him as a god.

When Alexander approached Nysa, the chief of the inhabitants, one Acuphis, came to see him with thirty of his priests. His intention was to ask Alexander to leave their town and their god alone. However, when they entered Alexander's tent to find him sitting still on the floor with his helmet on his head and a spear in his hand, he surprised them so much that they fell to the ground and prostrated themselves before him as if he were a god himself. After this, Alexander bade them to arise and to not be afraid . . .
Accordingly, he guaranteed the people of Nysa their freedom to govern themselves.[8]

It seems that Alexander had been taken for Skanda, the Hindu god of vigour, health and beauty. Skanda was also a war god and he was often depicted sitting cross-legged, wearing a plumed helmet and holding a spear. He was also supposed to be fair-skinned. It is doubtful that the people of Nysa had ever seen a white European, let alone one who resembled the depictions of Skanda. Also, Alexander was clean-shaven, as was the god, whereas the native tribesmen and the Persians they already knew all had beards. As luck would have it, the temple at Nysa was actually a shrine to Skanda, and Alexander's visitors were the god's priests.

It may have been no coincidence that Alexander was sitting cross-legged in the regalia of the Hindu god. Someone could have advised him that it would be a clever ruse. If so, then the most likely person is Roxanne. India was a place of mystery to Europeans and to most Persians too, and Roxanne seems to have become enthralled by this exotic land. According to the *Historia*, she was excited by plants and animals she had never seen, captivated by the local customs and intrigued by the Hindu religion.[9] In fact, in a couple of months, she had already learned enough about the culture to know exactly what god was being venerated in Nysa, when nobody else in the army did. When

Roxanne accompanied Alexander to the temple they found a sacred grove surrounding a statue of the seated god. The third-century Greek biographer Philostratus, describes the shrine.

> The mountain on which Nysa stood was covered to the very top by beautiful plantations, divided by neat pathways. When they ascended it they found a temple dedicated to Dionysus. Here there was a polished, white stone statue of the god, in the form of a youth, seated at the heart of a grove of sacred trees and vines. These trees had grown together to form a roof above the god which protected it from the rain.[10]

Philostratus says that the deity was the Greek god Dionysus, which is exactly what Alexander and his men first thought, as Dionysus was often depicted in white marble statues as a youthful man. However, so was Skanda, in his aspect as god of health and beauty. According to the *Historia*, Roxanne quickly put everyone right.

> Alexander's advisors told him that this was Dionysus and that the god himself had built the shrine when he came to India. From her learning the queen [Roxanne] knew that this was Skanda, called Karttikeya by some.[11]

In Hindu religion, Skanda was the son of the supreme deity Shiva. This was extremely convenient as it fitted in with Alexander's propaganda that he was the son of the chief god of every land. To Europeans he was Hercules, son of Zeus; to Egyptians he was Horus, son of Ammon; and in Persia he was Mithra, son of Oromasdes. Now he could be Skanda, son of Shiva.

Skanda appears to have been the main god worshipped along the Indus Valley. Many ancient shrines to the deity have been excavated in the region of what is now the Punjab. In fact, although modern shrines to Skanda are no longer found in the western Punjab of Moslem Pakistan, in the eastern Punjab of Hindu India there are temples to Skanda still in use today. Just as in Alexander's time, they are open-air shrines, where statues of the god are surrounded by groves of the sacred *shudha* trees. The orange-like fruit of the *shudha* is considered sacred to Skanda and, when burned, its smoke has an intoxicating quality believed to induce mystical visions. It is clear that Alexander became regarded as an incarnation of Skanda by far more of the population of the Punjab than Nysa alone. Strangely, the Persian version of Alexander's name was Xanda; a name that sounded very similar to the Indian Skanda. This was, in fact, the name by which many of the Indians began to call him. Not only do a number of ancient Sanskrit writings refer to him as such, but Skanda is the name by which Alexander is known in parts of the Punjab even today.[12]

In April 326 BC the bridge over the Indus was completed; the main army joined with Hephaestion's force and Alexander led his troops across the Indus. Within a few days they were in the Gandarian capital of Taxila, near what is now Islamabad, the capital of Pakistan. Here the king, a man named Ambhi, welcomed Alexander and requested an alliance to fight his enemy, Puru, the king of the neighbouring kingdom of Pauravas. Alexander agreed and remained in Taxila for about a month, preparing for the attack.[13]

During the stay in Taxila, Alexander instructed the Greek scholars who accompanied him to find out as much as they could about India. None of them had taken the trouble to learn the local language and they needed to employ a chain of interpreters. The Bactrians spoke to the Gandarians, and then interpreted for the Persians, who in turn interpreted for the Greeks. Roxanne, however, who already knew Greek, Bactrian and Persian, had learned to speak the Gandarian dialect enough to dispense with any interpreters. Alexander therefore asked her to translate directly for the Greek scholars. She must have been secretly laughing at the kind of questions she was asked to interpret. To begin with, they asked where they could find the giant ants that were supposed to inhabit India. Another ridiculous question concerned the colour of the Indian's semen, which they assumed was black because of their dark skin. It is not recorded what answer was given, but the scholars eventually concluded that it must be white 'because they had white teeth'. In fact, so ignorant were the Greeks that some of them even came to the conclusion that they were in Africa because of the crocodiles and elephants they had seen.[14] The Greek philosophers had long before worked out that the world was round, although they considered it to be at the centre of the universe. Alexander's Greek scholars wrongly assumed that they must have travelled all the way around the world and if they continued a little further east that they would end up back in Egypt. They had no idea that they would have to cross the whole of India, China, the Pacific, the continent of America and the Atlantic before they reached western Africa. Some of the Greeks and Macedonians even began to refer to the Indians as Africans; this is ironic, because, when the Europeans eventually discovered America eighteen centuries later, they too thought they had travelled all around the world and called the Native Americans Indians.

Roxanne soon became exasperated by the Greeks' self-centred view of the world. On one occasion, when they thought that a golden sculpture of two men embracing depicted the mythical Greek heroes Achilles and Patroclus, who were said to have been lovers, Roxanne had to educate them that they were in fact two local gods. According to Alexander's officer Hieronymus of Cardia, who was present during the Indian campaign, Roxanne informed her husband that, if he really wanted to find out about India, he needed the help of a native scholar and not the pompous, ignorant Greeks. Anyone else would have probably been executed for such a remark, but Alexander agreed. In fact, when his scholars complained that the new queen was interfering with their work, he simply laughed. It seems that he enjoyed seeing them being outshone by a slip of a girl. Alexander gave Roxanne permission to find someone she considered was right for the job as adviser on Indian affairs, and the person she found was a local Hindu priest named Kalyana.[15]

Kalyana was a Brahman, a Hindu sage, who was a devotee of the god Skanda in the temple at Taxila. The temple at Taxila was one of the most important cultural centres in what was then India. In fact, it was said that the most famous Hindu book, the *Mahabharata*, was written there. The site where the temple stood is now called Bhir Mound and has been excavated by archaeologists to reveal the oldest-known Hindu shrine. Kalyana was fascinated by the Europeans and was as keen to learn about them as Roxanne was to learn about Indian culture. The two struck up a close friendship; she taught Kalyana everything she had learned about the Greeks and he taught her about the Hindu religion and its practices. In fact, as far as we know, Roxanne was the only person in Alexander's entourage who was the slightest bit interested in the local practices of Yoga and meditation. Kalyana, for his part, not only became familiar with western ways, but he picked up the Greek language as quickly as Roxanne had learned the Gandarian dialect.[16]

Roxanne, however, did manage to interest Alexander in some remarkable feats that the Brahmans were able to perform. An account of Alexander's fascinating encounter with Hindu mysticism was written down by the military engineer Aristobulus and cited by the Greek geographer Strabo, who wrote around the time of the birth of Christ.

Aristobulus says that he saw two of the Brahmans; and that the elder had head shaved but that the younger had long hair, and that both were followed by disciples; and that when not otherwise engaged they spent their time in the market-place, being honoured as counsellors and being authorised to take as gift any merchandise they wished . . . And they came up to the table of Alexander, ate dinner standing, and taught him a lesson in endurance by retiring to a place nearby, where the elder fell to the ground on his back and endured the sun's rays and the rains (for it was now raining, since the spring of the year had begun); and that the younger stood on one leg holding aloft in both hands a log about three cubits in length, and when one leg tired he changed the support to the other and kept this up all day long.[17]

So impressed was Alexander by the Brahmans that he asked Kalyana to join him as his Indian adviser when he continued his advance.

At the beginning of summer, Alexander marched southeast into the kingdom of Pauravas and into his first real battle with an Indian army. Many centuries after Alexander's time, the inhabitants of northeastern India converted to Islam, and after the Second World War the area gained independence from the rest of predominantly Hindu India and became Pakistan. However, in Alexander's time eastern Pakistan was not only Hindu but also a part of India. The kingdom of Pauravas, what is now the eastern Punjab, is still a part of India today. This area of roughly 150 kilometres from north to south and the same from east to west was, in fact, the only part of what is now India that Alexander actually invaded.

After spending the winter in a freezing wasteland, the army entered an area of subtropical jungle. The *Historia* vividly describes this new and perilous terrain.

There were trees so thick that the roads could not be left and the air was filled with flies that sucked the blood of the men and horses too. Many of the soldiers were overcome by heat and others died of fever. Some were even swallowed by the mud when they fell into the swampy ground through which they travelled, and others were bitten by deadly snakes and creatures for which they had no name.[18]

The troops had to endure such conditions for over 200 kilometres until they finally reached open country to come face to face with Puru's army. The sight of the king of Pauravas must have been a daunting one. Plutarch records that he was a giant of man.

Porus [the Greek name for Puru] was four cubits and a span high, and when he was upon his elephant, which was of the largest size, his stature and bulk were so answerable, that he appeared to be proportionately mounted, as a horseman on his horse.[19]

A cubit was just over fifty centimetres, which means that Puru was over two metres – six foot, six inches – tall. His elephant was apparently formidable too.

This elephant, during the whole battle, gave many singular proofs of sagacity and of particular care of the king, whom as long as he was strong and in a condition to fight, he defended with great courage, repelling those who set upon him; and as soon as he perceived him overpowered with his numerous wounds and the multitude of darts that were thrown at him, to prevent his falling off, he softly knelt down and began to draw out the darts with his trunk.[20]

Alexander's army may have been far superior in numbers and equipment (35,000 to Puru's 20,000), but they had never fought against elephants before. Puru's elephants and their riders were placed in front of the Indian infantry and Alexander's cavalry horses were terrified by the huge animals and refused to go anywhere near them. Unable to deploy his cavalry directly, Alexander was forced to open the battle with an unsupported phalanx advance. However, when Puru decided to order a chariot attack from the left wing of his force, the Macedonian cavalry were able to engage them and force their way through to the rear of the enemy lines. At the same time, Alexander ordered the Persian archers in his army to shoot showers of arrows at the elephants, causing them to turn and stampede back on the Indian infantry. The Indians were now under assault from all sides: the enemy's cavalry in the rear, its infantry in front, and their own elephants crushing them underfoot. Puru was a brave warrior and fought on until his entire army was wiped out or forced to flee. Although wounded, however, he was taken alive.[21]

Alexander respected Puru's bravery and allowed him to live. According to Justinus:

Porus, covered with a number of wounds, was made prisoner, and was so grieved at being defeated, that when his life was granted him by the enemy, he would neither take food nor suffer his wounds to be dressed, and was scarcely at last prevailed upon to consent to live. Alexander, from respect to his valour, sent him back in safety to his kingdom.[22]

This unexpected display of clemency was not the only act of benevolence that Alexander performed after his victory over Puru. He began to play the role of peace broker and persuaded the people of Gandara and Pauravas to forget their squabbling and cease their regional conflicts. He even encouraged Puru and the Gandarian king Ambhi to reconcile their personal differences and become friends. Although these two kingdoms were to be a single part of Alexander's empire, he wanted it to be a truly multicultural province. He founded a new provincial capital, which he intended to be a cosmopolitan city, and left behind a few thousand Macedonian and Greek veterans to build it together with the Indians. Even the name he gave this new settlement shows a sentimental side of Alexander's character that had not been seen for years. According to Plutarch, he named it after his horse Bucephalus, who had recently died.

Some little time after the battle with Porus, Bucephalus died, as most of the authorities state, under cure of his wounds, or, as Onesicritus says, of fatigue and age, being thirty years old. Alexander was no less concerned at his death than if he had lost an old companion or an intimate friend, and built a city, which he named Bucephalia, in memory of him.[23]

It seemed that Alexander had undergone a refreshing change of attitude. Why he reverted to his old self is unclear, but it was probably to do with Roxanne. He was madly in love with this intelligent and lively young woman who seems to have reawakened his youthful spirit. Indeed, Roxanne seems to have had a positive affect on Alexander's entire entourage. Apart from a few Greek scholars, who no doubt hated being outshone by a teenage girl, she was the darling of the Macedonian court. Even the cold-hearted Seleucus, who was in love with her cousin, seems to have curtailed his bloodlust.

Sadly, however, all this was not to last. Alexander soon became restless and impatient to move on further into India. To the immediate east of Pauravas was the powerful kingdom of Magadha, and Alexander decided this would be his next objective. In June, as he left with his army, he passed a group of Brahman priests who surprised him by jumping up and down and stamping their feet on the ground. According to Arrian:

Through his interpreters, Alexander asked them what was meant by this strange behaviour and they answered saying: 'King Alexander, a man can only possess as much of the earth as we are standing on. Like all of us, you are but a man, even though you have conquered and taken so much from others. You will soon be dead, and then you will own just as much of this earth as it will take to bury you'.[24]

Whether this was intended as a general statement or was a specific prediction regarding Alexander's fate is unknown. However, if it was a warning, then perhaps Alexander should have heeded it. The campaign into Magadha was to prove a disaster that almost cost Alexander his crown.

Magadha was separated from Pauravas by a number of tributaries of the Indus and crossing them was no easy job; the mountain snows had melted, swelling them into foaming torrents. Somehow the army managed to cross two of them, and a town called Sangala was taken. How far into India Alexander had travelled is uncertain, but Sangala may have been Chandigarh, the modern capital of India's Union Territories – only 250 kilometres north of Delhi. However, this was as far as Alexander would reach. In July, when the monsoon rains began, the army refused to travel any further in the stifling, humid heat.

When Alexander ordered his men forward, the infantry simply stood their ground. Furious, Alexander summoned their commander Coenus to find out what was happening. Coenus seemingly had no control over his troops and informed Alexander that there was nothing he could do. His men were not prepared to go any further into a country that no one had ever heard of and for no conceivable purpose. If Alexander pushed them any further, Coenus warned him, he would have a full-scale mutiny on his hands. Alexander immediately sent for his cavalry commander Craterus and ordered him to restore order in the infantry, but he was told that there was no way the cavalry would charge its own men. Alexander still had the support of the Hypaspistes, but they would have no chance against the entire army. Coenus implored him to accept that his expedition into India was over.[25]

Alexander had never faced such a predicament before and threw what can only be described as a childish tantrum. He screamed at Coenus for his lack of courage and told him to gather his officers. When they arrived, he told them that he was going to advance into India regardless, and if his army wouldn't follow him then he would go on alone. 'Go back and tell your families that you left your king amongst his enemies,' he dared them, and stormed off into his tent. For hour after hour he waited for the army to change its mind, all the time expecting that someone would come and tell him that his men were ready to advance, but no one came. After two days, Alexander realised that the army had called his bluff. If he was going to go into India, then he really would have to go alone – or at least with so few troops that they would be wiped out in a matter of weeks.

Alexander had no intention of committing suicide. However, if he backed down, he would not only look ridiculous, but also would lose total respect.[26]

It seems that it was Roxanne who came up with an idea to get her husband out of the embarrassing corner he had painted himself into. There had been an eclipse of the moon a few weeks before, and she knew that in Hindu tradition it was considered a bad omen. She suggested he call for Kalyana and ask him for his opinion. He would confirm what she said and then Alexander could tell his men that he had decided to go no further because the priest had advised against it. This he did, and emerged from his tent with the announcement that he had decided to return to the west as the omens were against them. At this, there arose a great cheer and Alexander's honour was saved.[27]

Roxanne had been both a devoted lover and an inspiration to Alexander and she had been the darling of the royal court. In fact, she had lived up to her name. In Sogdian her name was Roshanak, meaning 'little star' – and indeed she was, to almost everyone she knew. She was loved and respected and she was queen of an empire that covered three-quarters of the known world. But her dream was not to last. When Alexander returned to Iran, he took a second wife, Statira, the daughter of the dead Persian king Darius III. This marriage may well have been political, but it devastated Roxanne – perhaps to the point that she decided to kill her husband and king.

Back in the summer of 326 BC, however, Alexander still had three years left to live – and a long journey home. After the near mutiny, he seemed to be back in full control. He immediately had Coenus dismissed as commander of the infantry and replaced by a veteran Macedonian soldier named Meleager. This seasoned infantry campaigner of around 55 was a loyal and trustworthy officer who had not been a part of the recent trouble. However, after he had been forced to turn back by his own army, Alexander began to victimise his European troops. In fact, so intolerable did his behaviour become that Meleager eventually had every reason in the world to want him dead.

SUMMARY OF CHAPTER EIGHT

Roxanne was Alexander's first wife and queen. After three years with Roxanne, however, Alexander took a second wife, the Persian princess Statira, daughter of the late King Darius. The historical sources all record that Roxanne was insanely jealous of this new bride, giving her a possible motive to murder her husband in revenge.

- During one of the last skirmishes of the Bactrian campaign Roxanne was captured by the Macedonian army. The sixteen-year-old daughter of a Sogdian chieftain, she is said to have been beautiful, intelligent and vivacious. Alexander appears to have fallen madly in love with her, because he married her almost at once. From all accounts, the feelings were mutual. There was certainly no political reason for the marriage as Roxanne's father was a minor figure of no real importance.

- In 327 BC the war with Persia was over and all of its once mighty empire was now under Alexander's control. With this added to his homeland of Macedonia, its adjacent countries and the Greek states, Alexander now ruled the largest empire the world had ever known. It should have been time to return home and call it a day, but for reasons best known to himself Alexander decided to push on into India.

- India was a place of mystery to Europeans, and to most Persians too, and Roxanne seems to have become enthralled by this exotic land. She was excited by plants and animals she had never seen, captivated by the local customs and intrigued by the Hindu religion. In the Punjab the conquerors encountered Hindu Brahmans and one of them, a priest named Kalyana, agreed to accompany Alexander as an interpreter and adviser on local affairs. Kalyana seems to have been fascinated by the Europeans – he was the only Indian who returned with them to the west. Keen to discover as much as she could about Indian culture, Roxanne struck up a close friendship with Kalyana and seems to have been quick to learn his language.

- In India, Roxanne was able to visit a number of Hindu temples and shrines. She seems to have understood more about the native religion than Alexander's own court scribes. On one occasion, when visiting a sacred grove in which there stood a white marble statue of a youthful god, the learned Greeks in Alexander's entourage believed it to be a depiction of the Greek god Dionysus, as the deity's images were similar. It was, however, as Roxanne pointed out, the Hindu god Skanda, the son of Shiva.

- Could such an endearing and seemingly spiritually minded a girl really have killed her husband three years later because he had taken a second queen? There is no indication that Alexander was actually in love with Statira, as his marriage to her seems to have been purely a political act to appeal to his new Persian subjects and bolster his claim to be their king. Nevertheless, Roxanne may have felt humiliated before the world, and it would not be the first time in history that an amorous young woman had been turned into a vengeful murderess by a love she thought betrayed.

9. MELEAGER – THE LONG MARCH HOME

Meleager had been a regular Macedonian soldier for over thirty years. Little is known of his early life, but he had seen service in the army of Alexander's father Philip three decades earlier. Before July 326 BC, Meleager had merely commanded a phalanx of 1,500 men and would have been the equivalent of a modern lieutenant colonel. However, when Coenus was dismissed for failing to control his men, Meleager was appointed commander of the entire infantry. It may have been that Alexander no longer trusted his more senior officers; alternatively, Meleager's promotion to general may have been to appease the troops. Meleager was a popular, grass-roots soldier – a seasoned veteran of considerable experience. Either way, his appointment suited both the king and the rank and file of his army, although it was obviously not popular with the Macedonian high command.[1]

Alexander, however, clearly bore a grudge against his army, particularly the infantry, although he could risk only limited and tacit recriminations. To begin with, as they withdrew from Sangala, he left behind around 5,000 men to found a Macedonian colony. These were obviously some of the troops Alexander felt he could no longer rely on, and he no doubt hoped they would never be heard from again. What happened to them in their settlement far inside India is not recorded, but it is interesting that there are tribesmen in the area of Chandigarh today who still claim descent from Alexander the Great.[2] Coenus himself may also have been surreptitiously dealt with: a few weeks after the near mutiny he was conveniently found dead – apparently after a fall from his horse.[3]

The easiest and most direct way to return to Persia and the west would be back via Taxila to Charika, where the expedition into India had started from. However, Alexander realised that, after only a few months, this would look as if his army had been defeated or forced to retreat. Such a perception may well have led to a rebellion in Gandara, so he decided instead to head west to the Indus and then follow the river south to the Arabian Sea. When the army arrived at one of the Indus' tributaries in September, Alexander ordered his admiral Nearchus to build a fleet of 800 ships to ferry part of his army and supplies down river. The rest would be divided into two – one part commanded by Hephaestion, the other by Craterus – which were to flank the fleet on either bank.[4]

In November the ships were ready and the army began its 1,000-kilometre trek south. Almost at once, the fleet ran into trouble when dozens of ships were smashed to pieces in a course of rapids and almost a thousand men lost their lives. However, for the next couple of months things went well, until January 325 BC when the army entered the territory of the Indian kingdom of Malava, around modern Multan. This was a relatively small kingdom and the massive army could easily have passed through with little or no trouble at all. Alexander, though, still saw himself as a conqueror and needed to demonstrate that he was not retreating, but instead occupying new Indian lands. Rather than make a quick and defensive drive south, Alexander ordered the army on the eastern bank to attack the Malavan capital. During the battle, which was an easy victory, Alexander was wounded by an arrow. When he fell, one of his bodyguards picked up his famous shield of Achilles and defended him with it, while Ptolemy and his men managed to carry him from the battlefield. Alexander should have been thankful he survived. Nevertheless, in reprisal, he ordered the Sogdian mounted archers, and some of his cavalry, to massacre the inhabitants of the surrounding villages. Alexander was so satisfied with the bloody slaughter that when the army moved on he left the Sogdian leader, Roxanne's father Oxyartes, behind as governor of this newly acquired province. Sadly, there were few people left alive for him to govern.[5]

Alexander's victory over the Malavans was to set a precedent for the rest of the journey down river. To the east of the lower Indus there was the much larger kingdom of Sindhu, which was divided into various tribal regions. The capital, in the area of modern Sukkur, surrendered immediately, but the tribal districts held out and for the next two months the army was involved in numerous battles to subdue the Sindhu towns. It is not known how many innocent inhabitants lost their lives, but the pointless exercise cost Alexander around 5,000 men. Most of these were his European infantry troops, and their commander, Meleager, must have wondered if Alexander had been deploying them as a punishment for their conduct the previous year. The hot, humid climate also took its toll and as many men again lost their lives to tropical diseases such as malaria.[6]

By April, the kingdom of Sindhu was completely subdued and Alexander finally decided to move on to the sea. No sooner than he did he received news that there was a revolt in Gandara. Apparently, the rebels had learned that Alexander had been forced to retreat from Magadha and they assumed that he had been defeated. In response, Alexander was forced to send an army of around 20,000 men back north, under the command of Craterus, to restore order. This was done quickly and effectively, and Craterus continued back to Persia the easy and direct way westwards. This was the way the entire army should have gone and now that the Gandarians had revolted anyway the entire trek south had been futile. The whole Indian campaign was turning into a fiasco. The trip down the Indus had cost well over 10,000 troops, not to mention the countless numbers of innocent Indians who had been mercilessly slaughtered. However, it was now the end of summer, and what remained of Alexander's army had finally reached the Arabian Sea.[7]

By this time Alexander seems to have been living in a world of make-believe. He was not only pretending that he had chosen to move south so as to invade more lands, but also now claimed that he had conquered all of India. As he stood on the shore at the mouth of the Indus, he pointed to the horizon, saying that somewhere beyond it lay Africa. According to him, he had virtually circumnavigated the globe and there was nothing else in the east left to conquer. No one in his army may have known how big India actually was, or what really lay beyond it, but even an uneducated common soldier would have known that the northern star was to their rear and Alexander was pointing south. If they really had travelled around the world then Africa would lie to the east. Alexander was clearly losing his mind, and the army, in particular Meleager's infantry, was suffering for it. Their ordeal, however, was far from over.[8]

Alexander decided to make camp to the north of the Indus delta at an Indian town called Patala. Here there was a river port where Nearchus began to prepare his fleet for the sea voyage home along the coast to the Persian Gulf. Nearchus, however, could only take about 20,000 men; the other 50,000 that remained would have to march over 700 kilometres west through the hot Gedrosian Desert before reaching the first Persian city of Pura (modern Bampur) in the province of Carmania. Alexander could have headed northwest, through the Bactrian province of Drangiana and back to Prophthasia, the city where he had had Philotas executed. His decision to lead his army directly west through the perilous Gedrosian Desert is something of a puzzle, but it may have been because the famous Persian king Cyrus the Great had tried to do it 200 years earlier and had failed. Plutarch tells us that Alexander wanted to do something that all military commanders thought impossible. Alternatively, it may have been because he had begun to fear that he had been away too long and his empire might collapse. Whatever his reason, the decision was loathed by his troops, who suspected that Alexander was doing it to punish them for their mutinous behaviour in India. Over half the soldiers that were forced to cross the desert during October and November 325 BC were the Macedonian and Greek infantry. And for two terrible months Meleager watched them die. Arrian describes the dreadful crossing:

> The suffering that the men had to endure on their sixty-day march though the desert was out of all proportion greater than had been their hardship in India . . . It was a disaster for all concerned and the blazing heat and lack of water caused first the animals to die. Even those mules and pack-horses that survived were often caught in the loose, deep sand, and the wagons that carried the supplies had to be abandoned with them as they too became caught . . . When all the supplies and animals were gone or butchered and eaten, then the men and the women and the children with them began to die . . . When the soldiers were sick or fell exhausted by thirst or from the harsh rays of the sun, there were no animals or wagons to carry them and those that still marched on were too fatigued to render assistance. There was nothing to be done but to leave them where they fell.[9]

Among the staggering, dying mass was the Hindu priest Kalyana, who had asked to accompany Alexander back to the west so that he could see this part of the world for himself. Remarkably, his Yogic training seemed to have made him almost invulnerable to the terrible heat. In fact, he did not even seem to suffer from thirst. He continued to walk, slowly, deliberately and upright for day after day. Before his crossing of the desert, Alexander is said to have asked such priests about their remarkable wisdom, and their answers concerning life and death were strangely relevant to the predicament he was now in. They are found in Plutarch's account:

> Then he [Alexander] went on and inquired what a man should do to be exceedingly beloved. 'He must be very powerful,' said he, 'without making himself too much feared.' The answer of the seventh to his question, how a man might become a god, was, 'By doing that which was impossible for men to do.' The eighth told him, 'Life is stronger than death, because it supports so many miseries.' And the last being asked, how long he thought it decent for a man to live, said, 'Till death appeared more desirable than life.'[10]

Alexander was now far more feared than he was loved by his men; he was killing more of them by trying to do what no leader had done before; he had made their lives a misery; and now, for many who just gave up and died in the sand, death indeed seemed more desirable than life. By the time they finally reached the other side of the desert as many as 17,000 people appear to have perished. Plutarch records that only about 33,000 survived the crossing.[11]

One last, ironic tragedy was to befall this unfortunate army. According to Arrian, on one occasion they finally found a stream where they could at last drink. They made camp for the night and hundreds were killed in a flash flood.

> There was yet another disaster, and perhaps the worst . . . In Gedrosia, it rains heavily in the monsoon season but the rain does not fall on the desert but in the mountains to the north. The rivers that run down from them become swollen by this rain. When the army made camp in the valley of such a stream, and were able to quench their thirst, in the night the stream grew to such a torrent that many were swept away while they slept. The tragedy is that it was mainly all the camp followers that died: the women and the children for whom the brave soldiers had given their rations of water so that they would survive.[12]

Not only had Meleager's men been decimated, but also many of those who had wives and families with them had lost them too. Alexander had once enjoyed the respect and unswerving devotion of soldiers such as Meleager. Now, since he had been given command of the infantry, Meleager had watched almost half of his men die needlessly and for no other reason than to satisfy the irrational whims of a man who seemed intent on killing them all. If this was not reason enough for Meleager to hate Alexander to the point where he contemplated his murder, then what happened soon after the beleaguered army arrived in Persia was to make Alexander's assassination almost a necessity.

By the end of 325 BC Alexander's army finally reached Pura, where they met up with Craterus and the force sent back to put down the revolt in Gandara. With Craterus' men, the army was now around 50,000 and Alexander decided to allow them all to celebrate. In fact, he decided that his march to the Persian capital of Persepolis would be a parade of triumph. In his account of Alexander's reign, Curtius describes the festivities.

Alexander sent ahead orders to the villages along the road to Persepolis that the route be strewn with flowers, and for flagons of wine to be left outside the doors of all the houses. He also had new wagons made and covered with coloured tents of the most costly material so that his favourite men could pass through in triumph. The royal company, with the queen and other members of his household, rode in front with garlands and wreaths of flowers on their heads, and a band of flute and lyre players led the way. The army then joined in the revels, drinking the wine from the doorsteps and following their king who was in a cart weighed down with as much gold as could be carried.[13]

For seven days these festivities continued, as the drunken army snaked its way along the road to what had been the capital of the Persian Empire. Curtius tells us that this staggering, drunken army was so inebriated that a band of as few as a thousand rebels could have wiped them out. After a week, however, the wine ran out and there was still 500 kilometres of hard marching through the hot Iranian plains before they reached Persepolis. It was lucky it was the middle of winter and there was plenty of water, or Alexander may have lost even more of his army to alcoholic dehydration.[14]

When Alexander finally arrived in Persepolis at the end of January 324 BC, he decided to visit the tomb of the founder of the Persian Empire, Cyrus the Great. It seems that he intended to tell the spirit of Cyrus personally that he had succeeded in leading an army across the Gedrosian Desert where Cyrus had failed. However, while he was here, Alexander was so inspired by the monument that he decided that he would be officially crowned as a Persian king. Arrian describes the tomb:

The monument stood in a splendid park with groves of trees and many various plants, around which flowed streams of running water. The tomb had a rectangular base built from the most precisely cut stone and above it was a roofed chamber, the only way into which was a small door that just one man at a time could enter . . . Inside there was a golden coffin which contained Cyrus' body, resting upon a couch with legs made from worked gold. It was spread with coloured cloth and a robe, the colour of amethyst and set with many precious stones.[15]

The robe had apparently belonged to Cyrus and Alexander decided to have himself crowned in it. Plutarch, in his work *The Life of Artaxerxes* (a Persian king who died in 359 BC), describes the Persian coronation ceremony:

> There is a temple dedicated to a warlike goddess [near the tomb], whom one might liken to Minerva, into which when the royal person to be initiated has passed, he must strip himself of his own robe, and put on that which Cyrus the first wore before he was king.[16]

He had himself crowned as Alexander I of Persia; and, so as not to be outdone by Cyrus, he also took the royal title Alexander the Great.

This may all have been for the benefit of his Persian subjects, but Alexander's European troops felt insulted. They had spent years fighting the Persians, only to have their king act like one of them. However, this was not the first time Alexander had behaved like a Persian king. Three years earlier, before his expedition into India, he had tried to introduce Persian customs to his court.

At a celebratory feast in Bactra, in the summer of 327 BC, when the Sogdian revolt had finally be quashed, Alexander introduced a practice known as *proskynesis*, which was the way Persian subjects bowed and prostrated themselves before their king. In Greece and Macedonia such a practice had never been accepted: courtiers stood in the king's presence, while army officers only greeted their monarch with the usual military salute of a fist against their chest. The only time that *proskynesis* was practised was in temples, before the statute of a god. According to Arrian, a Persian noble suggested the idea to him at the feast.

> The Macedonians would better honour their king with divine honours, he said. There was no doubt that when Alexander departed the world then he would be honoured as a god. Surely it would be better if he were honoured as such during his lifetime.[17]

The man clearly wanted to ingratiate himself to Alexander, and probably doubted that Alexander would take him seriously. Apparently, however, he did, and immediately ordered all those at the banquet to prostrate themselves before him. The Macedonian soldiers could not believe what he was asking them to do and hesitated. Most, no doubt, thought he was joking. However, when they failed to obey he became furious, but one man spoke out. This was his royal scribe Callisthenes.

Then Callisthenes spoke up saying: 'I believe that there is no honour befitting a man that Alexander does not deserve. However, there must be a distinction between the honours paid to mortals and the honours paid to gods . . . Alexander has more than proved himself to be the bravest of the brave, the most royal of kings and the greatest of generals . . . but even Heracles did not receive divine honours from the Greeks while he lived . . . Do not adopt such foreign ways, I implore you, Alexander; do not forget Greece. It was for the sake of Greek ways that you undertook this expedition.' . . . Alexander was furious at these words, though the Greeks and Macedonians applauded them.[18]

Nevertheless, Alexander ordered the guests to each approach in turn and bow before him. Apparently everyone did as they were told, but, when Callisthenes refused, the king had him arrested for insubordination. (He was replaced by Eumenes, who kept the royal diaries and was present at Alexander's last feast.)

A few weeks later, when Alexander further behaved like a Persian king, it almost cost him his life. Alexander was out hunting a wild boar, but he was so drunk that he fell from his horse and the creature turned to attack him. Luckily, one of the young courtiers acted quickly and saved Alexander's life by spearing the animal to death. In Persian court ritual, the king was meant to be the first to kill an animal in a hunt. Alexander was livid at what he considered an insult by the youth and, rather than show his gratitude, had him whipped. The boy was the son of a Macedonian nobleman and whipping was a punishment reserved for slaves. Evidently, other courtiers were so incensed by the punishment that they conspired to kill Alexander in his bed while he slept. He was only saved because he was so drunk that he collapsed and failed to return to his tent. When the plot was discovered the courtiers were executed, along with Callisthenes, whom Alexander accused of being behind it.[19]

This close call seems to have curtailed Alexander's ideas about acting like a Persian monarch, and when the army set off for India things returned to normal. Now, however, three years later, after his coronation as Persian king, Alexander formally reinstated the practice of *proskynesis*. This was almost too much for the Greek and Macedonians to take. They had set out to Hellenise the Persian Empire, and implant the Greek culture of southeastern Europe, only to find that their king had gone native and was expecting them to behave like Persians.

Alexander's first public act after the coronation was to hold a completely Persian-style court. He appeared in his throne room in the regalia of a Persian king: wearing a splendid robe, with a sceptre in his hand and a golden crown on his head. No Greek or Macedonian monarch had ever appeared in this way before. Alexander was setting a fashion that was to entrench itself into the traditions of European royalty that lasts to the present day. At the time, however, it shocked all the Europeans who were subjected to what they considered to be a crude Persian ritual. One by one, they each had to prostrate themselves before the king and bow and touch their foreheads in the traditional Asian manner.

What happened next, however, was to add injury to insult. Alexander summoned the Persian nobles and asked them if they had been treated fairly by their Greek and Macedonian governors while he had been away. At first, they all said they had, but once they realised that Alexander seemed genuinely concerned for their wellbeing the complaints came one after another.[20] Alexander then summoned the European governors of Parthia, Media and Aria, who had recently arrived in Persepolis, and presented them with the charges that they had ill-treated their subjects and had plundered their temples. According to Arrian, Alexander found them guilty, and had them put to death and replaced by Persians.[21]

In March, Alexander moved on to the city of Susa where he rendezvoused with Nearchus and the 20,000 men who had returned from India by boat. These had been mainly the cavalry and their horses that Alexander wanted to avoid losing in the crossing of the Gedrosian Desert. Alexander had obviously been waiting for this moment to make an announcement that was to stun Meleager and the Macedonian infantry. The army was now 70,000 strong, but less than half of them were Greeks and Macedonians. Incredibly, Alexander now decided to send 10,000 of them home.[22]

There can be little doubt that many of them would have been happy to see their homeland again, but for Meleager and the other infantry officers this was the worst snub of all. Since the near mutiny in India, the infantry had been made to suffer, and many suspected that this was Alexander's revenge. There could no longer be any suspecting about it: Alexander was clearly planning to get rid of his European infantry completely. The Macedonian phalanx had once been the backbone of the army, but it was now down to just 20,000 men. This was now going to be cut in half and, worse still, replaced by freshly trained Persians. As Alexander was informing Meleager and his officers of his decision, word got out and hundreds of soldiers surrounded them, shouting that they were being betrayed. According to Justinus, Alexander lost his temper and attacked the chief rabble-rousers with his own bare hands.

At last, when he could produce no effect by words, he leaped unarmed from his tribunal among the armed multitude, to lay hands on the authors of the mutiny; and not a man daring to oppose him, he led thirteen of them, whom he had seized with his own hand, to punishment.[23]

Alexander ordered the Bactrian archers to surround the mob and shoot any man who moved while he had the thirteen hanged. As Justinus says, the rest of the Europeans did nothing: the Macedonian infantry were in the minority. The Persians, who now made up the bulk of Alexander's army, were firmly on his side, as were the Hypaspistes and the European cavalry, who had had a relatively comfortable voyage back, compared to the terrible ordeal suffered by those who had crossed the Gedrosian Desert.

After this, Justinus tells us, Alexander began a full-scale purge of the army; he dismissed many of his senior Greek and Macedonian officers – on the excuse that they were growing old – and ordered a further 11,000 European auxiliary troops to return home.

He then addressed himself, in a public speech, to the auxiliary troops of the Persians apart from the Macedonians. He extolled their constant fidelity, as well as to himself as to their former kings; he mentioned the kindnesses which he had shown them, saying that 'he had never treated them as a conquered people, but always as sharers in his successes; that he had gone over to the usages of their nation, not they to those of his; and that he had mingled the conquerors with the conquered by matrimonial connexions. And now,' he added, 'he would entrust the guardianship of his person, not to the Macedonians only, but also to them.' Accordingly, he enrolled a thousand of their young men among his bodyguard; and at the same time incorporated into his army a portion of the auxiliaries, trained after the discipline of the Macedonians. At this proceeding the Macedonians were much dissatisfied, exclaiming that 'their enemies were put into their places by their king' . . . but he released eleven thousand veterans more.[24]

Alexander even dismissed Craterus, the commander of the cavalry, presumably because he had been unable to order his men to charge the infantry during the trouble in India, and replaced him with Hephaestion.

Whatever his private thoughts, through all of this Meleager remained loyal to his king and persuaded his demobilised troops to go home quietly. However, despite the fact that he had been an exemplary soldier and leader of his men through the most difficult times, Alexander failed to honour Meleager when he rewarded the other senior officers that remained. At a lavish ceremony in Susa in the summer of 324 BC, Alexander placed golden diadems on the heads of Hephaestion, the new commander of the cavalry, Seleucus, the commander of the Hypaspistes, and even the foreign commanders of his army. This was the equivalent of the highest military medal. However, Meleager was conspicuously left out. He had been in the thick of every recent action, had lost more troops than anyone else and had remained steadfastly loyal to his king. Hephaestion, on the other hand, had never once distinguished himself, and his previous commands usually involved little more than leading the baggage train or building bridges. Even the army he had been commissioned to lead down the Indus had been on the western bank and away from the action seen by Meleager and his infantry on the east. Meleager was the most experienced soldier left in the entire army and he was not only commander of the Macedonian phalanx, but also – in theory at least – of the entire allied infantry. Not only was Hephaestion bestowed with the honours that rightly belonged to Meleager, but Alexander also appointed him his grand vizier. This was the Asian equivalent of a prime minister, a position that had never existed in Alexander's empire, and effectively made Hephaestion Alexander's supreme deputy.[25]

At one time Alexander had respected his officers and, although many of them were aristocrats, rather than common men, he never appointed anyone to a position for which they were unsuited. Now, all this had changed and Hephaestion had been given the highest command simply because he was Alexander's friend. After the ceremony, the festivities went on long into the night, and Alexander and Hephaestion drank themselves stupid together in the king's bedchamber of the royal palace.[26] Somewhere outside, Meleager may have been drowning his sorrows with his men. Alexander's failure to bestow honours on Meleager was an insult to the entire Greek and Macedonian infantry, and it is almost certain that there was talk that Alexander had gone too far.

Soon after, Alexander announced that he intended to make Babylon the new capital of his empire. However, a rebellion in Media in the north of Persia forced him to lead an army to Ecbatana to put down the revolt. Knowing that it would not take him long, he ordered that Meleager and the Macedonian infantry go ahead to Babylon and prepare for his arrival once order had been restored. It was fairly obvious to everyone that this would be Meleager's last commission and the Macedonian infantry's final assignment. As soon as Alexander joined them in the city, he would almost certainly order them home. If the proud Macedonian infantry had any role to play in this massive new empire, then Alexander would have to die. It is likely that many of Meleager's officers tried to persuade him to get rid of the king. When Alexander arrived in Babylon the following year, the feast on 1 June was the first opportunity Meleager had to act. Despite everything that had happened, did Meleager remain loyal till the end, or had he finally decided to slip poison into Alexander's wine?

When Meleager and his troops departed for Babylon, one person seems to have believed that Alexander did not have long to live. This was Kalyana, the Hindu priest.

According to Arrian, Kalyana had never had a day's illness in his life, but when he was in Susa he fell sick. No details of the illness are recorded, but whatever was wrong with him, Kalyana seems to have known it was fatal and asked Alexander to help him end his life. Evidently, it was the custom among the priests of the god Skanda to be burned alive on a funeral pyre once they knew their end was near. Although everyone was horrified by the idea, Alexander agreed to his request. According to an eyewitness account of the macabre event, made by the admiral Nearchus and cited by Arrian, the priest died with the most incredible serenity.

> He was carried onto the pyre, for he was too ill to walk, and with great ceremony laid himself down. All the troops stood around watching with astonishment to see him give no sign of pain as the flames began to rise. Then before he died, as if merely falling asleep, he turned to the king and said: 'Alexander, we shall meet again in Babylon.'[27]

Was this just a prediction that Alexander would die in Babylon, or had Kalyana known that someone already had plans to assassinate him there? One way or the other, Alexander should have heeded these words.

And among those who went ahead to Babylon, it was not only Meleager and his troops who had every reason to want Alexander dead. There was also his new wife Statira. Statira was the eldest daughter of the dead Persian king Darius. She had been in Susa since Alexander left her there as a child in 331 BC. She was now sixteen and of marrying age. As well as becoming Persian king, Alexander had decided to found a new Persian dynasty, and to this end married Statira during the ceremony when he honoured his senior officers. It was clearly a political marriage, and Alexander appears to have had no interest in her as a women. In fact, he spent his wedding night getting drunk with the best man, Hephaestion. However, it may also have been a foolish marriage. Statira had sworn that she would one day kill Alexander to avenge her father's death.

SUMMARY OF CHAPTER NINE

When Alexander died, Meleager was the overall commander of the infantry and one of the three most senior officers in the army. His motive for the murder may have been to ensure the survival of the troops under his command.

- Alexander's spectacular military achievements were due in part to the open dialogue he had always encouraged with his men. He treated them with respect and in return received their unswerving devotion in battle. A seasoned infantry officer of around 55, Meleager shared a deep admiration for his commander-in-chief. However, once he had defeated the Persian Empire Alexander began to change.
- It began when Alexander started to behave like a Persian king, expecting his courtiers to prostrate themselves before him – a royal greeting that was alien to Macedonian culture. This was so unlike the familiar Alexander that, when he first ordered his entourage to bow down to him, his court scribe Callisthenes thought he was joking and refused. Everyone realised Alexander was deadly serious when he had the man arrested and killed. The king was also growing increasingly paranoid. He had his cavalry commander Philotas executed on the merest suspicion of disloyalty and ran his replacement Clitus through with a spear for daring to criticise him.
- Alexander's officers quickly learned to keep quiet, but the rank and file of the Macedonian infantry came close to mutiny in the late summer of 326 BC. They had conquered much of the western Punjab, but the Indian campaign was taking its toll. In the stifling monsoon heat, when the king ordered the army deeper into the subcontinent they refused to go. The infantry commander Coenus confronted Alexander with his troops' verdict that it was a pointless war and Alexander reluctantly backed down. However, a few weeks later Coenus died under mysterious circumstances. Whether or not this was Alexander's doing is unknown, but, when Meleager replaced Coenus as chief infantry general in September 326 BC, he must have

considered his promotion a mixed blessing. How long would he survive?

- More soldiers fell to disease and the elements during the return journey to the west than had died in the Indian campaign: firstly on the long march down the Indus Valley, and then during the crossing of the merciless Gedrosian Desert. By the time they finally reached the Persian city of Susa in March 324 BC, there could have been few Macedonian troops who still loved their king.
- In the summer of 324 BC Alexander demobilised 10,000 Macedonian infantry, ordering them home and replacing them with a contingent of Persians. Incredibly, three-quarters of Alexander's soldiers were now Persian and, when the Macedonian infantry protested, he threatened to deploy the Persians against them and had thirteen officers executed for mutiny. Meleager survived the purge but he must have felt his position, even his life, to be under threat. Alexander needed what remained of his Macedonian infantry until he reached Babylon, but he had plans to replace them all. It seems that Meleager had every reason in the world to wish Alexander dead.

Left Bust of Alexander the Great. The young Macedonian king was handsome and athletic, and his eyes of different colours were said to have been captivating to men and irresistible to women. Not only was Alexander arguably history's most successful soldier, he was an ancient trend-setter. His unusual habit of shaving his facial hair established the clean-shaven fashion in Europe that was to last well into Roman times. (Mary Evans Picture Library)

Below A first-century Roman Mosaic at Pompeii depicts Alexander (left) and Darius III (top centre) at the battle of Issus. In November 333 BC, the Macedonians defeated the mighty Asian army and the Persian king fled the battlefield. (Mary Evans Picture Library)

Left Artist's impression of the Hanging Gardens of Babylon – one of the Seven Wonders of the World. This may have been the splendid palace where Alexander held his last banquet and died in June 323 BC. (Mary Evans Picture Library)

Right Alexander did not die a warrior's death in battle, but expired as helpless as a baby in his own bed. What caused this strong, young ruler of half the known world to die mysteriously at the very height of his power? Was he poisoned by a member of his court? (Mary Evans Picture Library)

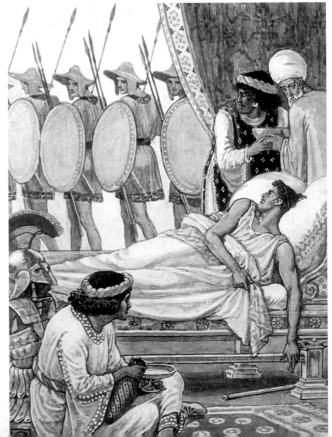

Above An ancient caravan stop near Gordium. Local tradition holds that it was here that Alexander solved the riddle of unravelling the legendary Gordian Knot. He cut it with his sword.
(Photograph: Yvan Cartwright)

Right The ruins of the palace of Persepolis in southern Iran. Once the greatest palace in the ancient world, this wonder of Persian architecture was plundered and senselessly burned by Alexander in a drunken rampage.
(Photograph: Mark Cockle)

Above Alexander with the family of Darius III. The women of the Persian royal family were taken captive after the battle of Issus. One of them was Darius's daughter, Statira, who swore to kill Alexander to avenge her father's death. (Mary Evans Picture Library)

Above Persian war-chariots. At the battle of Arbela, Alexander ordered his infantry to frighten the enemy horses by banging their spears against their shields. The terrified animals turned and stampeded back through the enemy ranks, and the Persian army was cut down by the scythes on the chariot wheels. (Mary Evans Picture Library)

Left The ruins of Aphrodisias in south-west Turkey. It was here that Alexander's son Heracles was finally made king in 309 BC. (Photograph: Deborah Benstead)

Right The Temple of Aphrodite in Aphrodisias. Was it here that Alexander's mother Olympias cleverly planned the death of her own son?
(Photograph: Yvan Cartwright)

Above The wilderness of Chak Chak in eastern Iran. This was the desert and mountainous terrain, once the Persian province of Bactria, where Alexander was forced to fight a long and arduous campaign. (Photograph: Mark Cockle)

Left One of the ancient Persian tombs near Persepolis, claimed to be the final resting place of Alexander the Great. (Photograph: Mark Cockle)

Above A Hindu temple such as the one Alexander visited at Nysa. In the Punjab, such magnificent shrines were sacred to the god Skanda, whose statues stood in groves of sacred Shudha trees. (Mary Evans Picture Library)

Above Rather than surrender, the Indian king Puru tells Alexander to take his life. Alexander was lucky to defeat the Indians. Their war-elephants terrified the Macedonian horses, and almost cost Alexander the entire campaign. (Mary Evans Picture Library)

Above The dwellings of the Magi in the Cappadocian city of Korama (modern Goreme). Was Alexander murdered on the orders of this ancient mystical sect? (Photograph: Deborah Benstead)

Below The Library of Celsus at Ephesus. Did its ancient archives hold a vital clue to reveal the identity of Alexander's murderer? (Photograph: Deborah Benstead)

10. STATIRA – A SENTENCE OF DEATH

Statira was born in 340 BC into the most incredible luxury. Her first name was actually Barsine but to distinguish her from the other Barsine, she is usually referred to as Statira. The royal palace at Persepolis was a marvel of huge staterooms, lavishly decorated with frescoes, tapestries and statuettes, connected by an endless maze of columned walkways. Amongst this splendid labyrinth there were dozens of courtyards, ornamented with beds of beautiful flowers and shaded by overhanging fruit trees. At the centre of each there was a trickling fountain of cool water and a gilded cage containing many exotic birds: the palace is said to have echoed to their song. It would have been a comfortable place for a child to play, as the floors of the royal chambers were covered with soft, intricately woven carpets. All around the palace there were balustraded balconies that looked out over the flat-roofed houses of the city below. From one of these, Statira must often have gazed in wonder at one of the most spectacular views in her father's empire: the magnificent gardens that surrounded the spectacular tombs of her ancestors that lay just to the north of the town. According to all accounts, Darius was a kind and loving father and Statira's mother, the queen, was said to be the most beautiful woman in Persia. This was the fairy-tale life that the little princess enjoyed until the age of seven, when her father set out to face Alexander at the battle of Issus in 333 BC.

Darius must have been confident of victory because he took his entire family with him. Not only did he take Statira, his wife, his mother Sisygambis and his youngest daughter Drypetis, but he also took his five-year-old son Cambyses, who was the heir to the throne. Just before the battle in November that year, the Persian king left them in the Syrian city of Damascus. Darius assumed that they would be safe, whatever the outcome of the battle, as they were 400 kilometres from the fighting. Even if he lost, they could return to the east well before Alexander's army reached them. However, the king made a drastic mistake: he left his royal treasury in the city too.

When Darius was defeated and fled east, Alexander learned about the treasury in Damascus and sent an advanced mounted force to the city to seize the gold before it could be shipped out. The garrison in the city was taken by surprise and everything was seized – including the royal family. However, Plutarch describes the considerate way in which they were treated by Alexander:

151

Word was brought him that Darius' mother and wife and two unmarried daughters, being taken among the rest of the prisoners, upon the sight of his chariot and bow, were all in mourning and sorrow, imagining him to be dead. After a little pause, more likely affected with their affliction than with his own success, he sent Leonnatus [one of his officers] to them, to let them know Darius was not dead, and that they need not fear any harm from Alexander, who made war upon him only for dominion; they should themselves be provided with everything they had been used to receive from Darius. This kind message could not but be very welcome to the captive ladies, especially being made good by actions no less humane and generous. For he gave them leave to bury whom they pleased of the Persians, and to make use for this purpose of what garments and furniture they thought fit out of the booty. He diminished nothing of their equipage, or of the attentions and respect formerly paid them, and allowed larger pensions for their maintenance than they had before. But the noblest and most royal part of their usage was, that he treated these illustrious prisoners according to their virtue and character, not suffering them to hear, or receive, or so much as to apprehend anything that was unbecoming . . . Nevertheless, Darius' wife was accounted the most beautiful princess then living, as her husband the tallest and handsomest man of his time, and the daughters were not unworthy of their parents. But Alexander, esteeming it more kingly to govern himself than to conquer his enemies, sought no intimacy with any one of them.[1]

The little princesses may have been beautiful, like their mother, but they were only six and seven years of age. If they had been older, Alexander may have married Statira at the time, so as to legitimise his claim on the Persian Empire. In fact, Darius actually offered Statira to Alexander as a bride in his letter in which he attempted to sue for peace. It may have been acceptable in Persia to marry someone so young, but in Macedonia a girl had to be at least a teenager before she could marry. It seems that Alexander decided to keep her on ice.

Statira apparently remained in Syria with her family until Alexander returned from Egypt to face Darius again in the autumn of 331 BC. The girl, now nine, and the rest of her family were put into wagons and joined the army as it marched east to meet the Persians at Arbela. On the way, Statira suffered a terrible double tragedy. Firstly, her mother died in childbirth. Plutarch describes Alexander's grief and Darius' sorrow at the death:

But the death of Darius' wife in childbirth made him soon after regret one part of this answer [in a threatening letter to the Persian king], and he showed evident marks of grief at thus being deprived of a further opportunity of exercising his clemency and good nature, which he manifested, however, as far as he could, by giving her a most sumptuous funeral. Among the eunuchs who waited in the queen's chamber, and were taken prisoners with the women, there was one Tireus, who, getting out of the camp, fled away on horseback to Darius, to inform him of his wife's death. He, when he heard it, beating his head, and bursting into tears and lamentations, said, 'Alas! how great is the calamity of the Persians! Was it not enough that their king's consort was a prisoner in her lifetime, but she must, now she is dead, also be but meanly and obscurely buried?' 'O king,' replied the eunuch, 'as to her funeral rites, or any respect or honour that should have been shown in them, you have not the least reason to accuse the ill fortune of your country; for to my knowledge neither your queen Statira when alive, nor your mother, nor children, wanted anything of their former happy condition, unless it were the light of your countenance, which I doubt not but the lord Oromasdes [the supreme Persian god] will yet restore to its former glory. And after her decease, I assure you, she had not only all due funeral ornaments, but was honoured also with the tears of your very enemies; for Alexander is as gentle after victory as he is terrible in the field.'[2]

Who the father of the child was is unknown, but it couldn't have been Darius, as he had not seen his queen for almost two years. Unfortunately, Darius' reaction to this is not recorded.

The second tragedy followed almost immediately, when Statira's seven-year-old brother Cambyses died. According to the *Historia*, he had always been a sickly child and the rough journey, coupled with grief over his mother's death, seems finally to have contributed to his demise. These sad blows for Princess Statira ironically also made her the most important person in the Persian Empire after her father. With no son to succeed him, and the queen dead, until and unless Darius married again and had another son, then whoever married Statira would be the legitimate Persian king.

After the Persian army was decisively beaten at Arbela and Darius again fled the battlefield, Alexander knew that Babylon and the Persian capital of Persepolis were his for the taking. Until this time, Alexander had apparently treated women and children with respect and had only

153

ever endorsed the killing of adult males. Even after the sieges of Tyre and Gaza, when Alexander had dealt out the most dreadful reprisals on the inhabitants of the cities, he ordered that no woman or child be hurt. Darius, it seems, had greatly respected Alexander for this, and Plutarch records that he had praised his enemy when the eunuch told him about the fair treatment of Persian women.

> [The eunuch told Darius] that he ought to look upon Alexander with love and admiration, who had given no less proofs of his continence towards the Persian women, than of his valour among the men. The eunuch confirmed all he said with solemn and dreadful oaths, and was further enlarging upon Alexander's moderation and magnanimity on other occasions, when Darius, breaking away from him into the other division of the tent, where his friends and courtiers were, lifted up his hands to heaven and uttered this prayer, 'Ye gods,' said he, 'of my family, and of my kingdom, if it be possible, I beseech you to restore the declining affairs of Persia, that I may leave them in as flourishing a condition as I found them, and have it in my power to make a grateful return to Alexander for the kindness which in my adversity he has shown to those who are dearest to me.'[3]

However, after Alexander's victory at Arbela, matters got tragically out of hand. When Alexander marched on Babylon, the city's inhabitants knew they stood no chance. According to Curtius, its Persian commander, Mazaeus, formally surrendered when Alexander assured him the city would be spared.

> When he arrived at Babylon, Alexander was met by Mazaeus, who came with his children to surrender the city. Alexander was happy that this was so, for the city walls were built to withstand a long siege. Since Mazaeus was an eminent man and a respected solider, his example induced others to leave the city to and surrender to the Macedonians. In return, Alexander warmly welcomed him and his children and promised that no harm would come to any who laid down their arms.[4]

Alexander, in a fabulous ceremonial chariot, led the army into Babylon through its famous Ishtar Gate. All along the streets inside the way was strewn with flowers by the population, who welcomed him as if he were a liberator. Alexander had promised that no woman or child would be harmed, but it seems that he lost control over his men, who went on a drunken rampage of rape and pillage. The Greeks and Macedonians had been told that the women of Babylon all served a goddess of love and the soldiers believed they could take whatever women they fancied. This mistaken Greek myth is recorded by Curtius.

> Alexander stayed in Babylon longer than he stayed anywhere before, because he lost the discipline of his troops. It was the fault of the belief they had in the moral corruption of the city . . . They had heard that men permitted their wives and children to have sex with anyone, so long as the act was paid for . . . and when women attend parties, they remove their clothes by degree so as to seduce the men and when finally naked they engage in perversions of every kind. It was even said that the youngest of girls regarded such prostitution as a sociable act.[5]

Once the troops discovered that their information was untrue, it was too late for them to control themselves and the result was a riot of sexual frenzy. For an entire night the men broke into homes and dragged the women, and even little girls, from their beds and raped them in the streets. The men attempted to fight off the attackers, but they were cut down as they tried. Alexander was appalled that his soldiers were disobeying his orders and commanded that his royal guard put a stop to it. Unfortunately, the royal guard were 'enjoying themselves' like everybody else. At one point things were so out of control that some of the soldiers tried to force themselves on the nine-year-old Statira and her eight-year-old sister, but Alexander's chief bodyguard Ptolemy managed to fight them off. By the time it was all over, the city was not only strewn with flowers, but with ravaged women and the bodies of their slain husbands and fathers.[6]

Alexander apologised to Mazaeus for what had occurred; he paid him off in gold and appointed him the governor of Babylonia. However, Alexander failed to discipline his troops; to do so would be to admit he had lost control. To the Persians and Babylonians, however, it looked as though he condoned the terrible carnage. Alexander left Babylon at the end of the year and did not see the city again for seven and a half years. As if by providence, when he returned in the summer of 323 BC, it was to be the city in which he died. Regardless of how well he had treated her, Statira must already have blamed Alexander for her mother and brother's deaths. One of Alexander's men must have forced himself upon the Persian queen because she had died in childbirth. As for the seven-year-old Cambyses: if he had not been made to travel in an army wagon for well over 500 kilometres, he might still be alive. The dreadful spectacle that Statira had witnessed at Babylon may ultimately have made her decide that this was a fitting place for Alexander to die. However, there were soon to be further personal tragedies that the unfortunate child was forced to endure.

When the army reached the Persian city of Susa in December, the garrison commander, Abulites, surrendered without resistance. Luckily, there was no repeat of the troops' dreadful behaviour in Babylon. Little seems to have occurred in the city, as Alexander was keen to move on to the capital of Persepolis where he believed Darius was. However, it was during an episode that occurred in Susa that we discover something interesting about Statira – she was remarkably tall. According to Curtius, when Alexander was in Darius' palace in the city, he sat on the Persian king's throne, only to find that his feet did not touch the ground. Darius is recorded as being an exceptionally tall man and it seems that his daughter took after him. When Alexander had left the room, Statira came in and she too sat on the throne, but *her* feet did touch the ground. Alexander may have been an outstandingly handsome man but he is said to have been short. Indeed, if Statira was taller than Alexander when she was only nine years old, she must have towered over him at the wedding ceremony seven years later.[7]

The city of Susa may have surrendered without a fight, but Persepolis did not. It appears that word about the atrocities in Babylon had reached the capital, and for ten days a small army of Persian defenders fought to the last man in a desperate but futile attempt to keep their city safe. When they were defeated, Alexander showed no admiration for the men who had fought so bravely to defend their homes, nor did he try to make amends for the horrors in Babylon by sparing the city when the governor surrendered. Instead, he told his men to do what they liked. It seems they had acquired a taste for rape and pillage and Alexander no longer cared. Only the royal palace and the necropolis (the royal burial site) was spared, and for three days it was a nightmare for the inhabitants of what had once been the capital of the largest empire in the world. The houses were plundered and the temples were looted, and many of the citizens chose to commit suicide rather than face the appalling horrors inflicted by the rampaging Europeans.[8]

The Greeks and Macedonians assumed that the war was over, but, when Alexander discovered that Darius was not in the city, he went berserk and began smashing up the palace throne-room. When the chief bodyguard Ptolemy managed to calm him down, Alexander decided to announce that he was king of Persia, regardless of the fact that Darius was still alive. It must have come as a relief to Statira to learn that her father still lived. All the same, it must have been a heartbreaking return to her beautiful home. The palace that had once echoed with the sound of birdsong now resounded with the screams of terror from the citizens who were being butchered in the streets outside. Never again would she hear her mother's lullabies in the royal chambers, or play with her little brother in the stately rooms. The palace that had once been her world of friends and family was now the barracks for the officers of a cruel, barbarian mob. Worst of all, the tyrant Alexander sat on her father's throne – a throne that even she was more suited to sit in than he.

If Statira hoped that things would one day return to the way they were, she was in for an awful shock. Alexander stayed in Persepolis for four months, hoping that the Persians would surrender and hand Darius over. When it failed to happen, he set off again, north to Ecbatana where the Persian king was attempting to assemble a new army. Before he left, however, he commanded that the palace be looted and burned to the ground. This was a completely senseless act of vandalism, which Plutarch explains that Alexander ordered when he was drunk.

> From hence designing to march against Darius, before he set out he diverted himself with his officers at an entertainment of drinking and other pastimes, and indulged so far as to let everyone's mistress sit by and drink with them. The most celebrated of them was Thais, an Athenian mistress of Ptolemy . . . She said it was indeed some recompense for the toils she had undergone in following the camp all over Asia, that she was that day treated in, and could insult over, the stately palace of the Persian monarchs. But, she added, it would please her much better if, while the king looked on, she might in sport, with her own hands, set fire to the court of that Xerxes who reduced the city of Athens to ashes, that it might be recorded to posterity that the women who followed Alexander had taken a severer revenge on the Persians for the suffering, and affronts of Greece, than all the famed commanders had been able to do by sea or land. What she said was received with such universal liking and murmurs of applause, and so seconded by the encouragement and eagerness of the company, that the king himself, persuaded to be of the party, started from his seat, and with a chaplet of flowers on his head and a lighted torch in his hand, led them the way, while they went after him in a riotous manner, dancing and making loud cries about the place . . .[9]

When the army moved on in May 330 BC, Statira was ten years old. She had begun her life in a dream world, but over the last year she had suffered in a way that no child should. She had watched her mother and brother die; she had witnessed innocent women and girls as young as herself raped before her eyes; she had seen her birthplace plundered and its people killed, and she had seen her beautiful home razed to the ground. If this was not enough to harden any girl's heart, then the death of her father was the last straw.

It may have been Bessus' men who killed Darius, but Statira blamed Alexander. Bessus had offered to hand over the captive Persian king, but Alexander knew full well that if he refused to accept him then the Bactrians would kill him themselves. Statira knew this too. Alexander, however, wanted to indulge the Persians he now ruled; so to lay the blame of their king's death squarely at Bessus' feet, he arranged a splendid state funeral for Darius. This won over some of the Persian nobility, but it did nothing to curtail Statira's anger. With the queen dead, and as his eldest child, Alexander let Statira decide on the manner of Darius' last rites. Usually, Persian kings were entombed, but Statira asked for her father to be cremated, as she feared that his tomb would be desecrated by the Macedonians, just as his palace had been. The *Historia* includes a moving and enlightening passage concerning the funeral.

> The princess [Statira] was only a child, but she shed not a single tear. She stood before the funeral pyre, upon which Darius lay, and set the flames with the torch she held. Still not one tear appeared in her eyes as she watched her father burn; nor did she utter a word until the flames had died. To her sister and before her servants, it is said she swore this oath: 'With this hand that I lit the flames, will I one day slay this king.'[10]

She referred, of course, to Alexander. From this passage we can gather that all emotion had been wrung out of the poor child, and all she had left was cold hatred for the man who had taken away almost everything she loved. Was she true to her word: was it her hand that put poison into Alexander's wine?

After the funeral, Alexander sent Statira and her sister Drypetis back to Susa, where they were to be brought up as Macedonian princesses. It seems that, even at this time, Alexander had plans to marry Statira once she came of age. When he finally returned from India, in 324 BC, Statira was sixteen, and this is exactly what he did. According to Arrian, after Alexander arrived back in Susa, in the summer of that year, he held a lavish wedding ceremony in which both he and his best friend and new deputy Hephaestion were married. Alexander married Statira and Hephaestion married Drypetis.

> Alexander also celebrated weddings in the city of Susa . . . He married Statira, Darius' eldest daughter, while Drypetis was married to Hephaestion. Drypetis was given to Hephaestion as she also was Darius' daughter and the sister of this new wife. Alexander hoped that the children of his friend would be the cousins of the children he hoped to sire. The marriages were held according to the custom of the Persians. Seats were placed for the grooms and after they had drunk well, each bride came and sat beside her husband to be. The men took their women by their hands and kissed them and the marriage rites began . . . Once they were married, the grooms each led their brides away.[11]

It is strange, but Alexander and Hephaestion seemed to have had absolutely no interest in the two young girls – who, by all accounts, were extremely beautiful. In fact, the two men spent their dual wedding night getting drunk together in Alexander's bedroom. The wedding must have been a bizarre and vile paradox for Statira; not only had she been forced to marry a man she had sworn to kill, but she had been insulted before the world when he did not even sleep with her on her wedding night. It might, at least, have made it possible for her to keep her oath. She would now be close enough to her enemy to kill him. However, it is possible that Statira had decided against killing her new husband. Not only would her children be his heirs, but also she was now a Persian queen. There was, though, another reason that she may have put the past to rest.

After Darius was killed six years earlier, the Persian king's mother, Sisygambis, was obviously as upset by her son's death as her grand-daughter, Statira. However, she did not want to see the girl grow up with nothing but anger in her heart. While they were in Susa, Sisygambis decided to introduce Statira to Zoroastrianism. It was not the country's official religion, but it had a large following in Persia and Babylonia. It taught a message of self-control and of peace, and Sisygambis apparently hoped that it would curtail her granddaughter's bitterness. Unlike most religions at the time, it taught there was a single, supreme god; but it was also virtually unique in that it afforded women the same religious rights as men. Women could become Zoroastrian priestesses and they could join in worship alongside the men. A

Zoroastrian priest was sent for and he apparently spent a number of years at the palace in Susa. Evidently, Statira's Macedonian minders saw no problem with the princess being taught Zoroastrian beliefs. However, after Alexander set off to the north, to put down the rebellion in the province of Media, in October 324 BC, this previously peace-loving religion was to give Statira a new and additional reason to kill the Macedonian king.[12]

Media was a centre of Zoroastrianism and its provincial capital of Ecbatana was the religion's holy city. In early 323 BC, as part of the reprisals for the revolt, Alexander ordered that a monument to the Zoroastrian founding prophet which stood in the centre of the city should be torn down; he desecrated temples, outlawed religious practices, executed priests and ordered the *Avesta*, the holy book of Zoroastrianism, to be burned. After this the Zoroastrian high priests took the unprecedented step of announcing that Alexander was the incarnation of their devil and issued a 'fatwa' against him, condemning him to death. There was now a religious contract out on Alexander's life, and every Zoroastrian was obliged to try to kill him if they could. If Statira had taken to Zoroastrianism and had found it helpful in suppressing her hatred of Alexander, then it now gave her a moral excuse to assassinate him. She had been sent on to Babylon with Meleager in autumn the previous year, before the death sentence was announced. The next time she is known to have seen him was at his final feast. If she had decided to carry out her religious obligation, then this seems to have been the first chance she had.

At the same time that Alexander was persecuting the Zoroastrians, he was giving yet another person at the feast a motive to kill him. This was his general Perdiccas – the last suspect on our list.

SUMMARY OF CHAPTER TEN

Statira is the only one of the eight suspects in Alexander's murder known to have openly threatened to kill him. As a child, she had sworn to avenge her father's death, for which she held Alexander responsible.

- Statira was the sixteen-year-old daughter of the Persian king Darius III who had been captured as a child after the battle of Issus in 333 BC. Along with her mother and sister, she had been well treated by Alexander and had been raised with a Greek education in the occupied city of Susa. When Alexander arrived back from India in 324 BC he decided to make Statira his second wife, presumably as a political act to secure his position as king of the Persian Empire.

- After his problems with the Macedonian army, Alexander needed the acceptance of the Persian aristocracy more than ever. Indeed, he was now acting more Persian than European. He not only insisted on the Persian form of royal greeting, he had taken to wearing the Persian royal vestments and crown. Moreover, he arrested and executed a number of Macedonian governors when he learned that they had ill-treated the native populace. Nevertheless, Alexander had continually insulted his conquered subjects in a deeply profane way – one that may have given Statira a further motive for murder.

- Statira promised to kill Alexander as a child, but she had another motive to assassinate the king. Although she had been brought up in the Macedonian style, she had been allowed to practise her native Zoroastrian religion. Although he had originally been tolerant of foreign religions, just a few months before he died Alexander began to persecute the Zoroastrians. He desecrated their temples, outlawed their religious practices, executed priests and ordered the *Avesta*, the holy book of Zoroastrianism, to be burned.

- Not everyone in Persia was Zoroastrian and it is doubtful its teachings would have mattered much to the average Persian soldier in Alexander's ranks. However, Alexander totally underestimated the depth of religious conviction amongst Zoroastrian zealots, and, when the equivalent of a fatwa was issued against him after he erected a blasphemous statue of a lion in the holy city of Ecbatana at the end of 324 BC, he failed to show any sign of concern. Alexander even ignored a number of Zoroastrian holy men who warned him about the religious death threat a few weeks before he died.

- Zoroastrianism taught the equality of men and women and, as a devout Zoroastrian, it was Statira's obligation to kill her husband if she could. For some months after the death sentence was passed, Alexander was in the field of battle putting down an insurrection in northern Iran, while Statira had been sent ahead to Babylon. The first chance she had to carry out what she may have considered her sacred duty was when Alexander joined her there in the summer of the following year – and within a few short weeks he was indeed dead.

11. PERDICCAS – THE LAST DAYS

Some four or five years older than Alexander, Perdiccas was the son of a Macedonian nobleman. He was not the most accomplished of soldiers, but he had one of the most varied careers of any officer in Alexander's army. The first we hear of him is as one of Philip's bodyguards at the time of the king's assassination in October 336 BC: it was Perdiccas who killed Philip's murderer, Pausanias, when he tried to escape.[1] As the avoidable death of the assassin prevented him from being interrogated to discover whether or not he had acted alone, if there was a conspiracy in which Alexander and his mother were involved, then Perdiccas may well have been part of it. He certainly supported Alexander's claim to the throne, as he was immediately promoted to the equivalent of a modern lieutenant colonel and given command of a phalanx battalion.

Perdiccas' first recorded military action was in the spring of 335 BC, the year after Alexander's accession, when he was part of the force sent to quash the uprising in Illyria. After the revolt was successfully dealt with, Perdiccas was in Greece, leading the battalion that stormed the rebellious city of Thebes in September of that year. When Alexander crossed into Asia Minor in 334 BC, Perdiccas went with him and played an important role in the battle of Granicus that June. By this time, Perdiccas had been in the front line of every major battle of Alexander's reign and had already been wounded twice. He was clearly a dedicated and fearless solider and came from the right aristocratic background to go far in the Macedonian army. Nevertheless, he was not to be promoted again for another nine years. The reason, it seems, is that he almost lost Alexander the battle for the harbour town of Halicarnassus, in southwest Turkey, a couple of months after the victory at Granicus. According to Arrian, Perdiccas' battalion failed to storm the walls of the town because they were drunk. It seems that, although Perdiccas was a fierce warrior, he was a bad commander who failed to control his troops.[2]

After the siege of Halicarnassus, Perdiccas was fortunate to retain his commission and continued with Alexander to Gordium, where the army spent the winter of 334–3 BC. For the next three years Perdiccas remained in the thick of the fighting – at Issus, Tyre, Arbela, and Persepolis – but once the army moved into Bactria, in the summer of 330 BC, he was left behind at Ecbatana as part of the force that secured the supply road from Europe. In December that year, when his

163

commander Parmenion was executed after Philotas was found guilty of conspiracy to kill Alexander, Perdiccas found himself in charge of this rearguard. He remained in Ecbatana, where he saw no more fighting for two years, but rejoined Alexander in 328 BC during the Sogdian campaign. Once Sogdiana was pacified, he continued on with the army into India, where his battalion was deployed to support Hephaestion's expeditionary force that built the bridge over the Indus.[3]

Until this time Perdiccas had been an infantry officer, but during the attack on Sangala, in the summer of 326 BC, he is recorded as commanding a cavalry squadron. A couple of months later, after the near mutiny when Coenus mysteriously died, he was back in the infantry under Meleager's command. When the army moved south down the Indus during 325 BC, Perdiccas was in the cavalry once more as one of Hephaestion's senior officers in the force on the west bank. This effectively made him the equivalent of a full colonel and was his first promotion since he had blotted his record at Halicarnassus nine years before. In fact, a year later, in August 324 BC, when the supreme cavalry commander Craterus was sent back to Macedonia, Perdiccas became a general and Hephaestion's deputy. Then, just two months later, he unexpectedly became commander of all Alexander's cavalry when Hephaestion suddenly died.[4] If Perdiccas was Alexander's murderer, then Hephaestion's death was the key episode that triggered events that gave him a number of possible motives.

In October 324 BC, after Alexander had sent his new wife Statira on to Babylon with Meleager and his men, the main army left Susa and marched north to the city of Ecbatana to put down a rebellion. Ecbatana was the capital of Media, and the governor of the province, Atarepata, was a Persian who had come over to Alexander's side after the death of Darius. The rebels were few in number, but they were conducting a hit-and-run, guerrilla campaign in the Median Mountains and were proving difficult for Atarepata to flush out. After the war in Sogdiana three years earlier, Alexander had troops who were expert at this kind of warfare and he was eager to help. As far as Alexander was concerned, this was to be little more than a minor excursion before he entered Babylon in triumph.[5] However, while he was attending a welcoming banquet organised by Atarepata, Alexander's second-in-command Hephaestion fell ill and died. There are few recorded details of Hephaestion's sickness, but what we know suggests that it was something unusual. According to the accounts, Hephaestion collapsed and was taken to his bedchamber, where he seems to have suffered convulsions, followed by a bizarre facial paralysis. The *Historia*, for instance, tells us that 'Hephaestion's face was frozen in a deathly grin, and though he could move his head and arms, his jaw was rigid and he could utter not a word'.[6]

Whatever killed Hephaestion, it did not take long. Justinus implies that he died the night he fell ill, 'in the course of those proceedings',[7] while Plutarch says it was 'shortly after'.[8] As Hephaestion had previously been in good health, the relatively quick death convinced Alexander that his friend had been poisoned and he brutally interrogated the servants. When Hephaestion's doctor insisted that the symptoms matched no known poison, Alexander flew into a rage and had him executed for daring to contradict him.[9] Somehow, Alexander was eventually persuaded that his friend had died of a natural illness, but not before at least half a dozen people had been executed.

Hephaestion had been Alexander's closest friend since childhood and, although Alexander's relationship with Barsine seems to have come between the two men for a while, after her departure from the scene they were as close as ever. Diodorus tells us that Alexander 'loved Hephaestion more than any other friend and was highest in his affections'.[10] Indeed, during the last few months they had been virtually inseparable. They had a joint marriage ceremony at Susa, and Alexander had made Hephaestion his deputy, even though there were far more able men for the job. Although he apparently accepted that Hephaestion had not been poisoned, the death seems to have completely unhinged Alexander's mind. For some time he had been showing signs of mental instability: he was increasingly living in a world of make-believe; he treated his army with contempt, and he expected to be greeted like a god. Hephaestion's death seems to have been the last straw that sent him over the edge into a complete psychological breakdown. According to Arrian, Alexander's reaction to the death was initially one of inconsolable grief.

> Alexander flung himself upon his friend's body and lay there crying for the whole day. Even that night he lay stretched out upon the corpse, sobbing . . . For two whole days after Hephaestion's death, Alexander ate no food and paid no attention to his bodily needs, but lay on his bed crying uncontrollably.[11]

When Alexander finally emerged from his hysterical grief, he commanded a special period of mourning by ordering the tails of all military horses to be clipped. It seems he had taken the idea from Homer's *Iliad*, where Achilles does the same to mourn the death of his friend Patroclus.

Ten years before, when Alexander portrayed himself as a reincarnated Achilles, he had chosen Hephaestion for the part of Patroclus at the festivities in Troy. According to Arrian, Alexander wanted the whole world to appreciate the similarity they bore to the ancient, mythical heroes.

> Hephaestion's death had been the greatest calamity for Alexander, and I am sure he would rather have been the first to die, than live to suffer the pain of loss, like Achilles, who would rather have died before Patroclus than to have lived to avenge his death.[12]

However, Alexander decided that this was not enough to honour his friend. According to Plutarch, he issued a series of orders that were clearly deranged. The first was to nail Hephaestion's doctor's body to a cross and have it erected in public, as a postmortem punishment for failing to save his master's life. He then forbade any kind of frivolity and ordered a mass slaughter of innocent civilians as a sacrifice to Hephaestion's spirit.

> The poor physician he crucified, and forbade playing on the flute or any other musical instrument in the camp a great while . . .
> Then, seeking to alleviate his grief in war, he set out, as it were, to a hunt and chase of men, for he fell upon the Cossaeans, and put the whole nation to the sword. This was called a sacrifice to Hephaestion's ghost.[13]

The Cossaeans were a tribe that lived in the mountains of Media. There was no evidence to implicate them in the revolt, nor had they given sanctuary to the rebels. Alexander nevertheless ordered them to be randomly massacred by the Hypaspistes, simply as a sacrifice to Hephaestion. If this slaughter of helpless men, women and children, who had been living peacefully under Macedonian rule, was not bad enough, Alexander then began to persecute the equally innocent Zoroastrians. It began when they refused to carry out Alexander's orders to put out the sacred fires that continually burned in their temples. According to Diodorus:

> He proclaimed that the Persians should immediately quench what they called the sacred fire, until the funeral of Hephaestion be over.[14]

These particular Persians were the Zoroastrians and their sacred flames represented a divine presence, similar to the menorah of the Jews. To put out these flames was unthinkable to the Zoroastrian priesthood, and they refused. Alexander was furious and ordered the temples to be sacked. A Zoroastrian text known as the *Book of Arda Viraf* refers to him desecrating temples, executing priests and ordering the *Avesta*, the holy book of Zoroastrianism, to be burned.

> And the holy book, the Avesta, was written in golden ink upon cow skins and in the archives, where Alexander burnt them . . . And he killed many priests and also the Magi [Zoroastrian mystics] and others who upheld the religion and their places of worship.[15]

The final straw for the Zoroastrians, however, was when Alexander ordered a monument to the religion's founder, the prophet Zarathustra, to be pulled down and replaced by the statue of a lion. The lion was the emblem of the Macedonian monarchy, but to the Zoroastrians the lion represented their devil Guzastag, the personification of evil who would be incarnated as a man in the world's final days. Certain members of the Zoroastrian priesthood perceived this blasphemous statue to be a sign that Alexander was this devil and took the unprecedented step of issuing a death sentence against him. Alexander appears to have scoffed at this religious contract on his life, but he nonetheless ordered the killing of a sect of Zoroastrian holy men known as the Magi.[16] The Magi were sworn to peace and appear to have had absolutely nothing to do with the threat on Alexander's life. Neither did another innocent victim of Alexander's purge: the Median governor Atarepata. Atarepata had been a Zoroastrian himself and Alexander gave orders that he be executed. However, Atarepata, suspecting he was in danger, had fled with his family into the Median Mountains.

Alexander decided to have Perdiccas take over completely from Hephaestion; not only as cavalry commander, but also as prime minister.[17] This decision to make Perdiccas his supreme deputy is a strange one. Perdiccas was not only Atarepata's friend; he was married to the man's daughter. Moreover, he had sympathy for the Magi that Alexander was persecuting.

Nine years earlier, in 333 BC, when Alexander's army left Gordium to march south towards Issus, they passed through the province of Cappadocia in central Turkey. Here they encountered the remarkable city of Korama, where they made camp for a few days. Now called Goreme, eleven kilometres northeast of modern Nevsehir, it is an area where, over millennia, the tufa-stone hills have been carved into the most spectacular shapes by wind and sand. These strangely contorted pinnacles of soft, yellow rock, which rise high above the surrounding desert, are honeycombed with an elaborate labyrinth of chambers and passageways, artificially cut into the cliffs almost three thousand years ago. When Alexander's army arrived here in 333 BC, this rock-cut city was home to a community of Zoroastrian mystics known as the Magi – a religious sect that seems to have greatly impressed Perdiccas.

The word Magi is the origin of the modern word 'magician'. However, the Zoroastrian Magi had nothing to do with magic or wizardry. They were, though, keen astrologers and interpreters of omens and dreams, which is why the term was later used by the Romans to apply to a sorcerer. Like all Zoroastrians, the Magi believed in the universal creator god, Ahura Mazda, and in an afterlife in which the dead would be rewarded or punished for their deeds in life, although they were far more devout and stringent in their beliefs. The Greek historian Herodotus, writing around a hundred years before Alexander's visit to Korama, describes the Magi in detail. Apparently, they were taught to live for the benefit of others, and were not even permitted to pray for anything for themselves – only for the good of the community. They lived as one with nature; they would eat no meat from an animal that was not killed with their own hands, and they refused to take a human life. In fact, they believed that their bodies should nourish nature after their souls had departed.

Herodotus describes the practice of excarnation: a funeral rite where the bodies of the dead are left until the flesh is devoured by wild animals before the bones are interred in tombs. In Korama, there were huge columns of weathered rock which the Magi hollowed out into chambers, open to the sky. Called 'towers of silence', these were where the corpses were left for their bones to be stripped clean by vultures.[18] These strange rocky pinnacles, shaped like elongated toadstools, can still be seen today and are called 'fairy chimneys' by the local Turks.

According to the Greek geographer Strabo (circa 64 BC–AD 23), the Magi of Korama also venerated fire.

In Cappadocia there is a sect of the Magi, who are also called the Pyrethaia [fire makers], and they have fire temples, in the centre of which is a fire that is always kept burning. Each day, for about an hour, they make incantations before these fires, holding sacred twigs and wearing turbans which reveal only their eyes.[19]

At this early stage in his campaigns, Alexander not only tolerated but also was enthralled by foreign religions. In fact, so much did he appreciate the Magi's doctrine of peace that he left them and the people of much of Cappadocia to govern themselves. He did not even bother to leave behind an occupation force or a military governor, as he wrongly assumed that all Cappadocians were committed to peace. A Persian governor named Ariatathes remained in charge and seems to have created a kingdom of his own right in the middle of Macedonian-held territory.

The Magi of Korama seem to have had a profound influence on Perdiccas. When he was stationed in Media between 330 and 328 BC, he struck up a close friendship with the governor Atarepata. Atarepata was a Persian aristocrat and a leading Zoroastrian. This is revealed by his name, which means 'keeper of the fire' – an honorary name given to the priest whose sworn responsibility it was to keep the sacred temple fires burning.[20] His friendship with Atarepata seems to have spurred Perdiccas' fascination with Zoroastrianism. When he became commander of the garrison in Ecbatana after Parmenion's death, he led an expedition back to Cappadocia and spent two months in the city of Korama. Although the excuse for the excursion was to assure that Cappadocia was not being used as a safe haven by Persian partisans, there was no military reason to spend so much time in the Magi's holy city.[21] Although it is unlikely that Perdiccas became a Zoroastrian himself, he must have empathised with their plight when Alexander began persecuting them in the autumn of 324 BC. Even if he didn't, then he certainly had sympathy for Atarepata and his family. Not only was the fugitive governor his friend; when Alexander's army returned to Persia from India, Perdiccas married Atarepata's daughter.[22] His wife and father-in-law were now in the mountains being hunted like animals by Alexander's terror troops, the Hypaspistes.

Why Alexander appointed Perdiccas as his second-in-command under these circumstances is a puzzle. He may simply have lost his grip on reality to such an extent that he failed to recognise him as a danger. It may, however, have been that he assumed that Perdiccas was like himself. Alexander had been fascinated by Zoroastrian mysticism but had no compunction ordering the deaths of the Magi, and he had married Statira, a girl in whom he appears to have had no interest, for purely political reasons. Maybe he assumed it was the same for Perdiccas. However, if this was Alexander's thinking, he was wrong. Perdiccas clearly loved his wife; after Alexander's death he had her rescued from the mountains and her father reinstated as governor of northern Iran. Furthermore, when he heard that Antigonus, the Macedonian governor of Phrygia (in northern Turkey), was attacking Cappadocia, he sent troops into the area to protect Korama and ordered that Antigonus face a military court.[23] However, in 324 BC, Alexander was either blissfully unaware of Perdiccas' sympathies, or was too wrapped up in his own delusions to care.

With the rebellion in Media savagely dealt with, Alexander finally moved on to Babylon in the later winter of 323 BC. By this time, Alexander's behaviour gave Perdiccas a second motive to assassinate him. According to Justinus, during this journey a Magi warned Alexander that he would die if he entered Babylon.

> When he was hastening to Babylon, therefore, to hold an assembly, as it were, of the states of the world, one of the Magi warned him not to enter the city, for that the place would be fatal to him.[24]

The Magi was a brave man because Alexander had ordered members of his sect to be killed on sight. However, Alexander not only spared him, but also for some reason or other he originally took notice of his warning.

> He accordingly avoided Babylon, and turned aside to Borsippa, a city on the other side of the Euphrates, that had been for some time uninhabited. Here again he was persuaded by Anaxarchus the philosopher, to slight the predictions of the Magi as fallacious and uncertain; observing that, 'if things were fixed by fate, they were unknown to mortals, and if they were dependent on the course of nature, were unchangeable'.[25]

The once-pragmatic Alexander, whose every action had at one time been based on political or military logic, was now chopping and changing his mind depending on the opinions of whatever mystic he encountered. This is a clear indication of Alexander's unstable and erratic state of mind. Even his own disturbed logic should have compelled him to ignore *anyone's* predictions. For many years Alexander had portrayed himself as the son of a god. According to Justinus, after the death of Hephaestion, Alexander decided that he was actually a god himself.[26] Why should a god take any notice of philosophy or predictions? A further indication of just how irrational Alexander had become is that he sent an envoy to the oracle at Siwa in Egypt to ask the god Ammon if Hephaestion could be made a god too.[27] If Alexander was a god, then why not ask Ammon himself? Alexander was the most powerful man on earth, but he was now clearly incapable of ruling. If it was Perdiccas who killed Alexander, then it may not only have been for the sake of his wife and father-in-law, or for the good of the Zoroastrians, but for the sake of the entire empire. If Alexander did not recover or die, then the entire Macedonian Empire might fall apart.

Perdiccas, however, may have had a more selfish motive to kill Alexander – power. Hephaestion's death unexpectedly left Perdiccas as the highest-ranking officer at Alexander's court, and he was not only appointed commander of the cavalry but took over the function of vizier. Against all the odds, an average soldier had found himself second-in-command of the largest empire the world had ever known. When Alexander returned to Babylon in the summer of 323 BC, he had still not named his heir. In the event of his death there would be great uncertainty about the succession his only son, the four-year-old Heracles, was illegitimate and his brother Arridaeus was considered mentally unfit. Perhaps this was even Alexander's intention, as it made the question of succession a problem for any potential assassin. At present, Perdiccas was the nearest thing to a successor, but his position was extremely precarious. There was always the chance that Statira or Roxanne would bear Alexander a son. In fact, in May 323 BC, it was even possible that Alexander would officially recognise his son Heracles, as he had invited him to court. If Perdiccas did have designs on absolute power, then his only hope would be to kill the king – and soon. Alexander finally entered Babylon at the beginning of May. He should have continued to heed the Magi's warning; he now had just over a month left to live.

Soon after Alexander's arrival in Babylon, the envoy he had sent to Egypt returned with the news that Hephaestion could be worshipped as a god.[28] Elated, Alexander held the funeral that he had been planning for months. After Hephaestion's death the previous October, Alexander ordered the body to be preserved and sent word to artisans in Babylon to construct a huge and elaborate funerary building. According to Diodorus, the funeral pyre was surrounded by a massive wooden stockade.

He levelled a place where the funeral pyre was to be built and constructed all about it great wooden walls . . . Upon the foundation there were many statues . . . of armed figures five cubits [2.5 metres] high, while the spaces between them were resplendent with red banners made from the finest felt. Above these, there stood huge torches fifteen cubits [7.5 metres] high with golden wreaths about their handles. At their flaming ends there were golden eagles with outspread wings and at their bases there were coiled serpents of silver. On the third level were carvings of hunted animals and on the fourth there were centaurs . . . the fifth was decorated with golden bulls and lions and the sixth was festooned with the flags and banners of all of Alexander's lands . . . And the height of this all was one hundred and thirty cubits [65 metres].[29]

This huge square edifice, each side some 200 metres long, had been under construction since Hephaestion's death, six months before, and the ornamentation had been stripped from the temples, palaces and even the city walls of Babylon. Hephaestion's funeral was the most spectacular that any Macedonian had ever received. By contrast, however, the feast held after the funeral was a small and relatively intimate affair at which there were only twenty people present. Although seven other people at the banquet that night all had motive and opportunity to murder Alexander, was it Perdiccas who ultimately committed the crime?

Around halfway through the evening, Perdiccas dared to question Alexander about the wisdom of his planned campaign into Arabia, sending the king into a familiar drunken rage. At this moment, Perdiccas' life hung by a thread. Alexander had killed many men – even his closest friends – for less. He had killed Parmenion, his most senior officer, and his sons Philotas and Nicanor, the cavalry and Hypaspistes commanders, on the merest suspicion of disloyalty; he had executed his scribe Callisthenes for daring to question his judgement; and he had run one of his closest friends, Clitus, through with a javelin for the slightest criticism of his actions. And all this had been when Alexander was relatively sane. Alexander's drunken rage at the banquet that night must have been a vivid reminder to Perdiccas that his end might come at any moment – on the point of a spear. If Perdiccas was the murderer, and he had been hesitating, this may have been the moment he decided to act.

There were, however, seven other people at the banquet that night with motives to murder the king. The question is – did one of them beat Perdiccas to it? Which one of the eight prime suspects really did kill Alexander the Great?

SUMMARY OF CHAPTER ELEVEN

In 323 BC Perdiccas was Alexander's second-in-command and when the king died he immediately took over the empire. Had Perdiccas assassinated Alexander in order to steal his throne?

- Some four or five years older than Alexander, Perdiccas was a competent but by no means outstanding soldier. However, he did have one of the most varied careers of any of Alexander's officers. He commanded an infantry unit until the death of Darius, he was a royal adjutant during the war in Bactria and he commanded a cavalry squadron during the Indian campaign. However, in the Punjab he suddenly found himself in the king's favour and was promoted to a more senior position. By 324 BC, the king had either killed or dismissed most of his best cavalry officers, so when Hephaestion was given command of the cavalry, Perdiccas became his deputy.
- In October 324 BC, only a few months after his promotion to cavalry commander and vizier, Hephaestion suddenly died. He fell ill during a celebration in the Median city of Ecbatana and was dead within a few hours. Although no one could prove it, Alexander believed he had been poisoned and, devastated by his friend's death, ordered the execution of several of Hephaestion's servants, including his doctor.
- Hephaestion's death unexpectedly left Perdiccas as the highest-ranking officer at Alexander's court and he was not only appointed commander of the cavalry but also took over the function of vizier. Against all the odds, a common, average soldier had found himself second-in-command of the largest empire the world had ever known.
- Perdiccas was clearly a brave soldier, but he lacked any real aptitude for senior command in battle and his appointment, although expedient, was almost certainly temporary. By June 323 BC, Alexander was preparing for a new campaign in Arabia and it is likely that Perdiccas would soon be replaced. No one else in the high command appears to have had much enthusiasm for another major war, and if Alexander were to die the chances were the plan would die with him – as indeed it did. If Perdiccas was aware of this, then it certainly gave him a motive for killing Alexander.
- There was, though, another motive for Perdiccas to murder his king. Alexander had still not named his heir. At present, Perdiccas was the nearest thing to a successor, but his position could change very quickly, particularly if Statira or Roxanne were to present Alexander with a son. Any hope Perdiccas might have had on taking power depended on Alexander dying sooner rather than later.

12. AN EMPIRE DIVIDED

It was the night of 1 June 323 BC, and the eight suspects were all at present at Hephaestion's funeral feast: Iollas, the butler, who may have acted on his father Antipater's behalf; Arridaeus, Alexander's brother; Barsine, the concubine; Seleucus, the chief of the feared Hypaspistes; Roxanne, the queen; Meleager, the infantry commander; Statira, Alexander's new wife and consort; and Perdiccas, the cavalry commander and prime minister. Before we can attempt to eliminate any of these from the list of suspects, we need to remind ourselves of their motives.

Antipater had secured Alexander the throne and had been responsible for creating the army with which he established his empire. He had remained behind in Macedonia to keep control of the European domains, making it possible for Alexander to concentrate on his conquest of the Persian Empire. For eleven years, he had executed this duty efficiently and with complete loyalty to his king. It is true to say that without Antipater there would have been no empire of Alexander the Great. By 323 BC Alexander was no longer the rational ruler he had once been; he was not only paranoid, but also he seems to have suffered a complete mental breakdown. In this state of mind, Alexander had begun to listen to his mother's accusations that Antipater was a traitor and was planning his overthrow. In his more rational days, Alexander had recognised these allegations for what they undoubtedly were: jealous rantings, prompted by personal rivalries and squabbles. Now, however, he had summoned Antipater to Babylon to face these allegations. Anyone, no matter how innocent, would have feared Alexander's irrational judgement. Antipater was now 76 years old, and may no longer have feared for his own life, but he would certainly have feared for his family. He would have been all too aware that seven years before, Alexander had killed his old comrade Parmenion and his two sons, Nicanor and Philotas, following equally unsubstantiated allegations. Antipater was unable to go to Babylon in person because of a rebellion in Greece, but sent his son Cassander instead. Nearly all the historical sources refer to rumours at the time that Antipater told his son to kill Alexander if he could not persuade him of his innocence. The story was that Cassander's brother Iollas, the royal butler, put poison into Alexander's wine on the night of Hephaestion's funeral feast.

Arridaeus was Alexander's older brother, who by rights should have inherited their father's throne. Not only did Alexander deprive him of

175

the kingship, but also he overshadowed him in every respect. He was cleverer, more powerful and far more handsome. Perhaps unwittingly, Alexander continued to humiliate Arridaeus before the world: he paid greater tribute to his friends, he prevented him from marrying and he stole the woman he loved. When Alexander was off conquering the world, Arridaeus was left behind with the overbearing stepmother who may even have ruined his health. All of this gave him ample motive to finally get his revenge. Only a few days before Alexander fell ill, Arridaeus arrived in Babylon to see his brother for the first time in ten years.

Barsine had been Alexander's devoted lover for six years. She had not only loved him, she had been a source of inspiration and had seemingly devised a number of invaluable political and military schemes. Yet despite all this, Alexander seems to have immediately abandoned her the moment he laid eyes on Roxanne. Not only did he apparently lose all interest in the poor woman, when he married Roxanne he also made her his queen – something he had never considered for Barsine. After witnessing the heartbreaking event of the royal marriage in 327 BC, Barsine had returned home to Asia Minor where she remained, not seeing Alexander again until he summoned her to Babylon so that he could see his son for the first time in four years. Jealousy may have given Barsine enough grounds to contemplate Alexander's murder, but she had an additional motive to assassinate him. Her four-year-old son Heracles was Alexander's only male child and, as such, a possible heir to the Macedonian throne. Heracles may have been illegitimate but, as Alexander had no other sons, there were many nobles who would undoubtedly proclaim him king if Alexander died. However, if either Roxanne or Statira gave birth to a son, then Heracles would be cut out entirely. If Barsine intended for her son to become king, then Alexander would have to die sooner, rather than later.

Seleucus was cold, ruthless and merciless. He was cunning too. He had worked his way to the top of the promotional ladder by cleverly orchestrating the disgrace and execution of his commander, and he made sure that no one stood in his way. That he was ambitious for total power cannot be doubted; he was by far the most successful of Alexander's successors. Hephaestion's funeral in Babylon gave Seleucus the perfect opportunity to seize control of the empire, as his crack troops were the only significant force inside the city at the time.

Like Barsine, Roxanne had the motive of jealously and revenge. She had loved Alexander and he had made her queen of the largest empire there had ever been. She had no doubt expected that together she and her husband would found the greatest dynasty the world had ever known. Sadly, Alexander had now destroyed her dreams by marrying a Persian princess. Roxanne may have been the vivacious darling of the Macedonian court, but she was no bimbo. She was highly intelligent and quite capable of planning her husband's demise.

Meleager was a soldiers' officer: a grass-roots warrior who had earned his men's respect and who respected them in turn. His Macedonian and Greek infantry had been the backbone of Alexander's army, but now their very existence was in question. In the last two and a half years they had been decimated by unnecessary conflict, avoidable disease and the pointless march through the Gedrosian Desert. Either Alexander had been deliberately making them suffer for their conduct in India, or he was no longer fit to command. Just a few months before the final feast, Alexander had sent half of them home to be replaced by the very Persians they had set to conquer. It was obvious to everyone that it was only a matter of time before Alexander got rid of his European infantry altogether. He was dressing like a Persian, behaving like a Persian and was creating a new Persian army. For the good of his men, and for the good of Macedonia, Meleager may have been impelled to murder Alexander. Besides which, if Alexander lived then Meleager may soon have found himself the victim of the kind of 'accident' that befell Coenus, his predecessor.

Statira is the only suspect known to have openly threatened Alexander's life. In fact, she swore to kill him to avenge her father's death. She had now been forced to marry the man she despised and had been humiliated before all her people when he spent his wedding night drinking with his friend. If all this was not motive enough for Statira to have murdered Alexander, his assassination had become her religious duty once the Zoroastrian priesthood had ordered his death.

Perdiccas had as many motives as anyone to murder Alexander. Firstly, for the sake of his wife and her father, his friend, who were being hunted like dogs on Alexander's orders. Secondly, for the sake of the Zoroastrian religion, which he respected, and which Alexander was persecuting to extinction. Thirdly, there was the motive of power and, last but not least, there was the motive of survival. Perdiccas was now second-in-command of the largest empire the world had known, but his position was almost certainly temporary, until Alexander began his new war in the west. As Alexander had a habit of replacing senior officers between campaigns, then the chances were that Perdiccas would soon be dismissed. If he wished to retain his status, and perhaps even his life, then Alexander would have to die. Alexander had still not named a successor and so, as prime minister, Perdiccas was the nearest thing to the empire's heir. If Alexander died now, Perdiccas might inherit the lot – if he lived, he would probably lose it all.

Alexander had ordered the flames that burned in the Zoroastrian temples be put out until after Hephaestion's funeral. According to Diodorus, the only time that the Zoroastrians ever did this was when a Persian king died. Alexander was now the king of Persia, so by ordering these fires quenched, he had, according to Zoroastrian belief, been inviting his own death.[1] He may as well have been, on the night of Hephaestion's funeral, by inviting so many people to the banquet with such obvious motives to kill him. The fact is that Alexander was now in such a state of mental instability that he seems to have been unable to grasp what was going on about him. He had been swinging between outright paranoia and the belief that he was an invincible god. It was a pity for him that he had not been in one of his paranoid moods on the night of 1 June 323 BC.

Antipater, Arridaeus, Barsine, Seleucus, Roxanne, Meleager, Statira and Perdiccas: they are the only characters in this historical drama that had both the opportunity to poison Alexander, at the feast and again a few days later, and the motive to commit the crime. However, which of them actually did murder Alexander the Great? As Alexander's assassin was presumably prepared to take advantage of the situation after he died, an examination of the immediate aftermath of his death may help us narrow down the list of suspects.

Alexander not only died without naming a successor, but also seems to have gone to his grave determined to provoke a civil war. Justinus gives an account of Alexander's last day.

> When his friends saw him dying, they asked him whom he would appoint as the successor to his throne. He replied, 'The most worthy' . . . But as if, by this reply, he had sounded the signal for battle among his friends, or had thrown the apple of discord amongst them, they all rose in emulation against each other, and tried to gain the favour of the army by secretly paying court to the common soldiers.[2]

Later that day, however, when Alexander could no longer speak, he gave his ring to Perdiccas, which was taken by some to be a sign that he had finally chosen his successor.

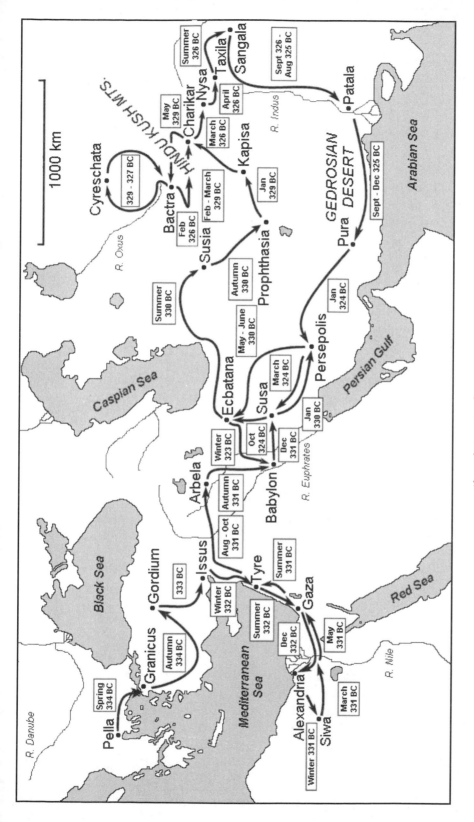

Alexander's route of conquest.

> On the sixth day from the commencement of his illness, being unable to speak, he took his ring from his finger, and gave it to Perdiccas, an act which tranquillized the growing dissension among his friends; for though Perdiccas was not expressly named his successor, he seemed intended to be so in Alexander's judgment.[3]

This only served to make matters worse, because a riot broke out the next day when Perdiccas produced the ring. Alexander died in the late afternoon of what is generally agreed to have been 11 June. As prime minister, it was up to Perdiccas to announce Alexander's death, and the following morning he erected the royal tent outside the main gates of Babylon and summoned all the senior officers of the troops camped around the city. Curtius gives an account of what happened.

> Alexander's friends, family and his generals were followed by a huge mass of soldiers; all of them were anxious to know to whom Alexander's crown would pass. Such was the size of the crowd that there was no order and no authority and everyone began pushing each other until the tent almost collapsed . . . At this moment Perdiccas came forward and set the royal throne for all to see, and on this he put Alexander's crown and robe and the ring he had given him the previous day. 'I return the ring which the king gave me by his own hand . . . We need a leader, and whoever that shall be should be up to you all to decide.'[4]

Justinus tells us that Perdiccas then made an announcement that seemed to surprise most people present: that Roxanne was pregnant with Alexander's child.

> Perdiccas gave his opinion that they ought to wait till Roxanne was delivered, who was now eight months gone with child by Alexander; and that, if she brought forth a boy, he should be appointed his father's successor.[5]

The fact that Roxanne was pregnant is noteworthy, as it appears to remove her from the list of suspects. If (as in fact it turned out to be) the baby was a boy, then he would be heir to the throne. Roxanne was an intelligent woman and must have reckoned on the possibility that if Alexander died before the birth then, with the matter of succession still wide open, one of Alexander's generals might seize the throne. If this happened, by the time her child was born the matter of Alexander's bloodline may have become irrelevant with a new king fully entrenched on the throne. Even if Roxanne did entertain plans to kill her husband, her pregnancy gave her every reason to want him to remain alive, at least until her child was born. If she did intend to kill Alexander then she would surely have waited until the child was born. If it was a boy, then she could kill Alexander then, before he had any more children by Statira.

The chaotic situation that transpired for many days after Alexander's death clearly rules out another suspect in Alexander's murder. According to Curtius, the chaos began when the admiral Nearchus objected to Perdiccas' suggestion that they should wait until Roxanne's baby was born.

> Nearchus then asked why, although it could not be doubted that only Alexander's bloodline was worthy of the throne, should they wait for a king to be born when the king already had a son by Barsine . . . Many of the troops disliked the idea and began to show their opposition by beating their spears against their shields. When Nearchus continued to press his proposal, the troops came close to rioting.[6]

According to Curtius, Meleager, whose troops had been dissenting, vehemently objected to the idea of either Roxanne or Barsine's child inheriting the throne. Not only would they both be the children of non-Macedonian women – a Sogdian and a Persian – but he suspected that Perdiccas intended to act as regent to the infants and so rule himself. Justinus gives the same account and reveals who Meleager proposed instead.

> There was then in the camp Arridaeus, a brother of Alexander, a person of courteous manners, and acceptable to everybody, not only on his own account, but on that of his father Philip.[7]

Curtius tells us that a dense crowd of riotous soldiers that had gathered around Meleager fell silent on hearing the suggestion.

> As if at the order of a single man, the gathering fell silent. Then they shouted in unison that Arridaeus be called and those that had decided to hold the meeting without his presence deserved to die . . . Meleager then brought Arridaeus to the tent and showed him to his men who all saluted him as king.[8]

The infantry were pleased with the idea but the cavalry, under Perdiccas' command, now came close to rioting themselves. So also did the Persians in the army, who preferred Barsine's son Heracles to be king as he would be the child of a woman from their own aristocracy. Justinus explains that it was Alexander's chief bodyguard Ptolemy who to tried to calm the situation.

> Ptolemy objected to Arridaeus as king . . . because of the extraordinary weakness with which he was affected, lest, while he had the name of king, another should exercise the authority; and said that it would be better for them to choose from those who were next in merit to the king, and who could govern the provinces and be entrusted with the conduct of wars, than to be subjected to the tyranny of unworthy men under the authority of a king.[9]

According to Curtius, Ptolemy went on to suggest that the same would apply if an infant son of Roxanne or Barsine was made king, as either of them would simply be puppet monarchs for someone else – presumably meaning Meleager or Perdiccas. Unfortunately, his suggestion that the best man be made king was nothing less than a call for civil war and again brought the proceedings close to a riot. However, it seems to have given Perdiccas the initiative, and one of his officers suggested that this best man for the job was Perdiccas himself.

> Then Aristonous rose and spoke, saying that when Alexander was asked to whom he was leaving his kingdom, he had said that it be the best man, and that he had expressed the wish that this be Perdiccas by giving him his ring. It was clear by this action that he intended for his power to be passed to Perdiccas.[10]

Perdiccas' cavalry obviously agreed with this argument, but it also won over many of the Persians who stood to gain more by serving under Perdiccas, as he was far more sympathetic to their camp than Meleager. He had announced an amnesty for the Zoroastrians and promised that he would reinstate his father-in-law Atrarepata as governor of northern Persia. They also knew that if Meleager took control then many of them would be dismissed from the army in favour of the Europeans. Curtius tells us that the larger part of the army accepted that Perdiccas should be king.

The assembly agreed that Aristonous' opinion was correct and they called for Perdiccas to pick up the king's ring. Perdiccas, wishing to appear reluctant to accept power, hesitated for a time, but the crowd implored him to accept.[11]

Perdiccas eventually alccepted, leading to more than a riot. Meleager led his infantry from the proceedings and prepared to face the cavalry and Perdiccas' Persian supporters in battle. Justinus describes what happened:

When the cavalry had also taken the oath [to accept Perdiccas as king] the infantry, indignant that no share in the deliberation had been granted to them, proclaimed Arridaeus, the brother of Alexander, king, chose him guards from their own body, and appointed that he should be called Philip, after the name of his father [his new throne name].[12]

Perdiccas and his followers withdrew to the Babylonian royal palace, where they prepared to defend themselves against Meleager's force.

The insurrection soon gathered strength, when it once began to have a head and regular management. The infantry rushed in a body, under arms, to the palace, with a resolution to cut the cavalry to pieces; but the cavalry, hearing of their approach, retreated in haste from the city, and after pitching their camp, began to threaten the infantry in return.[13]

This was a sensible move because the infantry would have had the upper hand in the city, whereas the cavalry would be seriously hindered from operating unless they were in open ground. Meleager responded by sending an assassination squad to kill Perdiccas, but the operation failed. However, just as it seemed that there would be an all-out battle, Ptolemy and Antipater's son Cassander came and stood between the rival factions and quietened things down by suggesting a compromise. They proposed that everyone accept Arridaeus as king but, as the man was not deemed suitable to govern by himself, Meleager and Perdiccas should be appointed as his coregents. The deliberations went on for some time, but in the end the compromise was accepted.

The cavalry, soon after, being reconciled with the infantry, agreed to have Arridaeus for their king. A portion of the empire was reserved for Alexander's son, if a son should be born [i.e. Roxanne's child]. These proceedings they conducted with the body of Alexander placed in the midst of them, that his majesty might be witness to their resolutions. Such an arrangement being made, Antipater was appointed governor of Macedonia and Greece; the charge of the royal treasure was given to Craterus; the management of the camp, the army, and the war, to Meleager and Perdiccas.[14]

Alexander's body was put back into storage, and for the best part of a week everyone began deciding upon who was to administrate various parts of the empire. The entire episode was a complete farce. According to Justinus, the new provincial governors were chosen by lot. While all this was going on, however, Perdiccas was busy making a pact with Seleucus, and eventually a joint force of cavalry and Hypaspistes seized power. Now firmly in control, Perdiccas ordered a purge of the infantry officers.

Perdiccas, who was still enraged at the authors of the late disturbance, suddenly gave notice, without the knowledge of his colleague, that there would be a lustration [purification] of the camp on the following day . . . Having drawn up the troops under arms in the field, he, with the general consent, gave orders, as he passed along, that the offenders, selected from each company, should be secretly given up to punishment.[15]

Various infantry officers were dragged from their beds and summarily executed, including Meleager, who was taken completely off guard. With Meleager dead, a final resolution was imposed by Perdiccas and Seleucus. The eventual state of affairs was that Arridaeus was king in name, with Perdiccas as his regent and supreme commander of all the empire's forces. For the rest, Antipater remained governor in Europe; his son Cassander was accepted as the new commander of the Greek and Macedonian infantry; Ptolemy, who had merely been the chief body-guard, somehow became governor of Egypt; Nearchus became governor of western Asia Minor (called Ionia); a Macedonian general named Antigonus was made governor of the east of the region; and Seleucus was appointed as prime minister and overall deputy leader.

The chaotic situation that lasted for a week after Alexander's death effectively eliminates Seleucus from the list of suspects in Alexander's murder. Seleucus was commander of the elite Hypaspistes. Why had it taken him so long to bring them into the action? When Alexander died, a week or so before, Seleucus' Hypaspistes were the only troops garrisoned inside Babylon. Even though there were only about 6,000 of them, they could easily have seized control in the virtual bedlam that ensued. They were the crack special force, whereas the rest of the army had broken into factions and had degenerated into a leaderless rabble. Unfortunately, however, they had been in no fit state to do anything. According to the *Historia*, when Alexander had first become ill at the banquet on 1 June, the Hypaspistes were all out celebrating after Hephaestion's funeral. The next day, when it seemed that Alexander's life might be in danger, Seleucus tried to whip them into shape, but most were too hung over to get out of bed. On Alexander's recovery from the first bout of sickness, they began celebrating again and drank themselves stupid for days. When Alexander died, they were not only incapacitated, but they were spread out all over the city. If Seleucus had been Alexander's murderer, then he would certainly have been prepared to take advantage of the king's death and would never have let his troops celebrate. There can be no doubt that Seleucus had designs on absolute power, as within three years he had taken control of the entire eastern empire, and so thoroughly entrenched himself in power that his dominion became the Seleucid Empire, named after him, which lasted for almost two and a half centuries. However, on both occasions that Alexander appears to have been poisoned, Seleucus was woefully unprepared. If he was not ready to exploit Alexander's death, then he was not expecting it, thus ruling him out as the assassin.[16]

The events immediately following Alexander's death also help us remove another person from the list of suspects. This is Antipater – or at least his son, Iollas, acting on his behalf. Most of the ancient sources refer to the rumours that Antipater had Alexander poisoned, but equally, most of them dismiss the idea. Diodorus, however, took them seriously:

> Antipater feared that Alexander might punish him for the crime of which Olympias accused him. So, by the hand of his own son, who was Alexander's butler, Antipater administered poison to the king. But many at the time dare not mention this drug because Antipater, and then his son Cassander, ruled in Europe after the king's death, and they feared what may happen to them if they spoke of it.[17]

Was Diodorus right? If Antipater and or his family had designs on power then this would be a ridiculous time to assassinate Alexander. Antipater was not in Babylon and his sons were in no position to secure control. Their only motive to kill the king at this time would be their immediate preservation. The entire question of Antipater's guilt therefore revolves around whether his eldest son Cassander managed to persuade Alexander that his father was innocent of Olympias' allegations of conspiracy. Cassander arrived in Babylon a few days before Hephaestion's funeral on his father's behalf and had an audience with Alexander. According to Plutarch, Alexander was furious to learn that Antipater had not come in person and began striking Cassander's head against the wall. He was lucky Alexander didn't have him executed on the spot. Instead, Alexander calmed down and ordered Cassander to be detained so that he could consider the matter and that he, his father and all his family would be severely punished if the allegations were found to be true.[18] The fact is that Alexander must have decided that Antipater was innocent or Cassander would not have been free to address the troops the day after Alexander's death. Indeed, Alexander would certainly not have continued to employ Antipater's other son Iollas as his butler if he still suspected his father of plotting against him. As Alexander must have accepted Antipater's innocence, the family no longer had a motive to kill him – at least, not at this time.

Of the eight people on the original list of suspects, we can seemingly eliminate three. However, this still leaves five, each of whom appears to have had both motive and opportunity to murder Alexander. When Perdiccas assumed control of the empire the situation was ostensibly stable for a while but was, in fact, highly precarious, with various parties still manoeuvring for power. Are there any clues during this period to help eliminate further suspects or to expose which one of them was Alexander's killer?

SUMMARY OF CHAPTER TWELVE

The events immediately after Alexander's death appear to eliminate three suspects from the list of eight. These are the Hypaspistes commander Seleucus, the European governor Antipater and the queen Roxanne.

- Alexander died in the late afternoon of what is generally agreed to have been 11 June. As prime minister, it was up to Perdiccas to announce Alexander's death, and the following morning he erected the royal tent outside the main gates of Babylon and summoned all the senior officers of the troops camped around the city. Justinus tells us that Perdiccas then made an announcement that seemed to surprise most people present; that Roxanne was eight months pregnant with Alexander's child.
- The fact that Roxanne was pregnant is noteworthy, as it appears to remove her from the list of suspects. If, as it turned out, the baby was

a boy then he would be heir to the throne. Roxanne was an intelligent woman and must have reckoned on the possibility that if Alexander died before the birth then, with the matter of succession still wide open, one of Alexander's generals might seize the throne. By the time her child was born the matter of Alexander's bloodline may have become irrelevant. Even if Roxanne did entertain plans to kill her husband, her pregnancy gave her every reason to want him to remain alive until her child was born.

- The chaotic situation that transpired for many days after Alexander's death clearly rules out Seleucus from the list of suspects in Alexander's murder. Seleucus was commander of the elite Hypaspistes. Why had it taken him so long to bring them into the action? When Alexander died, Seleucus' Hypaspistes were the only troops garrisoned inside Babylon and they could easily have seized control in the virtual bedlam that ensued. However, they had been in no fit state to do anything. When Alexander died they had been drinking themselves stupid for days. They were not only in incapacitated, but they were spread out all over the city.

- If Seleucus had been Alexander's murderer then he would certainly have been prepared to take advantage of the king's death and would never have let his troops celebrate. However, on both occasions that Alexander appears to have been poisoned, Seleucus was woefully unprepared. If he was unprepared to exploit Alexander's death, then he could not have been expecting it, and if he was not expecting it then he cannot have been the assassin.

- Antipater's motive for killing Alexander depends completely upon whether his son Cassander managed to persuade Alexander that his father was innocent of Olympias' allegations of conspiracy. The fact is that he must have done or Cassander would almost certainly have been arrested; in fact he was free to address the troops the day after Alexander's death. Moreover, Alexander would certainly not have continued to employ Antipater's other son Iollas as his butler if he still suspected his father of plotting against him. As Alexander must have accepted Antipater's innocence, the family no longer had a motive to kill him.

13. SYMBOLS OF SUCCESSION

The two largest and most powerful groups of citizens in Alexander's massive empire were the Europeans and the Persians. In the circumstances that existed when Alexander died, the interests of these peoples could be said to have been represented by two characters: Meleager and Statira.

Meleager was the only general in Alexander's army to have complete sympathy with the European cause. Not only were his soldiers the grass-roots Greek and Macedonian backbone of the army, but in the deliberations following Alexander's death Meleager had proposed that Arridaeus be made king because he was the one candidate with a purely European bloodline.

Statira, on the other hand, was the heir to the Persian king Darius. It would be through her that the ancient Persian bloodline could continue. Meleager and Statira were the only two suspects on the list to have already been in Babylon when Alexander arrived in May 323 BC. In fact, they had been there for nine months. If either of them had planned Alexander's assassination, this should have been plenty of time to prepare for the aftermath of his death. Is there any evidence, therefore, in the events that occurred after Alexander died to suggest that either of them had such plans?

Meleager, for certain, would have made careful preparations if he had planned to kill the king. It would be no good getting rid of Alexander only to have him replaced by a Persian or someone with Persian sympathies. Meleager was the most experienced general in Alexander's army apart from Antipater, who had spent the entire war back in Macedonia. The previous year, 10,000 of Meleager's own troops had been sent home. These were all men who had fought with Meleager for eleven years and were fiercely loyal to him. If he intended to take control of the empire then these troops would be ideally placed to help secure Europe. They were hardened veterans with far more experience than anyone back in Greece or Macedonia and would each be worth three of any soldier at home. Alexander had put them under the temporary command of Craterus and it would not have taken much to persuade him to support such a scheme. Craterus had been the army's most senior officer before he had been replaced by the inexperienced Hephaestion, and then the far-less-able Perdiccas. He had every reason to want Alexander gone. Indeed, his very life may have depended on it. He had been cavalry commander at the time of the near mutiny in India and was present when Coenus, his opposite number in the infantry, had conveniently met with a sudden death. Moreover, Craterus' immediate predecessors, Philotas and Clitus, had both been killed by Alexander on a whim. The chances were that it would not be long before Alexander would order Craterus' death. One way or the other, his career was over and his power was a thing of the past as long as Alexander lived. Meleager could probably count on his support. (If not, with 10,000 of his own men under Craterus' command, he would not be difficult for Meleager to remove.)

However, even though Meleager would have his 10,000 troops, taking control of Europe would not be easy. They would be facing Antipater. Antipater had remained loyal to Alexander throughout the entire war with the Persian Empire. If he had ever considered seizing power, he could have done so at any time at home while Alexander was far away in the East. No one could have known that Alexander would suddenly begin suspecting Antipater of conspiracy because of his mother's allegations. Antipater may have been old, but he had been the most brilliant soldier in the entire empire and had been responsible for creating the army that made Alexander's conquests possible. Furthermore, his troops would not only be fresh, they would be making a defensive stand in their own familiar territory, while Meleager's troops had not seen Europe in over a decade. It would be unlikely that the Macedonian troops at home would have sympathised with a coup by Meleager. They had no first-hand experience of Alexander's Persian behaviour or his mental instability; neither had they been made to suffer since the Indian campaign. The Macedonian home troops only knew the Alexander of old, and would no doubt fight fiercely against anyone who was thought to be stealing his throne. If Meleager wanted to secure Europe then he would need to make certain that these troops were occupied elsewhere.

To this end, Meleager's best shot would be to enlist the support of those Greeks who would be happy to see Alexander go: in particular the Thebans and Athenians who had once suffered at Alexander's hands. In fact, the Greeks of these cities did lead a massive revolt at exactly the time Alexander died. Justinus describes the rebellion:

> While these transactions were passing in the east [the deliberations in Babylon, following Alexander's death], the Athenians and Aetolians proceeded with all their might to prosecute the war which they had begun in the life of Alexander [shortly before he

died]. The cause of the war was, that Alexander, on his return from India, had written certain letters to Greece, according to which the exiles from all the states, except such as had been convicted of murder, were to be recalled. These letters, being read before all Greece, assembled at the Olympic Games, had excited a great commotion; because many had been banished, not by legal authority, but by a faction of the leading men, who were afraid that, if they were recalled, they would become more powerful in their states than themselves. Many states therefore at once expressed open discontent, and said that their liberty must be secured by force of arms.[1]

As Justinus says, this was a rebellion that had already started, so it cannot have been a spontaneous reaction to Alexander's death. In fact, Antipater's intelligence had already warned him of such a threat, which is why he had sent his son to Babylon to answer Alexander's summons on his behalf. It could, therefore, have been orchestrated by Meleager, who might well have struck a deal in return for the Greeks' support. Justinus' account certainly suggests that the Greek rebellion was planned well in advance by someone.

The Athenians, in consequence, collecting an army of thirty thousand men and two hundred ships, went to war with Antipater, to whom the government of Greece had been assigned; and when he declined to come to battle, and sheltered himself within the walls of Heraclea, they besieged him there . . . Meanwhile Leosthenes, the general of the Athenians, was killed, while he was besieging Antipater, by a dart hurled at him from the wall as he was passing by. This occurrence gave so much encouragement to Antipater that he ventured to break down the Athenian rampart. He then sought assistance from Leonnatus [the commander of the Macedonian forces in Asia Minor], who was soon reported to be approaching with his army; but the Athenians met him in battle array, and he was severely wounded in an action of the cavalry, and died. Antipater, though he saw his auxiliaries defeated, was yet rejoiced at the death of Leonnatus, congratulating himself that his rival was taken off, and his force added to his own. Taking Leonnatus' army under his command, therefore, and thinking himself a match for the enemy, even in a regular battle, he immediately released himself from the siege, and marched away to Macedonia. The forces of the Greeks, too, having driven the enemy

191

from the territory of Greece, went off to their several cities [and the war continued].[2]

The fact that the Greeks managed to muster an army of 30,000 men shows that it was no spontaneous uprising, and must have been planned for some time. The fact that it occurred at precisely the time Alexander died suggests that the two events could well have been linked. And the only person in a position to orchestrate both Alexander's death and the Greek uprising was Meleager.

Gaining control in Europe, however, would only have been a part of Meleager's objective. He would also need to secure the east. There were some 30,000 battle-ready troops stationed in Bactria alone, and these would be a formidable threat to anyone who wished to seize power. Fortunately, many of these were Greeks and Macedonians and they were under the command of a Greek general named Philon, the military governor stationed in the city of Bactra. Diodorus tells us that the moment Alexander died, Philon set out with an army to march on what had been Alexander's forces in northern Persia.

There were many Greeks who had been settled by Alexander in what were called the Upper Satrapies [northern Bactria] who pined after the Greek ways of life. These customs had been denied them in these distant parts of the east and Alexander had impelled them to embrace the Persian way of life. While Alexander was alive, they submitted to the king, but once he was dead they rose up in revolt. Together they chose Philon the Aenian as general, and raised a force of 20,000 foot soldiers and 3,000 horsemen.[3]

This appears to have been the entire European force that Alexander had left behind in Sogdiana and northern Bactria. They immediately marched west where Perdiccas' supporter Peithon, the new Median governor appointed by Alexander, met them with a much smaller army of around 10,000 men.

The uprisings in Greece, and the rebel attack from the east, would have played right into Meleager's hands if he had been planning a coup. All he needed was to secure the middle ground in Babylonia and he would have stood a good chance of seizing the entire empire. To this end, he already had 10,000 troops in Babylon and nine months to prepare them for the showdown. The rest of the army outnumbered them but they would be divided into various factions and unready to fight. The Persian contingent would undoubtedly have wavered for a time regarding who they would back – as proved to be the case – and the only real threat were the Hypaspistes which, as it turned out, were completely unprepared. Even if they had been fully operational, the infantry had had nine months to get themselves ready. Besides which, they could form the phalanx which the Hypaspistes, as heavy infantry, could not. In a battlefield situation, the Macedonian infantry would have the upper hand.

Meleager could well have taken Alexander's empire on the king's death, but the fact is he didn't. Although, at first glance, it seems that he could have orchestrated the rebellions in Bactria and Greece, and therefore have been responsible for Alexander's death, the events that then transpired appear to discount the possibility that Meleager had anything to do with it. In Media, where the Bactrian rebels were fighting, things went badly wrong. They outnumbered Peithon's army by more than two to one; nonetheless, they were defeated. It turned out that although there were over 20,000 troops under Philon's command, they were completely disorganised. Not only did the Bactrian forces arrive in dribs and drabs; when they did turn up no one appears to have known the battle strategy. In fact, according to Diodorus, once it seemed that Peithon had the upper hand, the Macedonians changed allegiance and fought against the Greeks who had been on their side.

> Peithon was greatly victorious in the battle and sent a messenger to the enemy, telling them to lay down their arms . . . Then the Macedonians broke faith with the Greeks on their side and set upon them unexpectedly and, taking them completely off guard, cut them down with their javelins . . . Peithon then came back to Perdiccas with the Macedonians who swore allegiance to him.[4]

This incompetent rebellion was clearly not organised in advance – or if it was, it was planned by a complete amateur. Meleager was an experienced commander and general; if he had planned the revolt of the Bactrian army and their march into Media, he would have made a much better go of it. Although the revolt in Greece faired better, this too was put down – and by Meleager's own troops. According to Justinus, Meleager's 10,000 infantry that had been sent home joined forces with Antipater and helped recapture the Greek cities.[5]

Not only does the fate of the eastern and western rebellions show that no overall strategy was involved, and therefore had not been organised by Meleager, but Meleager seems to have been even less prepared for Alexander's death than Seleucus. If he had expected Alexander to die, then the infantry under his command at Babylon could easily have defeated Perdiccas' cavalry before the Persians were persuaded to join them and Seleucus' men sobered up. However, as we have seen, they were a disorganised, riotous rabble. As with Seleucus, if Meleager had anticipated Alexander's death, he would have been far more prepared. And like Seleucus, this lack of foresight seems to rule him out as the assassin.

Whatever Meleager's personal feelings about Alexander, he must have decided to remain loyal to his king and not utilised the opportunity to kill him. Unfortunately, this ultimately cost him his own life. When Perdiccas took control, he ordered Meleager seized and had him murdered when he sought sanctuary in a temple.[6]

If there had been evidence that Meleager had orchestrated the rebellions in Greece and Bactria, it would have suggested that he had anticipated Alexander's death. It is clear, however, that he had not. But what about Statira? Is there any indication that she had been a part of a wider conspiracy to assassinate the Macedonian king?

As a child, Statira had sworn that she would one day kill Alexander. She may, of course, have decided against it over the years, but the Zoroastrian death sentence passed on Alexander gave her an additional reason to murder him. The feast on the night of Hephaestion's funeral is the first chance we know of that Statira had the opportunity to act. Alexander had not slept with her after their marriage at Susa in the late summer of 324 BC and she had been quickly sent on to Babylon. Like Meleager, she had had a good nine months to plan Alexander's death if she still intended to kill him. We do not know everything Alexander was doing during his short time in Babylon, but he seems to have been busy planning his new campaign and there is no indication that he had much to do with Statira until the night of the feast.

Statira may have wanted Alexander dead for her own reasons, but she would also have wanted to see her country restored to Persian rule. If she had decided to kill her husband, then the chances are that she involved others in the plan: in particular, someone who could ensure that she became queen after Alexander's death. Alternatively, as she was one of the few Persians who could get close enough to Alexander to poison him, someone else may have devised the plot and put her up to it. There were thousands of Persians who wanted Alexander dead, and for as many reasons. Can any of them be linked with Statira in the circumstances following Alexander's death?

Although there were a large number of Persian troops and junior officers in Alexander's army, the king had died before appointing any of them to the most senior positions. By far the most important Persian still to survive, apart from Statira, her sister and her grandmother (the last surviving members of the royal family), was Atarepata, the ex-governor of Media. He had been hiding out in the Median Mountains for over six months, being hunted by the Macedonian troops. Once Perdiccas gained control of the empire, he immediately had Atarepata pardoned. However, as Peithon, the new governor of Media, had backed Perdiccas and defeated the rebel forces from Bactria, the new leader could not fully reinstate his old friend. Instead, the province was divided between them and Atarepata got the north of the region. Atarepata was not only a leading Persian aristocrat; he also seems to have been the patriarch of the Zoroastrian faith. His Persian name, 'keeper of the fire', meant that he was an important Zoroastrian priest, and a Zoroastrian text called the *Denkard* ('Religious Acts') praises Atarepata as a great holy man who saved the religion from the pagan Europeans.

> There was much confusion in those times amongst the peoples of Persia. They had no ruler of their own or high priest of their religion . . . until the time when the blessed and immortal Atarepata came.[7]

The oldest surviving copy of the *Denkard* dates from the ninth century AD, but a much earlier indication that Atarepata was a highly revered figure is that he gave his name to the entire region of northern Media. When Seleucus took over what had been Alexander's eastern empire, Atarepata's province remained independent and took the name Atropatena (land of Atarepata), which it continued to be called for hundreds of years. Today it is called Azerbaijan and its citizens still regard Atarepata as their country's founder. As both an important Persian political figure and a leading Zoroastrian, Atarepata could well have been involved in a plot to murder Alexander. However, there is nothing in any of the historical sources to suggest a link between him and Statira at any point following Alexander's death.

The only other Persian in a position of high status who attempted to capitalise on Alexander's death was Ariatathes, the ruler of Cappadocia. When the Macedonian army had passed through this region of central Turkey in 333 BC, Alexander had decided to let it remain virtually independent and allowed the provincial governor Ariatathes to stay in power. He had assumed that all of the area's citizens were like the Magi of Korama and committed to a doctrine of peace. However, he was wrong: Ariatathes eventually claimed that he had been divinely chosen

195

by the Zoroastrian god Ahura Mazda as a divine warrior to take over the empire. Over the next few years Ariatathes set up what was, for all intents and purposes, a kingdom within an empire, and the moment Alexander died he led his own private army into the province of Phrygia in northern Turkey. Antigonus, the Macedonian commander of the province, retaliated and sent troops to sack the city of Korama. When Perdiccas heard of this, he was furious and ordered Antigonus to be arrested. However, he managed to escape. Although Perdiccas was sympathetic to the Magi and to the Zoroastrian religion generally, he had to do something about Ariatathes, whom he feared was capable of seizing Phrygia and hence control the main routes to Europe and the Dardanelles. Ariatathes was defeated by Perdiccas and Justinus describes the dreadful fate he and his followers chose for themselves and their families.

> Perdiccas, in the meantime, making war upon Ariatathes, king of the Cappadocians, defeated him in a pitched battle, but got no other reward for his efforts but wounds and perils; for the enemy, retreating from the field into the city, killed each his own wife and children, and set fire to his house and all that he possessed; throwing their slaves too into the flames, and afterwards themselves, that the victorious enemy might enjoy nothing belonging to them but the sight of the conflagration that they had kindled.[8]

Ariatathes seems to have been a dangerous leader and clearly a religious fanatic, but did his plans for conquest include any kind of arrangement with Statira? It seems doubtful. Ariatathes believed that he was chosen by his god to rule alone; if anything, he would be happy to see the old Persian bloodline come to an end.

If Statira was Alexander's murderer and she collaborated with someone she hoped would secure her position as queen of the empire, then it does not appear to have been a Persian. What, then, of the Europeans? The Greek and Macedonian military leaders who contested for power after Alexander's death were known as the Diadochi, meaning 'successors'. Is there any evidence that any of them were in collusion with Statira?

Although Roxanne did give birth to a son, to be named Alexander, it was too late for him to inherit the throne that had already been given to Arridaeus. Nevertheless, it was Perdiccas, as Arridaeus' regent, who held the true reins of power. He managed to rule virtually unopposed for eighteen months before problems arose. Antipater was still governor in Europe and wanted to secure his family's position by offering his daughter Nicea to Perdiccas. Perdiccas, who was already married to Atarepata's daughter, decided it would be a good idea to accept this second wife, as it would strengthen his ties with Antipater's influential family. However, according to Justinus, before the marriage took place, Perdiccas changed his mind and decided he would marry Alexander's sister Cleopatra instead.

> Soon after, that he might secure royal support to his present power, he turned his thoughts to a marriage with Cleopatra, sister of Alexander the Great, and formerly wife of the other Alexander [the Molossian chief who was now dead], her mother Olympias showing no dislike to the match. But he wished first to outwit Antipater, by pretending a desire for an alliance with him, and therefore made a feint of asking his daughter in marriage, the more easily to procure from him young recruits from Macedonia. Antipater, however, seeing through his deceit, he courted two wives at once, but obtained neither.[9]

If Perdiccas were to marry a daughter of Philip, their son would be first in line of succession, as Arridaeus had no sons himself. Antipater clearly had plans for his own family in this respect, but there was another danger he foresaw. Perdiccas had been ruling from Babylon, but he had announced that he would come to the Macedonian capital of Pella, where Cleopatra was living, for the marriage. This would give Perdiccas an excuse to bring troops with him. What made matters worse is that Perdiccas also announced that he was having Alexander's body moved to Macedonia to be buried in the royal cemetery at Aegae. Until this time, Alexander had been interred in a splendid rock-cut tomb in the Persian royal cemetery at Persepolis. If he were to be reburied in Macedonia, it would mean a special military ceremony at which a large part of the army would be present. Antipater suspected that when Perdiccas and his troops arrived for the burial, he would use the opportunity to get rid of Antipater and his family. Antipater, however, took the initiative and sent his own army, under the command of Craterus and Cassander, to stop Perdiccas' troops in Asia Minor. Alexander's empire was now officially in a state of civil war.[10]

At this time, Ptolemy, who was governor in Egypt, decided to take advantage of the situation and offered his support to Antipater. He probably hoped that Perdiccas, not wanting to fight a war on two fronts, would come to an arrangement to grant him total autonomy in Egypt in return for his assurances to remain neutral. However, he was wrong. Perdiccas valued the wealth of Egypt and sent an army under the command of Seleucus to attack the country, while his main force continued north towards Europe. Until this time, Arridaeus, his sister, and the daughters of Antipater had been the political pawns; it was now that Roxanne and her child were brought into the power game and so, bizarrely, was Alexander's corpse.

According to Justinus, Arridaeus, Roxanne and her child were in Cappadocia with Perdiccas' army that was on its way to Europe: initially for Alexander's burial, and now on its way into battle. Learning of this, Antipater sent an elite squadron of cavalry, under the command of Craterus, to snatch the royal family so that he could pronounce himself regent to Alexander's brother and marry Roxanne to one of his sons. Ptolemy, for his part, was more interested in Alexander's body that was also on its way to Europe. It was being taken through Syria to the Mediterranean coast, where the intention had been to send it by sea to Macedonia. Presumably to use it as a bargaining tool, Ptolemy decided to steal the corpse and despatched a contingent of troops to intercept the burial detail.[11]

In December 322 BC, Alexander's body was in the Syrian city of Damascus, where it was apparently being kept until the fighting was over. There are various accounts of what happened, but the general outline of events is that Ptolemy's men managed to pay off the troops who were guarding the body and returned with it to the coast.[12] However, when the body was found to be missing, another of Perdiccas' officers gave chase and a fight for Alexander's remains ensued. Ptolemy's men won, but during the struggle to get hold of the corpse its head was torn off. Unknown to anyone, Antipater had sent his own men to snatch the body and they arrived by boat at the same time Ptolemy's men were loading the corpse onto a ship somewhere near Tyre. Like Ptolemy, Antipater apparently believed that possession of the corpse would somehow legitimise his claim to rule the empire. What happened next is a mystery, as the accounts vary as to what became of the body. In one version Antipater's men seized it and took it back for burial in Macedonia; another says that it was retrieved by Perdiccas' men and taken back to Persepolis; and the most popular is that Ptolemy's men escaped with it and took it back to Egypt.[13] Even in Egypt there were two separate legends as to where it was eventually buried. Some say that it was interred in the temple of Ammon in Siwa, whereas others say that it was placed in a mausoleum in Alexandria. The last of these became the most fashionable story and a mausoleum in Alexandria was claimed to be Alexander's tomb by the Egyptians until well into Roman times.[14]

It is ironic that the most famous soldier who ever lived should have had such an undignified epitaph. His body was left lying in a hot storeroom after his death; it was wheeled in and out during the deliberations between the generals; it was buried, exhumed, moved halfway across the Middle East, fought over, ripped apart, sewn back together, and ended up goodness knows where. Even the mummified body in Alexandria, which was claimed to be Alexander's remains in Roman times, had its nose accidentally pulled off by the emperor Augustus.[15]

By the beginning of 321 BC, the possession of Alexander's body had become academic. The fate of the empire was going to be decided on the battlefield and the alliance against Perdiccas began cementing their agreements with a new series of political marriages. Antipater gave his daughter Euridice to Ptolemy and his daughter Phila to Craterus, while Nicea, who was to have been married to Perdiccas, was married to the Macedonian general Lysimachus. Antipater's son Cassander was supposed to have been married to Roxanne, but after the attempt to seize her failed he decided to marry Alexander's sister Cleopatra instead, although this marriage never went ahead.

Although the more important war would be fought in the north, for some unknown reason Perdiccas decided that he would personally join his deputy Seleucus in the battle for Egypt. Even stranger, is that he gave command of the northern army to Eumenes. Eumenes had once been a cavalry officer in Alexander's army, but when the king died he was an old man and was serving as the royal secretary. Perdiccas' choice to give him control of his main force may have been strange, but it turned out to be a sound one. In the late winter of 321 BC, Eumenes somehow managed to defeat Antipater's army that had been sent to Asia Minor, and its commander, the highly experienced Craterus, was killed in the fighting.[16]

For some reason, even though he was not involved in the fighting in Asia Minor, Perdiccas decide to postpone his march to Egypt. It was May 320 BC before he finally arrived to face Ptolemy. This gave his enemy plenty of time to prepare, and twice Perdiccas' army tried and failed to cross the Nile and reach the Egyptian capital of Memphis. When he attempted the crossing for a third time and thousands of men were killed in a shower of arrows and flaming missiles, catapulted from the western bank, the deputy commander Seleucus exploited the opportunity to seize control of the demoralised army and had Perdiccas killed.[17]

On taking power, Seleucus declared an end to the fighting and immediately opened negotiations with both Ptolemy and Antipater. A conference was held in the Syrian town of Triparadisus, where an agreement was reached. Although there was still some fighting afterwards, the final settlement resulted in the establishment of three independent states.

Macedonia and the European part of Alexander's empire remained under the control of Antipater, who reached an agreement with Seleucus to make no demands on Asian territory so long as the royal family, Arridaeus, Roxanne and her baby boy, were returned to Macedonia. Here, Antipater accepted Arridaeus as Macedonian king but appointed himself as his new regent, and when he died in 319 BC his son Cassander took over as king, after marrying a daughter of Arridaeus.

Ptolemy not only got to keep Egypt, he was also granted Gaza, Judah and Palestine, whereas the largest part of Alexander's empire was kept by Seleucus, which included nearly all of what are now Iran, Iraq, Syria and Afghanistan. Seleucus even took the Indian part of the empire, although in 316 BC he surrendered it to the Indian king Chandragupta, who conquered the entire Indus Valley. Asia Minor was the only region not fully under anyone's control and was fought over by the Asians and Europeans for many years.[18]

With the empire divided, Alexander's ultimate legacy was that he had spread Hellenism, classical Greek culture, ideals and way of life, throughout much of the ancient world. Until the eastern expansion of the Roman Empire in the second century BC, what became known as the Antigonid Alliance continued to rule in Greece and Macedonia and the Seleucid Empire thrived in Asia. Ptolemy's descendants continued to rule in Egypt until the last of them, the famous Cleopatra, committed suicide before the country was annexed by the Romans in 30 BC.

During the period when Alexander's empire was being fought over and carved up, many hapless symbols of succession had been exploited by the Diadochi. Antipater's daughters were being married off to everyone, as were Alexander's sister and niece; Arridaeus was dragged about like a puppet on a string; Roxanne and her child were carted around all over the Middle East; even Alexander's corpse was involved. Yet during all this, no one seems to have had the slightest intention to use Statira as a means to power. Plutarch tells us that, soon after Alexander's death, the poor girl was murdered by Roxanne, and with Perdiccas' permission.

Roxana [Roxanne], who was now with child, and upon that account much honoured by the Macedonians, being jealous of Statira . . . killed her and her sister, and threw their bodies into a well, which they filled up with earth, not without the knowledge and assistance of Perdiccas.[19]

Unlike Alexander, none of the Diadochi, or the Persian aristocracy, had any interest in the old Persian bloodline. As Plutarch says, even Statira's sister Drypetis was killed. According to Diodorus, the last member of the Persian royal family, Statira's grandmother Sisygambis, took her own life and no one cared.[20]

All this suggests very clearly that Statira was not part of a larger plot to kill Alexander. If she was his murderer then she acted alone. What's more, she appears to have made no plans for the aftermath of his death. Although Statira must still remain on the list of suspects, she is an unlikely candidate for Alexander's assassin.

With Meleager and Statira removed from the list, we are left with three remaining suspects: Perdiccas, Arridaeus and the first of Alexander's women, Barsine. Unlike Statira, Barsine *was* dragged into the deliberations that followed Alexander's death. Her son Heracles was suggested as Alexander's heir by the admiral Nearchus. Nearchus had a good personal reason for wanting Barsine's son to become king. He was married to Barsine's daughter from her marriage to the Persian general Mentor. But is there any evidence that Barsine had actually been involved with Nearchus in a conspiracy to murder Alexander?

SUMMARY OF CHAPTER THIRTEEN
The aftermath of Alexander's death seems to eliminate two more suspects, Meleager and Statira.

- If Meleager had planned to kill Alexander, he would have made careful preparations. He was one of the most experienced generals in Alexander's army. The previous year 10,000 of Meleager's own troops had been sent home. These were all men who had fought with him for eleven years and were fiercely loyal. If he intended to take control of the empire then these troops would be ideally placed to help secure Europe. In fact, a rebellion did take place in Greece at the time Alexander died and these troops could have formed an alliance with them.
- Gaining control in Europe would only have been a part of Meleager's objective. He would also need to secure the east. There were some

30,000 battle-ready troops stationed in Bactria and these would be a formidable threat to anyone who wished to seize power. Diodorus tells us that the moment Alexander died their commander Philon set out with an army of 20,000 men to march on what had been Alexander's forces in northern Persia. Here, Perdiccas' supporter Peithon faced them with an army only half that size.

- The uprisings in Greece and the rebel attack from the east would have played right into Meleager's hands if he had been planning a coup. All he needed was to secure the middle ground in Babylonia and he would have stood a good chance of seizing the entire empire. To this end, he already had 10,000 troops in Babylon and nine months to prepare them for the showdown.

- Meleager could well have taken Alexander's empire on the king's death, but the fact is he didn't. In Media things went badly wrong for the rebels. They outnumbered Peithon's army more than two to one; nonetheless, they were defeated. It turned out that although there were over 20,000 troops under the Philon's command, they were completely disorganised. This incompetent rebellion was clearly not organised in advance. Although the revolt in Greece faired better, this too was put down – by Meleager's own troops.

- Not only does the fate of the eastern and western rebellions show that no overall strategy was involved, and therefore had not been organised by Meleager; Meleager seems to have been even less prepared for Alexander's death than Seleucus. If he had expected Alexander to die then the infantry under his command at Babylon could easily have defeated Perdiccas' cavalry before the Persians were persuaded to join them and Seleucus' men sobered up. However, they were a disorganised, riotous rabble. If Meleager had anticipated Alexander's death, he would have been far more prepared. Like Seleucus, the fact that Meleager had not foreseen that Alexander would die means that he cannot have been the assassin.

- As for Statira, there is no evidence that she had sought backing from any of the major players in the event of Alexander's sudden death. In fact, after the murder, she was completely friendless, meeting her grisly fate at the hands of Roxanne with no one willing or able to protect her.

14. THE AEGEAN DREAM

Nearchus was the only one of Alexander's military successors to propose Barsine's son Heracles as heir to the throne. There is no direct evidence to link Nearchus with Alexander's murder, but if he was involved in a conspiracy to make Heracles king then the events following 11 June 323 BC might hold clues to expose him. One place, in particular, where there might be evidence to implicate Nearchus in such a plot would be the region of the Aegean Sea where he assumed power after Alexander's death. It was here that Nearchus had become closely associated with Barsine's family.

The Aegean is separated from the Mediterranean to the south by an arc of islands, the largest of which is Crete. To the western side of the Aegean is Greece, to the north, Macedonia, and to the east, Asia Minor (modern Turkey). This sea, about the area of the United Kingdom, is dotted with dozens of islands, such as Santorini, Naxos and Kos, which are famous today as holiday destinations. For a few hundred years, until around 1350 BC, the Aegean, its islands and its coastline was dominated by the Minoan civilisation based on the island of Crete. It was one of the most advanced civilisations in the world, rivalling even Egypt, until it was taken over by the Mycenaean culture from Greece. By 1000 BC this too had declined, but by then the entire area was populated by a common people referred to as the Hellenics (meaning of Greek origin). By 500 BC the Aegean coastline was dominated by various states that mainly spoke Greek and had a common Greek culture. These were: the Greeks proper, in mainland Greece and most of the islands; the Macedonians in the north; and the inhabitants of western Asia Minor, known as the Ionians. By the time Alexander's father Philip came to the Macedonian throne in 359 BC, the Ionians were part of the Persian Empire, although their cities still retained Hellenic culture and enjoyed a certain amount of autonomy. Greek Asia Minor, or Ionia as it was called, was divided into four provinces, namely, from north to south: Phrygia, Lydia, Caria and Lycia.[1]

For generations, both the Greeks and Macedonians had dreamed of reuniting the Hellenic world of the Aegean into one empire, and this had been Alexander's father Philip's intention. He had secured Macedonia and its neighbours, and had gained control of most of Greece and some of the Aegean islands. Furthermore, he had already despatched an army under Parmenion's command to annex Ionia at the time he was assassinated. When Alexander became king he continued this Ionian campaign, and his generals appear to have assumed that Asia Minor was to be the extent of his ambitions in the east. After Darius was defeated at the battle of Issus in 333 BC, Asia Minor was completely under Macedonian control, and the weakened Persians would have stood little chance of retaking it. Alexander's army had no problem controlling this new Aegean empire. Indeed, most of the Ionians regarded Alexander as a liberator, which is why he had portrayed himself as Achilles, the legendary hero who fought to reunite the Ionians with the Greeks many years before.

If Alexander had halted in Asia Minor he could have consolidated his position and moved against the Persians at some later time, as their empire was already in serious decline. He could have campaigned in the west and taken Italy and Rome and established a secure Hellenic empire based in Europe: his successors would have been in a good position to create a huge empire that might have lasted for generations. However, when Alexander moved on through Syria, Phoenicia and into Egypt, and then decided to conquer the entire Persian Empire, he stretched his forces too far, too thinly and too fast. When he died, his empire broke apart and the Greeks and Macedonians were left weak and depleted of resources. From this, they never really recovered and it was left to the Romans to take the initiative; a century and a half later they conquered Macedonia, Greece and Ionia. The massive Roman Empire – that eventually stretched from Britain to Egypt and from Morocco to the Black Sea – was established over many generations and lasted for hundreds of years. If Alexander had not been so greedy, then the Western world of today might have been the legacy of the Greeks rather than the Romans.

Anyone who really thought about it could have foreseen that Alexander's empire could not possibly last. It had been established far too quickly and Alexander was the only thing holding it together. His empire was bound to break up the moment he died. Even if he had lived, and had not considered expanding his empire still further, the Greeks and Macedonians lacked the manpower to control it for long. Alexander had relied more and more upon foreign troops that had not been ruled by the Europeans long enough to have incorporated their culture or, more importantly, for new systems of government to become entrenched. The only hope this empire had was to break apart into more manageable divisions – which is exactly what happened.

Ptolemy was quick to grasp this perception when he became governor of Egypt. When Alexander's successors met in Triparadisus after

Perdiccas' death in 320 BC, Ptolemy was offered the regency as a compromise settlement that was acceptable to Antipater and Seleucus. However, he wisely refused. Although he was turning down the chance to be ruler of all of what had been Alexander's empire, he realised that it could not be controlled. Egypt, however, was already firmly in his power and he knew he could hang on to it. He was right, as his dynasty continued to rule for over two and a half centuries. When Seleucus gained Asia, Antipater remained in power in Europe and Ptolemy kept Egypt, but much of Asia Minor was left in the balance. Nearchus, however, still had control of Ionia and initially managed to keep well out of the hostilities that had been going on between the other protagonists.[2] It seems that here, he and Barsine were attempting to found a new Aegean Empire – and one that had a good chance of survival.

Nearchus, who was about five years older than Alexander, was born on the island of Crete. His father Androtimus was an important Cretan aristocrat who sided with the Macedonians against the Greeks and joined the court of King Philip. When Nearchus was a teenager he was sent to attend Aristotle's school along with Alexander and here the two men became close friends.[3] It was at this time that Nearchus first met Barsine and her brother Pharnabazus, when they were living in Macedonia after their father Artabazus had fled from the Persian Empire.

Although they were Persians, Artabazus' family had lived in Asia Minor for a number of generations and empathised with the Hellenic culture of the Ionians. In 358 BC, Artabazus was the most influential aristocrat in Asia Minor, and on the death of the Persian king Artaxerxes II he made an alliance with the Athenians from mainland Greece and led a successful revolt against Persian rule. For a few brief years he managed to found a separate state in Asia Minor in which the Greeks and Persians shared power and enjoyed equal rights. In 353 BC, however, the new king Artaxerxes III managed to reconquer the region, forcing Artabazus and his family to flee to Macedonia, where they were made welcome by Philip. Ten years later, the Persian king needed support against potential rivals and invited Artabazus to return to Asia Minor, which he did, being made governor of Phrygia. Barsine was then married to the most important general in the Persian army, a man named Mentor, and when he died in 340 BC she married his brother Memnon, who became commander of the Persian forces in Asia Minor. Around this time, her brother Pharnabazus was appointed commander of the Persian Mediterranean fleet. When Alexander crossed the Dardanelles to begin his campaign in 334 BC, not only was Barsine's father the governor of the larger part of Asia Minor, and her brother was the top Persian admiral, but also her husband was supreme commander of all the Persian forces in the region.[4]

When the invasion of Asia Minor began, Alexander put Nearchus in command of the navy. He was therefore fighting against Barsine's brother, while Alexander was doing battle with her husband. Alexander probably hoped, or even expected, that the Artabazus family would capitulate. Not only had the Macedonians given them sanctuary, but Barsine's husband was an Ionian from the island of Rhodes. Alexander was fighting a fellow Hellenic, while Nearchus was sailing into battle against an old friend. Although the Artabazus family did eventually change sides, for the time being they remained loyal to the new Persian king, Darius.

Pharnabazus' navy had to sail from Egypt, Phoenicia and Cyprus, and arrived too late to prevent Nearchus seizing a number of Aegean islands that had been under Persian control. However, even after Alexander's forces won their decisive victory at Granicus, Memnon managed to hold the Persian naval base at Halicarnassus in Caria long enough for his brother-in-law to evacuate the town by sea.[5] In August 333 BC Memnon died fighting to retake the Aegean islands, and command of the Persian forces that remained in Asia Minor went to Artabazus. When the Persians were decisively beaten at the battle of Issus three months later, Artabazus retreated to the east with his king, and all of Asia Minor belonged to Alexander.

Alexander had now achieved the Hellenic dream: he had created a unified Aegean empire. Nevertheless, to hold on to it he needed to control the sea. Pharnabazus still had a huge fleet in the Mediterranean that was far superior to that of Nearchus. Nearchus' main naval base was now on the island of Crete, whereas the bases of the Persian fleet were in Syria and Phoenicia. These had to be taken if the Aegean empire was to be secured. Alexander's army therefore marched south and conquered the area by the summer of 332 BC. Deprived of their eastern Mediterranean ports, and without the support of the Phoenician sailors, the Persian fleet was soon defeated and Pharnabazus captured.[6]

Alexander had now secured the united Hellenic empire that had been dreamed about for centuries. With historical hindsight this should have been the end of the war with Persia, and Nearchus and most of the generals assumed that it would be. Perhaps even Alexander himself considered this for a while, as he decided that he would marry Barsine following her capture after the battle of Issus. Anyone who intended to rule a peaceful Ionia would need to consider the interests of both the

Greeks and Persians of the area, as Artabazus had done two decades earlier. Barsine was the daughter of the man who had been the most influential figure in the region's recent history; she was someone with whom both these peoples could identify. As did Memnon and his brother before, Alexander realised the political importance of a marriage with Barsine. However, for various reasons, the marriage did not go ahead; not least of these was Alexander's decision to move on into Egypt. He now had plans for a much larger empire and ruling the Aegean was only a small part of his scheme. Nevertheless, Barsine stayed with him. When he took Egypt and moved on eastward, he left Nearchus behind as commander of the Aegean islands and overall governor of Asia Minor.

At this time many Greek and Macedonian officers thought that Alexander was marching into disaster; the Persians had infinitely more soldiers and resources. If Alexander's army were to be wiped out, what would become of the empire in the Aegean? Nearchus must have known that it stood an excellent chance of survival, no matter what happened to Alexander and his main army. In the Aegean, it was sea power that counted for more than anything and Nearchus now had total superiority on the waves. If Alexander did lose, then he would do so only after further weakening Persian land power. The Persians would have little chance of retaking the important Ionian harbour cities that could be continually reinforced from Greece and Macedonia by sea.

In fact, it is doubtful whether Darius would have had the slightest intention of attempting to retake Ionia. Apart from anything else, after losing his western empire and fleeing the battlefield, he would have had enough problems maintaining his authority at home. If this happened, then Nearchus would be the one person in Alexander's empire who was in a position to rule the Aegean and Ionia. He was, in fact, the first man from Crete to command the Aegean since the time of the Minoans. Although there is no specific reference to Nearchus' thoughts in 331 BC, when Alexander crossed the Euphrates and headed into the heartland of the Persian Empire, he must have realised the unique position he was in.[7]

As it turned out, Alexander succeeded against all odds in totally defeating Darius at the battle of Arbela and moved on to take Babylon, Susa and the capital of Persepolis. In 330 BC, even after Darius was dead, Alexander continued on into Bactria. By this time, with the Aegean Sea firmly under his control, Nearchus had established his provincial capital in the Phrygian city of Pergamum, in northwest Asia Minor – the home of Barsine's family. Although Barsine was away with Alexander, she had left her only child, an eleven-year-old daughter from her first marriage to Mentor, at Pergamum in the care of her relatives. The child's name goes unrecorded, but this is the girl Nearchus would eventually marry. Nearchus must have developed a close friendship with the Artabazus family at this time, some of whom he already knew from his youth.

With the death of Darius, Artabazus and his son Pharnabazus openly came over to Alexander's side in the war against the new Persian leader Bessus (although they may have been in league with him for some time). When Alexander defeated Bessus and captured Bactra in the summer of 329 BC, he made Artabazus governor of Bactria.[8] By the end of that year Alexander was drawn into a further campaign in Sogdiana and sent word to Nearchus to bring around 10,000 Greek reinforcements from Europe and Asia Minor. When he set off for the new campaign, Alexander left two-thirds of his army behind in Bactra under Nearchus' command. For almost a year, between the summers of 328–7 BC, Bactria was left completely under the control of Nearchus and Artabazus: Nearchus commanded the Greek and Macedonian army, and Artabazus commanded the Persian allies and had overall jurisdiction as civil governor.[9] As the two men shared power during this time without any friction or disagreements, they clearly got on well.

Throughout this period Barsine appears to have stayed with her father in Bactra and sometime in early 327 BC she gave birth to Alexander's first son, Heracles. However, just a few weeks later, when the Sogdians were finally defeated, Alexander met and married Roxanne. It is not known whether the events were connected, but when the embittered Barsine decided to return home to Pergamum, her father offered Alexander his resignation as Bactrian governor. Alexander accepted it – apparently because Artabazus, who was now in his mid-sixties, claimed he was too old for the job – and Artabazus returned home with his daughter. Alexander seems to have lost all interest in Barsine. He had no problem with her leaving; he did not even mind her taking his only son.

What happened to Nearchus is unknown, but he probably returned with Barsine and Artabazus to resume command in Asia Minor. However, the following year Alexander called him back to the east to build and command a fleet of ships on the River Indus. For the next two years, Nearchus commanded the fleet that sailed down the Indus and then shipped half of Alexander's army back west via the Arabian Sea and Persian Gulf. Eventually he was reunited with Alexander in the Persian city of Susa in March 324 BC. At this time Nearchus was also reunited with Barsine's daughter, who was now seventeen, whom he immediately married. This was no marriage of convenience, as the girl had travelled all the way from Pergamum, almost 2,000 kilometres away, to be with him. When Alexander set off north to Ecbatana, to put down the revolt in Media, Nearchus returned to the Persian Gulf and led his fleet up the River Euphrates to Babylon, arriving there the next spring, about the same time as Alexander. Shortly after his arrival he again met Barsine, whom Alexander had summoned to Babylon.[10]

From all this it is very clear that there was a long-standing and deep link between Nearchus and the Artabazus family. By the time of Alexander's death he was married to Barsine's daughter, and after the king died he immediately proposed Barsine's son as heir. The question is: if Barsine was Alexander's murderer, was Nearchus somehow involved?

Nearchus had undoubtedly remained loyal to Alexander throughout his reign; if he had harboured schemes to overthrow him, he could have attempted a coup while he commanded the army in Bactria. An alliance with Artabazus, the commander of the Persian allies and the governor of Bactria, could well have brought Alexander down. Nearchus had not suffered, as the infantry had, in the unnecessary battles in the Indus Valley; and neither he nor his sailors experienced the horrors of the march through the Gedrosian Desert. Nearchus seems to have remained loyal to his king to the end. However, Barsine wanted her son to inherit the throne and for this to be achieved she not only had to kill Alexander, she would need someone with power and influence to back the claim. It was obvious that Meleager would not support the succession of a half-Persian monarch and that Perdiccas would back Roxanne, while Seleucus was clearly not the kind of man to trust. Nearchus, however, was ideal. Not only was he now Barsine's son-in-law, and would therefore be a member of the royal family if Heracles became king, but if the empire fragmented then he would be the perfect person to establish a smaller – but much safer – empire based on the Aegean.

Nearchus was an experienced admiral who could easily control the Aegean Sea. In fact, he had no rival in this respect. The only other man with any real experience as an admiral left alive in the empire was Pharnabazus, and he was Barsine's brother. Nearchus certainly had the respect of the Ionians and had been governor of Asia Minor for some time. The Persians in Asia Minor would be loyal to Barsine's father, and an alliance through marriage between Nearchus and the Artabazus family already existed. If the empire did fall apart and her son was not accepted as Alexander's successor in the rest of the dominions, then he almost certainly would be in Asia Minor. An Aegean Empire with a son of Alexander and Barsine as king, and Nearchus as regent and protector, would undoubtedly be popular in Ionia, and the Aegean islands. It would probably have had support in Greece. After all, the Athenians had allied themselves with her father three decades earlier. As a native of Crete, Nearchus would certainly have liked the idea of an Aegean Empire, such as his ancestors the Minoans had ruled a thousand years before.

If Barsine had decided to murder Alexander, then she would almost certainly have had to include Nearchus in her plans for the aftermath of the assassination – with or without his knowledge. Is there therefore any evidence in the events after Alexander's death to suggest that Barsine really was the assassin?

According to Curtius, few troops in Babylon liked Nearchus' idea that Heracles be made king, and the matter was dropped. However, when the deliberations were finally over and Perdiccas came out on top, Nearchus was granted governorship of Ionia and the Aegean islands and he immediately departed for the region with Barsine, her child and his wife. When the war started between Perdiccas, Ptolemy and Antipater, Nearchus remained neutral. After Perdiccas was killed in 320 BC, Ionia lay between the European empire, where Antipater ruled as regent to Arridaeus, and the Asian empire, under the control of Seleucus. To the east, however, another empire was emerging under Antigonus, the governor of eastern Asia Minor who had fled from Perdiccas after the massacre of Korama. He had seized control of Eumenes' army that Perdiccas had sent to fight Antipater and he now had 60,000 troops under his command. Antipater, Seleucus and Antigonus all accepted Ionian independence and Nearchus remained in power; not only on the mainland but also retaining many of the Aegean islands. Unfortunately, Nearchus' neutrality was not to last long – a year later he was forced to take sides.[11]

In the autumn of 319 BC Antipater died of old age and, for some reason, on his deathbed he made an old Macedonian general named Polyperchon his successor. According to Diodorus:

> While he was on his deathbed, Antipater appointed Polyperchon as his successor and as the regent to Arridaeus . . . Antipater appointed his son Cassander as Polyperchon's deputy . . .
> Cassander, however, was angered by the arrangement and that the authority of his father should pass to a man who was not related by blood . . . and he left the capital [Pella] and plotted to seize the country for himself.[12]

It was not long before Cassander organised an effective revolt, seized control in Macedonia and pushed Polyperchon and his army south into Greece. At the same time, Antigonus decided to invade Seleucus' territory in southern Media and Bactria, and to keep Cassander from exploiting the situation and attacking his rear, he made a pact with the Macedonian, offering to help him defeat Polyperchon in Greece. For this, Antigonus needed Nearchus' navy. Although Nearchus would have much preferred to stay out of it, Antigonus now had an entire army on the Ionian borders. Nearchus had little choice but to ally himself with Antigonus and lead his fleet against the eastern coast of Greece.[13]

By 316 BC Antigonus had secured Media and most of Bactria, while Cassander was firmly in control of Macedonia and much of Greece. Polyperchon, however, managed to hold on to the Peloponnese Peninsular (in southern Greece), and this is how things remained for two years. In 314 BC, unable to defeat Seleucus in the heartland of his empire, Antigonus turned his attentions westward and decided to invade Macedonia. To this end, he now allied himself with Polyperchon against Cassander, and Nearchus now found himself fighting alongside the man he had reluctantly been sent to attack.[14]

In the autumn of 313 BC, a peace treaty was finally agreed between Antigonus and Cassander, and Polyperchon once more found himself isolated. As part of the treaty, Antigonus agreed to attack Polyperchon, and Nearchus was again expected to change allegiance. However, by this time, both Nearchus and Polyperchon were fed up of being used as pawns in a larger power struggle and decided to make an alliance themselves. A conference of the two parties was held in the city of Aphrodisias, in Caria in southern Ionia. Here Nearchus and Polyperchon agreed that by uniting they could control much of the Aegean. Cassander had for years been unable to defeat Polyperchon in southern Greece, while Ionia was, for the time being, safe from attack by Antigonus, who was fighting Seleucus' forces for the second time, and which were now far more formidable. It seemed that they were in a strong position to establish a secure Aegean empire. The problem was, who would be leader? In the end a compromise was reached in which Barsine's son Heracles, now fourteen, would be king and Artabazus (who seems to have been in retirement until this time) would be regent. Polyperchon and Nearchus would share equal powers as his deputies. At last, the Greeks and Ionians were part of a united kingdom, and one ruled by Alexander's eldest son. It may not have been a complete Aegean empire, as it did not include Macedonia and northern Greece, but it was a significant start. Antigonus was being defeated by Seleucus, who had no designs on Asia Minor, and Cassander lacked the naval power to wage war in the Aegean. The new kingdom was called Anatolia – a name that the Romans later used for Turkey – and for four years it remained an independent alliance of Ionian provinces, Aegean islands and Greek city-states. Barsine's hope that Heracles would one day succeed Alexander was now as much of a reality as could ever have been hoped.[15]

While Heracles was still a young teenager, the experiment worked, but in 309 BC he turned eighteen and was nearly old enough to rule alone. This began to trouble Polyperchon, who suspected that Nearchus, as the young king's brother-in-law, would use his influence for Ionian, rather than Greek, interests. Rather stupidly, Polyperchon decided to seek help from his longstanding enemy Cassander. Cassander was himself unhappy about a son of Alexander ruling in Asia Minor, and agreed to offer assistance to get rid of the boy. However, what Cassander wanted more was to see the end of Polyperchon and his control of southern Greece. Polyperchon seems to have naively thought that Cassander would send an army to depose Heracles, get rid of Nearchus, put him in charge and happily return home. He was grossly mistaken. Cassander despatched an army all right, but it never returned home.[16]

Heracles was in the Ionian capital of Pergamum in the northeast of the region when Cassander's army, under the command of the Macedonian general Lysimachus, crossed the Dardanelles, a hundred kilometres due north of the city, while Polyperchon's fleet landed a Greek army on the Mediterranean coast, some fifty kilometres to the west. The two armies took the Ionians completely by surprise while Nearchus was away visiting Crete. What happened to Artabazus, the regent, is unknown, but Heracles was seized along with his mother. Polyperchon may have been naive but he was not a heartless man. He had expected that Heracles would simply be deposed and sent into exile. However, once Cassander heard that Pergamum had been taken, he sent orders that Barsine and Heracles should both be killed. According to Justinus:

> Cassander sent secret orders that Heracles should be put to death, together with his mother Barsine, and that their bodies should be privately buried in the earth lest the murder should be betrayed by a regular funeral.[17]

By the end of the fourth century BC Antigonus had been defeated by Seleucus, who fully established the Seleucid Empire in the East, and

Cassander remained in control in Macedonia. After the murder of Barsine and Heracles, Polyperchon managed to retreat to southern Greece where he hung on to power for a couple more years. However, although Barsine and Heracles were dead, the Ionian kingdom survived. Lysimachus, the general Cassander had sent to Ionia, remained there and when he died his deputy Philetaerus founded an independent dynasty, known as the Attalid kings. These were to successfully rule, not only Pergamum, but most of Ionia for the next two centuries until it was annexed by the Romans.[18] Nearchus never returned to Ionia. Instead, he remained on the island of Crete where he retired to write his memoirs. His original work no longer survives, but the section that deals with the events after Alexander's death was used by Arrian. Unfortunately, Arrian's work concerning this period is mostly lost, although extracts do survive in other later works. However, they reveal nothing further than is already known about the period following Alexander's death.

Throughout all of this, it had been Alexander's brother Arridaeus, rather than Heracles, who was seen by most parties as the symbol of succession. Perdiccas, Antipater, Polyperchon and Cassander had all used him as a puppet. But was he really as hapless as these leaders seem to have imagined? Although Statira and Barsine must remain on the list of suspects, there is no evidence to suggest that either of them were part of a larger conspiracy. However, when we delve deeper behind the scenes of the Macedonian court, we find that Arridaeus may have been involved in an extremely elaborate plot indeed.

SUMMARY OF CHAPTER FOURTEEN

There are only four suspects left, and one of these is Barsine. If she had been Alexander's assassin then a possible motive would have been to secure the throne for her son. Nearchus was the only one of Alexander's military successors to propose Barsine's son Heracles as heir to the throne.

- One place in particular where there might be evidence to implicate Nearchus in Alexander's assassination would be the region of the Aegean Sea where he assumed power in Ionia after Alexander's death. It was here that Nearchus had become closely associated with Barsine's family. By Alexander's death he was married to Barsine's daughter, and after the king died he immediately proposed Barsine's son as heir.
- Barsine wanted her son to inherit the throne and for this to be achieved she not only had to kill Alexander, she would need someone

with power and influence to back the claim. Nearchus was ideal. Not only was he Barsine's son-in-law, and would therefore be a member of the royal family if Heracles became king, but if the empire fragmented then he would be the perfect person to establish a smaller, but much safer empire based on the Aegean.

- Eventually, in 313 BC, Nearchus did establish an Aegean kingdom with Heracles as king. However, as the boy was only fourteen, Nearchus remained in power as governor in Ionia, while the Macedonian general Polyperchon held power in southern Greece.

- In 309 BC Heracles was in the Ionian capital of Pergamum in the northeast of the region when Cassander's army crossed the Dardanelles, a hundred kilometres due north of the city, while Polyperchon's fleet landed a Greek army on the Mediterranean coast, some fifty kilometres to the west. The two armies took the Ionians completely by surprise while Nearchus was away visiting Crete. Heracles and Barsine were seized and killed.

- If Barsine had entertained hopes that Heracles would rule in her homeland of Ionia then there certainly seems to have been no organised plan made between her and Nearchus. If there had been, then Nearchus could have proclaimed Heracles king on a number of occasions over the next few years – which he did not. After his proposal that Heracles be made king on Alexander's death, he dropped the idea. It was ten years before Heracles was finally made king and only then as a compromise forced on Nearchus by Polyperchon. If Barsine killed Alexander and intended her son to become king, there is no evidence that anyone else, including Nearchus, was involved. Like Statira, if she was Alexander's murderer then she probably acted alone.

15. A WARRIOR QUEEN

Arridaeus was made king after Alexander's death, but he suffered from some kind of psychological problem which was deemed to render him unfit to govern alone. First Perdiccas, then Antipater, Polyperchon and Cassander all followed one another as his regents and ruled on his behalf. Whatever was wrong with Arridaeus, it seems to have been intermittent and at times he was completely sane. Indeed, he was perfectly all right at the time Alexander fell ill, as he helped officiate at the ceremonies during Hephaestion's funeral on the day of the ill-fated feast. According to Curtius, during the deliberations that followed Alexander's death, Meleager, when proposing Arridaeus as king, said:

> You are forgetting Arridaeus, the son of King Philip and Alexander's brother; only recently he accompanied the king in performing the religious ceremonies which makes him Alexander's sole heir.[1]

Arridaeus had his own motives for killing Alexander; but if he did murder his brother, did he act alone? It was his stepmother Olympias who sent him to Babylon. Could she somehow have been involved?

There can be little doubt that Olympias was an ambitious and calculating woman with a vicious temper, and she was, as we have already seen, directly involved in the deaths of many people over her lifetime. However, would she have killed her own son? She had certainly fallen out with Alexander after he had met up with Barsine, following the battle of Issus in 333 BC. Alexander, for his part, had become fed up with his mother's meddling (she had originally insisted on accompanying him on his campaigns in Greece). In fact, Alexander went so far as to give another woman, Ada the queen of Caria, the title of 'mother'. According to Plutarch, around the end of that year Olympias complained: 'When will Alexander leave off slandering me?'[2]

Olympias remained behind in Macedonia and, over the next eleven years, mother and son occasionally exchanged letters, and at times they appeared to have reconciled their differences. Alexander appears to have tried to make things up by sending her gifts. However, by 323 BC, although Alexander no longer bore her ill will, Olympias was furious that she was not allowed power of her own to rule in Europe. According to Plutarch:

To his mother he [Alexander] sent many presents, but would never suffer her to meddle with matters of state or war, not indulging her busy temper, and when she fell out with him on this account, he bore her ill-humour very patiently.[3]

Olympias was certainly hungry for power. Plutarch relates that just before Alexander died she and her daughter Cleopatra were conspiring to take over from the European governor, Antipater.

Even at home, Olympias and Cleopatra had raised a faction against Antipater, and divided his government between them, Olympias seizing upon Epirus, and Cleopatra upon Macedonia.[4]

Plutarch goes on to say that even though Olympias had support in her homeland of Epirus, and Cleopatra had the support of the aristocracy in Macedonia itself, Alexander did not take either of them seriously as threats to his power.

When Alexander was told of it, he said his mother had made the best choice, for the Macedonians would never endure to be ruled by a woman.[5]

In dismissing her in this way, Alexander infuriated his mother. However, there was another reason Olympias was angry with her son. He now expected his subjects to embrace Persian religion. If Plutarch is right, Olympias was priestess of the Greek god Dionysus and this threatened not only her sect but her religious authority.

Philip's passion for her; and whether he feared her as an enchantress, or thought she had commerce with some god, and so looked on himself as excluded, he was ever after less fond of her conversation. Others say, that the women of this country [Epirus, where Olympias came from] having always been extremely addicted to the enthusiastic Orphic rites, and the wild worship of Bacchus [the Roman name for Dionysus] . . . Olympias, zealously, affecting these fanatical and enthusiastic inspirations [rites], to perform them with more barbaric dread, was wont in the dances proper to these ceremonies to have great tame serpents about her, which sometimes creeping out of the ivy in the mystic fans, sometimes winding themselves about the sacred spears, and the women's chaplets, made a spectacle which men could not look upon without terror.[6]

Olympias did have both personal and political motives to kill her son, and it seems that she may also have had religious ones. If she did manipulate Arridaeus' jealousy of his brother to get him to kill Alexander, it may not have been the first time Olympias got someone else to murder one of her relatives in such a way. Plutarch accuses her of manipulating the bodyguard Pausanias to kill her husband Philip.

But the disorders of his family, chiefly caused by his new marriages and attachments (the troubles that began in the women's chambers spreading, so to say, to the whole kingdom), raised various complaints and differences between them, which the violence of Olympias, a woman of a jealous and implacable temper, made wider, by exasperating Alexander against his father. Not long after this, Pausanias, having had an outrage done to him at the instance of Attalus and Cleopatra [Olympias' daughter], when he found he could get no reparation for his disgrace at Philip's hands, watched his opportunity and murdered him. The guilt of which fact was laid for the most part upon Olympias, who was said to have encouraged and exasperated the enraged youth to revenge.[7]

If Plutarch is right, then Olympias and her daughter Cleopatra had worked together to get rid of Philip. By the summer of 323 BC Olympias and Cleopatra were working together to oust Antipater in Europe: if they really wanted secure power in Macedonia then they would also have to get rid of Alexander. Olympias certainly had motive and she had the opportunity, if she could persuade Arridaeus to kill his brother. She also, it seems, had the means – Olympias would have known exactly how to poison Alexander.

Alexander seems to have been killed with one of the alkaloid vegetable toxins from the poisonous plants such as aconite, hemlock, henbane, thorn apple and belladonna. Whoever poisoned him must have known something about these plants – or at least was involved with someone else who did. There is no evidence that Arridaeus had any knowledge of poisons, but Olympias certainly had. According to Plutarch, her training as a priestess (or an enchantress, as he calls her), made Olympias an expert with drugs, which he accuses her of using on Arridaeus.

Arridaeus, who was Philip's son by an obscure woman of the name of Philinna, was himself of weak intellect, not that he had been originally deficient either in body or mind, on the contrary, in his childhood, he had showed a happy and promising character enough. But a diseased habit of body, caused by drugs which Olympias gave him.[8]

Plutarch tells us that Olympias often visited the temple of the love goddess Aphrodite at Aphrodisias in Caria (in southern Asia Minor). The temple at Aphrodisias was famous for the drugs it manufactured and sold, which were said to increase sexual performance. In fact, the word aphrodisiac, meaning any sex-enhancing substance, took its name from the town. The second-century historian Apollonius of Caria writes that the priestesses of Aphrodite made a drug from the belladonna plant which was said to be the best aphrodisiac there was. The active ingredient was a chemical called atropine and the belladonna seeds were ground down to concoct the love potion. Indeed, the name belladonna, meaning 'beautiful lady', came from the fact that the plant was sacred to the goddess Aphrodite. However, its use as an aphrodisiac required very small quantities of atropine: in larger doses it was fatal, which is why it has the common name of deadly nightshade. Is it simply a coincidence that belladonna, we concluded earlier, is the most likely poison to have been used on Alexander?

If Olympias did manipulate Arridaeus to poison Alexander then she may have covered her tracks by accusing others of the crime. When suspicions were voiced that Alexander may have been poisoned, it was Olympias who blamed Antipater.

At the time, nobody had any suspicion of his being poisoned, but upon some information given six years after, they say Olympias put many to death, and scattered the ashes of Iollas [Antipater's son – Alexander's royal butler], then dead, as if he had given it him.[9]

Justinus also says that Olympias accused Antipater of poisoning Alexander.

The author of this conspiracy was Antipater, who, seeing that his dearest friends were put to death, that Alexander Lyncestes, his son-in-law, was cut off, and that he himself, after his important services in Greece, was not so much liked by the king as envied by him, and was also persecuted with various charges by his mother Olympias; reflecting, too, on the severe penalties inflicted, a few days before, on the governors of the conquered nations, and hence imagining that he was sent for from Macedonia, not to share in the war, but to suffer punishment, secretly, in order to be beforehand with Alexander, furnished his son Cassander with poison, who, with his brothers Philippus and Iollas, was accustomed to attend on the king at table . . . Iollas, who used to taste and mix the king's drink, had the poison ready in cold water, which they put into the drink after it had been tasted.[10]

Eventually Olympias stopped accusing Antipater and his family and began to blame others. The entire thing, however, may have been to divert suspicion from herself. In fact, Olympias' original accusations against Antipater, that he was conspiring against Alexander, not only made him look guilty when Alexander died, but also might have provided her with a reason to send Arridaeus to Babylon to poison her son.

Olympias certainly had the motive, means and opportunity to kill Alexander by proxy, and could have concocted an extremely clever plan, not only to murder him but also to blame and get rid of Antipater at the same time. In the end Alexander seems to have accepted Antipater's innocence of the earlier claims made against him by Olympias, and Antipater managed to survive to remain ruler in Europe. Olympias certainly wanted Antipater out of the way, and when her son was dead she soon allied herself against him. Is there any evidence during the tumultuous period following Alexander's death to further implicate Olympias in her son's assassination?

When Alexander died it was Perdiccas who took power, although Arridaeus did become king in name. Nonetheless, Antipater remained firmly entrenched as governor in Europe. To strengthen ties with Perdiccas, Antipater offered him his daughter in marriage. However, fearing an alliance between the two, Olympias suggested that Perdiccas marry her daughter Cleopatra. Justinus writes that Perdiccas saw this as a move towards securing the throne for himself, as it would mean that he would become the king's brother-in-law, and he agreed.

Soon after, that he might secure royal support to his present power, he turned his thoughts to a marriage with Cleopatra, sister of Alexander the Great, and formerly wife of the other Alexander, her mother Olympias showing no dislike to the match.[11]

Perdiccas set off to Macedonia to marry Cleopatra, taking Arridaeus with him. Antipater, however, suspecting that Perdiccas intended to oust him from power the moment he arrived in Macedonia, declared war and sent an army under Cassander and Craterus to stop him in Asia Minor. Justinus tells us that Perdiccas had agreed to give Olympias power in Macedonia if she helped him defeat Antipater by mustering the people of her home country of Epirus to his side.

> Perdiccas, as the aspect of affairs was unfavourable, called Arridaeus . . . then in Cappadocia . . . to a consultation concerning the management of the war. Some were of opinion that it should be transferred to Macedonia, to the very head and metropolis of the kingdom, where Olympias, the mother of Alexander, was, who would be no small support to their party, while the good will of their countrymen would be with them, from respect to the names of Alexander and Philip.[12]

When the war started Olympias and Cleopatra went to Epirus as Perdiccas had hoped. The governor of Epirus – the Molossian tribal leader Alexander – had been Olympias' brother and Cleopatra's incestuous husband. He had died shortly before and Olympias was accepted as regent and acting tribal chief for his young son Aeacides. It seems that the plan was for Olympias to wait for Perdiccas to defeat Antipater in Asia Minor, before she deployed the army of Epirus against Macedonia. Perdiccas' army, under the command of Eumenes, did manage to defeat Craterus and Cassander in Asia Minor: Craterus was killed and Cassander retreated into Macedonia. However, unfortunately for Olympias, in 320 BC Perdiccas was killed and replaced by Seleucus, while Eumenes' army was seized by Antigonus who sent Arridaeus to Antipater as a part of a nonaggression pact. When Antipater died the next year and Cassander fought with Polyperchon for control of southeast Europe, Olympias allied herself with Polyperchon.

In Celtic society women could and did fight alongside men in battle, and Celtic queens often led armies. Olympias was to be no exception. It seems that as a Molossian princess she had been given warrior training as a girl and she now intended to put this experience to good use. While Cassander was forced to lead his main army south into Greece to fight Polyperchon, Olympias led a Molossian army into Macedonia.

By now Arridaeus had married Cassander's sister Eurydice. As queen of Macedonia, Eurydice not only dominated her husband, she seems to have controlled her brother the regent as well. According to Justinus, it was she who had persuaded Cassander into fighting Polyperchon in the first place.

> In the meantime Eurydice, the wife of king Arridaeus, when she learned that Polyperchon was returning from Greece into Macedonia, and that Olympias was sent for by him, being prompted by a womanish emulation, and taking advantage of her husband's weakness, whose duties she took upon herself, wrote in the king's name to Polyperchon, desiring him 'to deliver up the army to Cassander, on whom the king had conferred the government of the kingdom' . . . Cassander, attached to her by such a favour, managed everything according to the will of that ambitious woman. Marching into Greece, he made war upon several cities.[13]

Now, Justinus tells us, with Cassander away, Eurydice had to face Olympias' army. In 317 BC the fate of the homeland of what had been the empire of Alexander the Great was being decided by two women. Moreover, they were women who both decided to lead their armies into battle. According to Justinus, they each stood at the head of their troops decked out in full armour. However, there was to be no battle, as the Macedonians immediately came over to Olympias' side.

> The Macedonians being moved, either by respect for the memory of her husband, or the greatness of her son, or by the indignity with which she was treated, went over to Olympias.[14]

With no army left to speak of, Eurydice and Arridaeus were both captured and taken in chains to the capital of Pella. Diodorus describes the awful fate that awaited them.

> But after Olympias had captured Eurydice and Arridaeus and had taken the whole kingdom without a fight, she showed no pity. At first she placed them under guard and treated them dreadfully by bricking them up in a small room and gave them just enough food and drink to survive upon through a narrow opening in the wall . . . Then, after they had suffered terribly for many days . . . she ordered that Arridaeus be taken out and stabbed to death.[15]

If Olympias had used Arridaeus to murder Alexander, he would be telling no one about it now. There can be no doubt whatsoever that Olympias was a particularly cruel and heartless woman: Diodorus' account of the manner of death she chose for Eurydice was the invention of a warped and sadistic mind.

> Eurydice would not submit to Olympias' demands that she openly declare that the kingdom belonged to her. Olympias therefore decided that she was worthy of greater punishment and sent her a sword, a noose, and some hemlock, and told her to use whichever of these she wished to kill herself before she starved . . . Eurydice prayed that Olympias should befall such a fate for her cruelty and after lovingly cleaning the wounds of her dead husband, ended her life by hanging herself with the rope.[16]

It seems that poor Arridaeus had died having finally found a woman who genuinely cared for him. Olympias was finally queen of Macedonia in her own right. But her short reign was a bloody one. According to Diodorus:

> After she had killed Eurydice and Arridaeus, Olympias killed Nicanor, Cassander's brother, and destroyed Iollas' grave, avenging, as she said, the death of Alexander. She also chose one hundred of Cassander's friends and had them slaughtered to a man.[17]

By 315 BC, however, Cassander managed to lead an army back from Greece and, according to Justinus, he forced Olympias to abandon the capital.

> But neither did Olympias reign long; for having committed great slaughter among the nobility throughout the country, like a furious woman rather than a queen, she turned the favour with which she was regarded into hatred. Hearing, therefore, of the approach of Cassander, and distrusting the Macedonians, she retired, with her daughter-in-law Roxanne, and her grandson Hercules, to the city of Pydna [on the Aegean coast to the south of Pella].[18]

When her own army began to desert, Olympias knew she was defeated and surrendered.

When the news of her retreat was brought to Cassander, he marched immediately, with the utmost expedition, to Pydna, and laid siege to the city. Olympias, distressed with famine and the sword, and the weary of a long siege, surrendered herself to the conqueror, stipulating only for life. But Cassander, on summoning the people to an assembly, to inquire what they would wish to be done with Olympias, induced the parents of those whom she had killed to put on mourning apparel, and expose her cruelties; when the Macedonians, exasperated by their statements, decreed, without regard to her former majesty, that she should be put to death.[19]

Cassander ordered that Olympias be stoned, bludgeoned and slashed to death, but, Justinus tells us, she died bravely.

Olympias, seeing armed men advancing towards her, bent upon her destruction, went voluntarily to meet them, dressed in her regal apparel, and leaning on two of her maids. The executioners, on beholding her, struck with the recollection of her former royal dignity, and with the names of so many of their kings, that occurred to their memory in connexion with her, stood still, until others were sent by Cassander to despatch her; she, at the same time, not shrinking from the sword or the blow, or crying out like a woman, but submitting to death like the bravest of men, and suitably to the glory of her ancient race, so that you might have perceived the soul of Alexander in his dying mother. As she was expiring, too, she is said to have settled her hair, and to have covered her feet with her robe, that nothing unseemly might appear about her.[20]

We know that Olympias was a manipulative woman who seems to have engineered Philip's death. We also know that she fell out with Alexander. She was the one who accused Antipater, and had various people accused of Alexander's murder. Everything the ancient sources tell us about Olympias reveals that she could well have been behind Alexander's assassination.

She had motive. She was a strong and shrewd woman from a background where women were valued for such attributes and held power in their own right: yet Alexander had forbidden her to be involved in politics and warfare. For this, she came to despise him. She clearly desired power and she attempted to oust Antipater in Macedonia during Alexander's absence. She cleverly manipulated wars to her advantage after Alexander's death, and may have devised a clever plot to blame Antipater for the murder.

She had opportunity. Olympias appears to have been quite capable of persuading Arridaeus to poison Alexander on her behalf: Arridaeus seems to have been easily influenced and had his own motives for killing his brother. Furthermore, Olympias may have orchestrated her husband Philip's assassination in a similar way.

She had the means. Olympias had knowledge of and access to the sort of poison that seems to have been responsible for Alexander's death.

Not only did Olympias have the motive, means and opportunity to kill her son, she was ambitious enough to have wanted her son's throne, and her actions after seizing Macedonia in 317 BC show that she was cruel and merciless when it came to gaining power. She had no compunction in killing her stepson, and perhaps her husband, so she could have had Alexander killed.

If Olympias did manipulate Arridaeus to poison her son then her attempts to accuse others of murdering Alexander would have been part of her plan to throw suspicion away from herself.

None of this actually proves that Olympias was behind Alexander's death, but Arridaeus, working on her behalf, is a far more likely suspect than either Barsine or Statira. However, there is one final suspect on the list – Perdiccas. Is there any evidence to prove that he may have been the one who murdered Alexander?

SUMMARY OF CHAPTER FIFTEEN

Arridaeus had his own motives for killing Alexander; but if he did murder his brother, did he act alone? It was his stepmother Olympias who sent him to Babylon. Could she somehow have been involved?

- Arridaeus was made king after Alexander's death but he suffered from some kind of psychological problem which was deemed to render him unfit to govern alone. First Perdiccas, then Antipater, Polyperchon and Cassander all followed one another as his regents and ruled on his behalf. Whatever was wrong with Arridaeus, it seems to have been intermittent and at times he was completely sane. Indeed, he was perfectly all right at the time Alexander fell ill, as he helped officiate at the ceremonies during Hephaestion's funeral on the day of the Alexander's last feast.
- There can be little doubt that Olympias was an ambitious and calculating woman with a vicious temper, and she was directly involved in the deaths of many people over her lifetime. However,

would she have killed her own son? She had fallen out with Alexander after he had met up with Barsine, following the battle of Issus in 333 BC. Alexander, for his part, had become fed up with his mother's meddling. In fact, Alexander went so far as to give another woman, Ada the queen of Caria, the title of 'mother'.

- Olympias was certainly hungry for power. By the summer of 323 BC she and her daughter Cleopatra were working together to oust Antipater in Europe. If they really wanted to secure power in Macedonia then they would also have to get rid of Alexander. Olympias had motive and she had the opportunity – if she could persuade Arridaeus to kill his brother.

- She also, it seems, had the means – she would have known how to poison Alexander. Alexander seems to have been killed with one of the alkaloid vegetable toxins from the poisons plants, such as aconite, hemlock, henbane, thorn apple and belladonna. There is no evidence that Arridaeus had any knowledge of poisons, but Olympias certainly had. According to Plutarch, her training as a priestess made Olympias an expert with drugs.

- The second-century historian Apollonius of Caria writes that the priestesses of Aphrodite made a drug from the belladonna plant that was said to be the best aphrodisiac there was. However, in larger doses it was fatal. Is it simply a coincidence that belladonna is the most likely poison to have been used on Alexander?

16. ESTABLISHING MEANS

Perdiccas had many motives to have murdered Alexander, not least of which was power. The king had died without naming an heir, so as vizier and Alexander's deputy Perdiccas was the nearest thing to a successor. Of all the suspects on the list, Perdiccas was the one to have initially benefited the most from Alexander's death. He became leader of the entire empire – in actuality, if not in name – and the way he achieved this appears to have been skilfully stage-managed.

Perdiccas' performance when he addressed the troops the day after Alexander died is reminiscent of Mark Anthony's famous funeral speech from Shakespeare's *Julius Caesar*. In this devious monologue, Anthony tells the hostile mob that he has come to bury Caesar, not to praise him. He holds nothing against Brutus and the others who murdered Caesar, as they are all honourable men. In reality, he intends to seize the Roman Empire for himself and cleverly brings the mob round to his side, until at last it is they who condemn the assassins and hail Anthony as Caesar's successor. When Perdiccas faced Alexander's army he did not tell them that he should be king. Rather, he appeared to be surrendering any right to succession. He placed Alexander's robe, crown and ring on the royal throne saying: 'I return the ring which the king gave me by his own hand . . . We need a leader, and whoever that shall be should be up to you all to decide.'[1] In fact, he goes further by suggesting that if Roxanne's unborn child turns out to be a boy then he should be king.[2]

Perdiccas knew that Nearchus would obviously propose Heracles, as he was the boy's brother-in-law, and that Meleager would propose Arridaeus, as he was the only purely European candidate of Alexander's bloodline. In fact, it didn't really matter to Perdiccas which of these three became king. None of them was capable of ruling alone, so someone would have to be regent, and that was the person who would have the real power. Perdiccas obviously wanted the regency himself, but he did not want to appear eager for the job. When the arguments about who should be king turned into a riot, it was one of Perdiccas' men, Aristonous, who proposed him for regent, as Alexander had given him his ring.[3]

Perdiccas 'reluctantly' accepted the responsibility and agreed that Arridaeus should be king: Meleager's idea – not his own. Not only had Perdiccas become regent when he was apparently prepared to relinquish any claim to being Alexander's successor, but he also had accepted his chief rival's proposal over his own. With the popular majority backing, it was not long before Perdiccas could get rid of Meleager altogether.

This was clearly a cleverly orchestrated seizure of power, which must have taken some planning. But was it a coup d'état? Did Perdiccas know in advance that Alexander would die, or was he just a quick thinker?

Perdiccas did not have a particularly illustrious career, and had only reached high rank in the army because better men were either dead, or had been murdered or dismissed by the paranoid and unpredictable Alexander. In fact, the only reason that Perdiccas was in the position to take over the empire after Alexander's death was that he became deputy leader upon Hephaestion's unexpected demise in October the previous year. If Perdiccas did have long-standing plans to seize the empire, then he would firstly have had to get rid of Hephaestion. Interestingly, Hephaestion did die suddenly, having previously been in good health, and Alexander himself originally suspected that his friend had been poisoned. Was this a coincidence, or could Hephaestion have died from the same poison that killed Alexander?

In the summer of 324 BC, Alexander made Hephaestion both his vizier and senior officer of the cavalry and Perdiccas became his second-in-command. Shortly after, Perdiccas was sent on to Media in command of an advanced force to assess the rebellion that had been reported there, and in October, Alexander, Hephaestion and the main army joined him in Ecbatana to put down the revolt. Here, Atarepata, the governor of the province, held a welcoming banquet for Alexander, during which Hephaestion became acutely ill. Although most of the historical sources mention it, there is no detailed description of the feast as there is with the one in Babylon where Alexander fell sick. Plutarch, for instance, simply says that Hephaestion fell 'sick of a fever'. He does, however, tell us what he had to eat and drink: 'He ate a fowl for his dinner, and drank a large draught of wine, upon which he became very ill, and shortly after died.'[4] All we know from the other sources is that Hephaestion collapsed and was taken to his bedchamber, where he seems to have suffered convulsions, followed by a peculiar facial paralysis. The *Historia*, for instance, tells us that, 'Hephaestion's face was frozen in a deathly grin, and though he could move his head and arms, his jaw was rigid and he could utter not a word.'[5]

Whatever killed Hephaestion, it did not take long. Justinus implies that he died the night he fell ill, 'in the course of those proceedings',[6] while Plutarch says it was 'shortly after'.[7] There is no detailed account of Hephaestion's fatal illness, but what there is makes it sound very similar to Alexander's sickness. Apparently, like Alexander, he suffered delirium and repeated convulsions. These symptoms could be caused by a number of natural diseases, but the reference in the *Historia's* account of Hephaestion's frozen jaw might link specifically to the accounts of one of Alexander's symptoms. All but one of the accounts of the last stages of Alexander's illness refer to him being conscious and capable of movement but being unable to speak. The *Historia*, for example, tells us, 'he recognised his officers and raised his head to speak to them, but could utter no word. From that moment until the end he spoke no more.'[8] I had assumed that this speechless condition was an effect of belladonna poisoning, which constricts the vocal cords. However, could it have been caused by something that specifically affected the jaw, as in Hephaestion's case?[9]

There is one illness renowned for causing a lockjaw condition such as Hephaestion seems to have suffered. That is tetanus, and a number of historians have suggested that this disease was responsible for Hephaestion's death. Tetanus is caused by the bacteria *clostridium tetani*, which is found in soil, dust and animal droppings. The infection usually enters the body through a puncture, wound or cut and it produces a highly poisonous neurotoxin in the blood that spreads to the nervous system. The symptoms of tetanus appear gradually, over a few days, with the patient showing signs of acute tiredness, lack of appetite and flu-like symptoms. This is followed by stiffness in the muscles of the neck and face, causing the jaw to become completely locked, preventing the patient from opening the mouth or talking. Known as trismus, this condition results in a grotesque facial expression called a sardonic grin (or *risus sardonicus*). Soon after, other muscles become affected, causing rigidity, spasms and convulsions. These can continue for three to four weeks before the patient may die from heart or respiratory failure.

Soldiers were, of course, particularly vulnerable to tetanus infection, and Hephaestion could well have contracted such a disease in the field. However, tetanus comes on gradually, over a day or so, with the patient losing appetite, becoming tired and feeling unwell, with symptoms similar to flu. Hephaestion's condition came on suddenly in one evening, during which he had enjoyed a hearty meal. Also, the lockjaw condition is one of the first symptoms of tetanus, affecting the sufferer well before the spasms and convulsions start a day or so later. Hephaestion's lockjaw was one of the last symptoms he suffered. Moreover, the illness seems to have killed him quickly, whereas tetanus is usually a long and drawn-out death. If the accounts are accurate, then Hephaestion cannot have died of tetanus.

The rapid onset of Hephaestion's illness, resulting in convulsions and a quick death, after he had been eating and drinking, could however have been caused by a toxic substance. Tetanus is one of the few diseases that emulate poisoning, as the spores of the *clostridium tetani* bacteria produce a dangerous neurotoxin similar to that found in alkaloid vegetable toxins, such as those that seem to have been responsible for Alexander's fatal condition: aconite, hemlock, henbane, thorn apple and belladonna. Could one of these have been used to murder both Alexander and Hephaestion? Before continuing, it is important to remind ourselves of the symptoms Alexander suffered.

According to the *Historia*, Alexander first began pacing agitatedly around the room, before his hands began trembling. Soon after, there was an aching or stiffness in his neck, followed by a sudden, sharp pain in the area of the stomach.

> He left the table and began to walk between the guests, but speaking to none of them, as if he were troubled by some important matter . . . with his hands trembling, [he] complained that it was as if a heavy yoke were upon his neck. When he stood again to drink . . . he shouted with pain as if struck through the stomach with an arrow.[10]

Diodorus adds that the pain was so severe that Alexander cried out 'as if struck by a violent blow'.[11] Justinus also says that Alexander cried out with the sudden, piercing pain, before collapsing. The pain then spread through his body and when touched anywhere on his skin it became so excruciating that 'he called for a sword to put an end to it, and felt pain at the touch of his attendants as if he were all over with wounds'.[12]

According to Diodorus, the pain increased during the night. 'None of them were able to do anything to help and Alexander's great and acute discomfort continued unabated.'[13] Plutarch tells us that Alexander also suffered from an intense thirst and fell into a state of delirium.[14] And according to the *Historia*, Alexander also endured uncontrollable tremors and convulsions, followed by periods of quiet and what appear to have been hallucinations.[15]

The next day, although Alexander had recovered somewhat, according to the *Historia*, 'he bade his attendants to leave him alone in darkness, as he was distressed at both their presence and by the light.'[16]

A few days later, after Alexander had virtually recovered, he fell acutely ill again. The *Historia*, for example, describes how the condition was similar to before: ' . . . the pain returned and the king was beside himself with agony and again he fell into fits and delirium'.[17]

This time Alexander failed to recover. According to Plutarch, he got progressively worse over the next few hours until he was bedridden and 'when the generals came into his chamber he was speechless and continued so the following day'.[18]

All the accounts agree that although Alexander could not talk, he was still conscious and able to move to some degree. For instance, Justinus recounts that Alexander was able to take his ring from his finger and give it to Perdiccas.[19] The histories all concur that for a few more hours Alexander lingered on, his breathing becoming more laboured, until he fell into a coma and died the following evening.

The Los Angeles County Regional Poison Center at the University of Southern California had concluded that these symptoms had been caused by an alkaloid neurotoxin from one of five poisonous plants – aconite, hemlock, henbane, thorn apple and belladonna – of which the most likely was belladonna. Although they would all have caused intense stomach pain, tremors, convulsions, delirium and extreme sensitivity of the nerves, belladonna poisoning causes three crucial symptoms that the others do not. All the historical sources make reference to fever, which might have been a way of describing any incapacitating illness, especially if delirium is involved. However, strictly speaking, fever means a high temperature, which would usually be caused by a bacterial or viral infection – not a reaction to a toxin. However, belladonna is amongst the few poisonous plants that do cause fever and results in the victim becoming hot and sweaty. The other two symptoms of belladonna poisoning are dryness of the mouth with intense thirst, and an eventual effect on the vocal cords, rendering the victim incapable of speech.

If Hephaestion had suffered from the same kind of poisoning then it seems to have resulted in lockjaw. I decided to contact the Poison Center again to ask them if any of the plants on the list they had given me could cause this condition. There was not one on the original list, they told me, but there was a vegetable alkaloid toxin that was uniquely renowned for rendering a person speechless by causing a lockjaw condition, similar to tetanus. This was the highly toxic substance, strychnine.

The symptoms of strychnine poisoning are very similar to those of belladonna poisoning, but there are three unique to strychnine that also matched Alexander's illness. Like the others, if ingested, strychnine causes stomach pains, but it can also lead to the tightening of the muscles of the solar plexus, resulting in extreme discomfort. Twice the Historia referred to the pain in Alexander's stomach, but the second time it specifically said that it was 'as if a knife had been thrust in and turned *beneath* his stomach'.[20] This is exactly where the solar plexus is. Another unique effect of strychnine amongst the other alkaloid toxins is that it causes sensitivity to light and noise. I had not previously considered it a symptom, but the *Historia* also said that, on the second day of his illness, Alexander 'bade his attendants to leave him alone in darkness, as he was distressed at both their presence and by the light'.[21] And finally, there was the most significant effect, lockjaw. The lockjaw symptom of strychnine poisoning is caused in exactly the same way that the neurotoxins produced by the *clostridium tetani* bacteria cause the condition in tetanus. Unlike tetanus, however, the lockjaw effect of strychnine poisoning occurs as one of the last symptoms, as happened with Hephaestion and also Alexander, if lockjaw was the cause of his inability to speak.

As Hephaestion could not have died of tetanus then, the Poison Center assured me, the only way he could have died so quickly from a condition that brought on lockjaw was by strychnine poisoning. Like Hephaestion, neither could Alexander have died from tetanus. His symptoms came on as rapidly as Hephaestion's, and if he did have lockjaw, it was one of the last effects of his illness. Although we are not told specifically that Alexander's jaw was locked, every other symptom he exhibited precisely matches the effects of strychnine poisoning – even more so than belladonna.

If the ancient accounts of Alexander's illness are accurate, and there is no reason to doubt them as they were all taken from eyewitness reports, then these were the symptoms Alexander suffered. Initially, agitation, tremors, aching or stiffness in the neck, followed by a sudden, sharp pain in the area of the stomach (specifically, just below the stomach). He then collapsed and suffered acute and excruciating agony wherever he was touched. Alexander also suffered from an intense thirst, fever and delirium, and throughout the night he experienced convulsions and hallucinations, followed by periods of calm. The following day, although he had recovered considerably, he could not stand the light or the presence of his servants. When he was taken ill for the second time, he did not recover and in the final stages of the condition he could not talk, although he could still move his head and arms. Ultimately, his breathing became difficult and he fell into a coma and died. When this is compared to the effects of strychnine poisoning, as described in *The Grant Dictionary of Toxicology*, we can see that they are identical in every way:

Strychnine interferes with inhibitory transmitters, which produce a state of muscle rigidity and stimulation. Soon after ingestion, the first clinical signs are uneasiness and restlessness, anxiety, muscle twitching and stiffness of the neck. After about an hour the solar plexus tightens causing extreme pain. Periods of delirium, hallucinations and toxic convulsion occur shortly afterwards, characterised by sudden contractions of the muscles followed by complete relaxation. The patient may be particularly sensitive to light and noise and can experience a painful reaction to pressure on the skin. Other symptoms include a temperature rise of $2 - 4$ C above normal, sweating, elevated blood pressure, episodic rapid heart rate, and intense thirst. The final stages of poisoning resemble tetanus with the jaw muscles being completely locked.[22]

The Poison Center assured me that there was no known poison other than strychnine that could have caused all the symptoms Alexander suffered. However, I was confused. Strychnine had not been on the list of alkaloid poisons they had originally given me. When I queried them, they reminded me that I had only asked them to provide a list of the poisons available in Europe, western Asia and the Middle East. Strychnine comes exclusively from the orange-like fruit of the *nux-vomica*, commonly called the strychnine tree, which is native only to parts of India. I had overlooked the fact that Alexander had recently returned from the Indian subcontinent.

The nearest place that strychnine could have been directly acquired by any of the suspects in Alexander's murder was the Punjab, which no one in Alexander's entourage had visited until the spring of 326 BC. Indeed, until this time, no European is known to have visited India and even the Persians knew little about it. Alexander and Hephaestion both seem to have died of strychnine poisoning, which by the wildest stretch of the imagination cannot have been a coincidence. Neither could it have been an accident, as the substance was completely unknown in the west at this time. Even in the places where it grows, the strychnine tree is rare in the wild. Whoever got hold of it must have done so for the explicit purpose of poisoning. But why go to the trouble of obtaining such a rare and exotic poison when they could have used something available far nearer home?

We know from all the sources that Alexander's physicians, although unsure of the exact nature of the malady, believed that the king had died of a naturally occurring illness. Presumably they would have been familiar with the effects of aconite, hemlock, henbane, thorn apple and belladonna. Administering a poison that produced such an apparent and unusual symptom as lockjaw might fool the doctors into thinking the victim had died of some form of tetanus. At the very least, if the poison was completely unfamiliar, no one would be able to prove poison had been used – death would probably have been put down to natural causes. Whoever killed Alexander was clever enough to use a poison that was unfamiliar to his physicians. Not only would this allay suspicions of murder, it would rule out the possibility of a known antidote. In hindsight, however, it helps us narrow down the list of suspects. To have known about or obtained strychnine, the murderer had to have been someone who was with Alexander during the Indian campaign.

So where were our four remaining suspects – Statira, Barsine, Arridaeus and Perdiccas – during the Indian campaign? Statira had been in Susa for the duration of Alexander's reign, well over 2,000 kilometres from the nearest strychnine tree, and Barsine had been almost 4,000 kilometres away in Asia Minor. Arridaeus and his stepmother had been even further away in Macedonia, and even though Olympias seems to have had a knowledge of drugs, it could not possibly have included strychnine. There was only one person on this list who had been with Alexander in India and that was Perdiccas. And, unlike the others, he had a motive to murder both Alexander and Hephaestion.

Everything seemed to fit. Alexander and Hephaestion both had to have died of strychnine poisoning and Perdiccas is the only remaining suspect to have had the motive and opportunity to kill them both (Statira, Barsine and Arridaeus were nowhere near Ecbatana when Hephaestion died) and he exclusively had the means – strychnine. The case seemed to have been solved – but there was one loose end. If Perdiccas was the murderer, how did he acquire the strychnine? The *nux-vomica* tree is rare, even in the parts of India where it grows.[23]

Remarkably, an ancient account of the campaign in India actually places Alexander in what has to have been a grove of strychnine trees. The third-century Greek biographer Philostratus refers to the shrine at Nysa that Alexander visited, which contained a statue of the Hindu god Skanda.

Here there was a polished, white stone statue of the god, in the form of a youth, seated at the heart of a grove of sacred trees and vines. These trees had grown together to form a roof above the god which protected it from the rain.[24]

As we learned earlier, Skanda was the main deity worshipped along the Indus Valley, and in the eastern Punjab of Hindu India there are temples to Skanda still in use today. Just as in Alexander's time, they are open-air shrines, where statues of the god are surrounded by groves of the sacred trees known as the *shudha kupilu*, or *shundha* for short. In Sanskrit (Ancient Hindi) *shudha kupilu* is the name of the *nux vomica* – the strychnine tree. The orange-like fruit of the strychnine tree, which contains the toxin, was and still is considered sacred to Skanda and, when burned, its smoke has an intoxicating quality believed to induce mystical visions.[25]

It was at such a temple that Alexander met the Brahman priest Kalyana who accompanied him as his interpreter and guide and travelled with him back to the west. As a devotee of Skanda, Kalyana would almost certainly have taken some of the dried strychnine fruit with him when he left the temple, as it played an essential part in his religious devotions. Strychnine can be fatal if ingested, but brief exposure to the smoke merely causes a state of heightened agitation and mild delirium. Nonetheless, there can be little doubt that Kalyana would have been all too familiar with its lethal properties. Kalyana himself cannot have been the murderer, as he died in Susa a few months before Alexander. However, it seems highly probable to have been from him that the murderer obtained the strychnine, or at least learned its deadly secret. Interestingly, Kalyana's own death was mysterious; and before he died he actually warned Alexander that he would die in Babylon.

Kalyana did not tell Alexander how he would die, nor did he name any potential assassin, so Alexander ignored the warning. Nevertheless, the priest was right, so had he known what someone intended to do? Indeed, had Kalyana himself been killed with his own sacred fruit in order to keep him quiet? Like Alexander and Hephaestion, he died suddenly after being in excellent health. According to Arrian, he had never before had a day's illness in his life. We have no account of the symptoms he suffered, but he evidently knew exactly what was wrong with him and knew that he would not recover. There was no known antidote for strychnine in the fourth century BC, and it is interesting that Arrian tells us that Kalyana decided to take his own life rather than suffer the undignified death he knew he would face.[26] Logically, if someone intended to kill Alexander with strychnine so that poisoning would not be suspected, then the one person they certainly had to eliminate was Kalyana.

This leaves us with a dilemma. Perdiccas appears to have had the motive, means and opportunity to have killed both Alexander and

Hephaestion. Yet if Kalyana was poisoned by Alexander's would-be murderer to keep him quiet, he cannot have been killed by Perdiccas. When Kalyana died in Susa, Perdiccas had been sent ahead to Media in command of an advanced reconnaissance force to gather intelligence about the rebels.[27] Indeed, he had been gone for over a month. If he had considered Kalyana a danger to his plans, he would have killed him before he left, rather than leave someone else to do it for him when he was gone.

Someone now appeared to have been a triple murderer. And a smart one too: strychnine emulated a condition previously only associated with tetanus – a common disease in the theatre of war. Although a modern doctor would recognise that many of the symptoms would not match tetanus, contemporary physicians would probably have put it down to a variation of the disease, since no other illness was known to cause lockjaw. More importantly, neither was any poison known in the West at that time. But if it wasn't Perdiccas, then who was it? He was the only suspect left in Alexander's murder. I must have been overlooking something. Someone I had already discounted must have been the true culprit. Whoever it was had to have been someone close to Kalyana. In fact, of all the eight suspects on the original list, there is only one who is known to have befriended the priest. This was one of the first people I had eliminated as the possible murderer – Alexander's queen, Roxanne.

SUMMARY OF CHAPTER SIXTEEN

If Perdiccas murdered Alexander to take over the empire, he would firstly have had to get rid of Hephaestion, his predecessor. Interestingly, Hephaestion did die suddenly, a few months before Alexander, and poisoning was originally suspected.

- Hephaestion collapsed during a feast and was taken to his bedchamber, where he suffered convulsions and delirium, followed by a peculiar facial paralysis in which his jaw was locked and he was unable to speak. Whatever killed Hephaestion, it did not take long as he seems to have died the same night he fell ill.
- There is one illness renowned for causing a lockjaw condition such as Hephaestion seems to have suffered. That is tetanus, and a number of historians have suggested that this disease was responsible for Hephaestion's death. However, tetanus comes on gradually, over a day or so, with the patient losing appetite, becoming tired and feeling unwell, with symptoms similar to flu. Hephaestion's condition came

on suddenly, after he had enjoyed a hearty meal. Also, the lockjaw condition is one of the first symptoms of tetanus, whereas in Hephaestion's case it was one of the last symptoms he suffered. Moreover, the illness seems to have killed him quickly, whereas tetanus is usually a long and drawn-out death.

- If the accounts are accurate, Hephaestion cannot have died of tetanus. His illness could however have been caused by a toxic substance. There is one poison that is uniquely renowned for rendering a person speechless by causing a lockjaw condition. This is the highly toxic substance, strychnine, an alkaloid vegetable toxin that comes from the fruit of the *nux-vomica*, commonly known as the strychnine tree.

- The effects of strychnine poisoning not only match Hephaestion's symptoms, but those of Alexander's illness. The symptoms of strychnine poisoning are almost exactly like those of the other five poisons that could have been used on Alexander: aconite, hemlock, henbane, thorn apple and belladonna. However, there are three unique symptoms of strychnine poisoning that also match those suffered by Alexander: intense pain in the solar plexus, sensitivity to light and noise, and lockjaw. All the historical sources report that although Alexander could still move towards the end of his illness he was unable to talk. Like Hephaestion, Alexander could not have died from tetanus. His symptoms came on as rapidly as Hephaestion's, and if he did have lockjaw, it was one of the last effects of his illness.

- Why was strychnine not on the original list of alkaloid vegetable toxins that could have killed Alexander? Because the list was only of plants that would have been available in Europe, western Asia and the Middle East. Strychnine comes exclusively from the *nux-vomica* tree, which is native only to parts of India. It had been overlooked that Alexander had recently returned from India.

17. THE MURDERER UNVEILED

It now seemed that Roxanne could be back on the list of suspects. However, she had initially seemed the least likely of the eight possible murderers. Although she had the motive of jealousy concerning Alexander's marriage to Statira, she was also expecting his child. If she intended to kill him in revenge, then why not wait until the child was born? Even though Roxanne may have wanted vengeance on Alexander, she would surely have considerer the future of her unborn child – or, for that matter, her own position of power. If, as it turned out, the baby was a boy, then he would be Alexander's only legitimate heir. Roxanne was clearly an intelligent woman and must have reckoned on the possibility that if Alexander died before the birth then, with the matter of succession still undecided, one of Alexander's generals would seize the throne. If this were to happen, by the time her child was born the matter of Alexander's bloodline would be irrelevant. If Roxanne had plans to murder her husband, she had every reason to want him to remain alive until her child was born. According to Justinus, she was eight months pregnant when Alexander died: she would only have a few more weeks to wait.[1]

Perhaps I had underestimated the extent of Roxanne's wrath. Indeed, it was only when I examined the period following Alexander's death that I realised that she was jealous to the point of frenzy. Shortly after Alexander died, Roxanne persuaded Perdiccas to arrest Statira on the grounds that she might become a focus of Persian opposition. According to Plutarch, when Roxanne had Statira alone, she murdered the girl with her own bare hands and threw her body down a well.[2] This not only proves that Roxanne was capable of cold-blooded murder; it shows just how furious she was. Perhaps she just couldn't wait another month.

Before Alexander's expedition in 325 BC, no one from the West had ever visited India. Olympias had been in Europe during and after the Indian campaign, and Arridaeus had come to Babylon directly from Europe. The same applies to Antipater and his son Cassander, while Antipater's other son Iollas had been head of the domestic household of the royal palace at Babylon until Alexander returned in 323 BC. Barsine had been in Asia Minor and remained there until she travelled to Babylon in the summer of 323 BC; while Statira had been under guard in Susa from 331 BC. Of the original eight suspects, only Perdiccas, Meleager, Seleucus and Roxanne accompanied Alexander to India.

Meleager and Seleucus, however, were both so woefully unprepared for Alexander's death that neither of them could possibly have been the assassin. Perdiccas and Roxanne are the only two suspects who could have obtained strychnine, learned of its poisonous properties and had the opportunity to murder both Alexander and Hephaestion. So which of them was most likely to have obtained the murder weapon?

The strychnine tree only grows at an elevation of over 400 metres and in moist rain forests, such as the Hindu temples of Nysa and Taxila, which were in the sub-tropical foothills of the Gandara Mountains. The tree does not grow in the lowland areas of the Indus Valley. When Alexander made the excursion to Nysa and Taxila in the spring of 326 BC, Perdiccas had accompanied Hephaestion ahead to the Indus as part of the advanced force that built the bridge over the river. For the rest of the Indian expedition, most of the army remained in the lowland swamps of the Indus Valley: in particular, the force that marched along the western bank. This was Hephaestion's command of which Perdiccas was a part. Roxanne, however, had been with Alexander when he visited Nysa and Taxila. In fact, one account puts her right in the middle of what has to have been a grove of strychnine trees. According to the *Historia*, when Roxanne accompanied Alexander to the Hindu temple at Nysa, she was the one who told the scribes the true name of the god whose statue was there.[4]

This shows that she must have visited a strychnine grove, as the statues of the god Skanda were always surrounded by these trees, which were considered sacred to him. There can be no doubt that the Skanda statue at Nysa was no exception, as the third-century Greek biographer Philostratus specifically describes it as being 'at the heart of a grove of sacred trees'.[5]

According to the *Historia*, Roxanne was excited by the plants and animals of India, captivated by the local customs, and intrigued by the Hindu religion.[6] In fact, in just a couple of months she had already learned enough about the culture to know exactly what god was being venerated in Nysa when nobody else in Alexander's entourage did. As we are told Roxanne was enthralled by the native flora, she was probably familiar with the properties of the strychnine fruit well before she returned to Babylon. Perdiccas, on the other hand, not only seems to have never been anywhere near a strychnine tree; he also appears to have been a hardened soldier with absolutely no interest in foreign culture whatsoever.

There is even more reason to believe that Roxanne could exclusively have learned about the poisonous properties of the strychnine fruit –

because she befriended the Hindu priest Kalyana. Kalyana was a Brahman, a Hindu sage, and a devotee of the god Skanda in the temple at Taxila. He was fascinated by the Europeans and was as keen to learn about them as Roxanne was to learn about Indian culture. The pair struck up a close friendship, and Kalyana taught Roxanne about the Hindu religion and its practices. In fact, as far as we know, Roxanne was the only person in Alexander's entourage who was the slightest bit interested in the Hindu religion.[7] Moreover, as a devotee of Skanda, Kalyana would have known all about the properties of the strychnine fruit. Neither Perdiccas nor Roxanne would have had a motive to murder Alexander during their time in India, so there would be no reason for either of them to have obtained strychnine to use as a poison. However, Kalyana almost certainly brought some of the dried strychnine fruit with him when he accompanied Alexander to the west, as he would need to burn it as part of his daily devotions. By the time either of them decided to kill Alexander, Kalyana would be the man to get it from. Not only did Perdiccas evidently have no connection with strychnine shrines, but he also could not have got to know Kalyana. He was ahead building the bridge when Alexander and Roxanne first met the priest, and he had been with the army on the west bank of the Indus on the return home, while Kalyana had been on the east bank acting as Alexander's adviser. After that, Perdiccas had returned to Persia by sea with Nearchus, whereas Kalyana had returned with Alexander through the Gedrosian Desert. Roxanne, on the other hand, seems to have got to know him very well indeed.

We now know that strychnine had almost certainly been used to murder Alexander, and the only person we know of who would have recognised the symptoms of strychnine poisoning was Kalyana. Kalyana was the only Indian recorded to have joined Alexander's court on the return to the west. Whoever murdered Alexander would first have to kill Kalyana if they wanted to keep him quiet. Not only did Kalyana die mysteriously after having been in good health, but also before he died he appeared to warn Alexander that he would die in Babylon. As it turned out, he was right. Some scholars have inferred this to have been a prophesy, while others, from the more pragmatic perspective, have suggested that Kalyana might have known that someone intended to kill him when he arrived in the city. Unlike Perdiccas, Roxanne had every reason to wait until Alexander arrived in Babylon before murdering him.

If Roxanne was Alexander's murderer then she must have decided to kill him after he married Statira. Recalling that whoever intended to kill Alexander with strychnine and get away with it had first to silence

Kalyana, it is interesting that it was immediately after this marriage that Kalyana died. Roxanne and Perdiccas are the only two possible suspects remaining, and Perdiccas could not have killed Kalyana as he was on his way to Media. Roxanne, however, was still in Susa when Kalyana died.

Kalyana's warning that Alexander would specifically die in Babylon further implies Roxanne's guilt.[8] Alexander's original plan had been to move on directly to the city, but news of a revolt in the north forced him to change his plans and march to Ecbatana, sending Statira ahead to Babylon. If Roxanne's plan was to murder Statira as well as her husband, which her eventual killing of the girl suggests was the case, then if she killed Alexander immediately the chances were that Statira would escape her clutches. With Alexander dead, some rival successor would almost certainly seize the girl and marry her to enhance his bid for the throne. Roxanne would need to be close to Statira when Alexander died and, as such, she would have to wait until he reached Babylon.

Is this how Kalyana had known that Alexander would die in that city? Just why Kalyana wasn't more specific in his warning we'll never know. Nevertheless, of the two remaining suspects, only Roxanne would have had reason to wait until Babylon to kill Alexander. Once Hephaestion was dead in October, Perdiccas could have killed Alexander at any time. Why wait until he was in Babylon?

Kalyana's death aside, Roxanne appears to be the only one of the eight original suspects with the motive, opportunity, *and* the means to have murdered Alexander. She was jealous to the point of frenzy, she was present on both occasions he was poisoned, and she was in the best position to have obtained the murder weapon – the strychnine. Furthermore, the one man who would have recognised the poison for what it was died mysteriously the moment Roxanne had been given the motive to kill her husband – immediately after his marriage to Statira. Roxanne is the only person who *could* have murdered Alexander the Great.

There is, however, a mystery that still remains. What had Hephaestion got to do with it all? Not only Alexander, but also Hephaestion, seems to have died of strychnine poisoning. This means that Alexander's murderer almost certainly murdered Hephaestion too. Perdiccas had good reason to kill Hephaestion, but why should Roxanne want him dead? Roxanne killed Statira and, according to Plutarch, she killed Statira's sister as well.[9] This is understandable. Roxanne was jealous of

Statira, and the girl and her sister were also both potential rivals. She did not want either of them left alive as the last survivors of the Persian royal bloodline. But why kill Hephaestion? There is also another puzzle. Roxanne had been with Statira and Alexander in Babylon for over four weeks before the feast on 1 June. She could have poisoned Alexander at any time. Why wait until the night of Hephaestion's funeral? Was the occasion somehow significant? Hephaestion must have been involved – but how?

As Roxanne had been insanely jealous of Statira, perhaps she was also jealous of Alexander's relationship with his best friend? Looking back on Alexander's life, it suddenly becomes clear just what kind of relationship this was. Alexander and Hephaestion appear to have been lovers.

The historical sources leave a number of clues that Alexander was bisexual. Plutarch, for instance, tells us that during the campaign in Asia Minor in 333 BC, one of Alexander's officers wrote to him asking if he would be interested in a couple of young slave-boys that were up for sale.

> Philoxenus, his lieutenant on the sea-coast, wrote to him to know if he would buy two young boys of great beauty . . .[10]

The fact that the boys are referred to as being 'of great beauty' implies that Philoxenus assumed that Alexander would be interested in them for sexual reasons. Evidence that Hephaestion was bisexual as well can also be inferred from the historical sources. This is graphically implied in the contemporary painting made by the artist Aetion of Alexander's marriage ceremony to Roxanne. According to the second-century Greek author Lucian of Samosat, beside Alexander in the picture, 'stands Hephaestion, his best man, who holds a blazing torch and leans against a young boy at his side'. The boy is naked.[11]

That closeness of Alexander and Hephaestion is described many times in the historical accounts of Alexander's reign. Plutarch, for instance, tells us that Hephaestion was so close to Alexander that he was the only one allowed to read the letters from the king's mother.

> She often wrote to him to this purpose, and he never communicated her letters to anybody, unless it were one which he opened when Hephaestion was by, whom he permitted, as his custom was, to read it along with him; but then as soon as he had done, he took off his ring, and set the seal upon Hephaestion's lips.[12]

The fact that Plutarch specifically refers to Alexander setting his ring upon Hephaestion's lips hints strongly that the two men were more than just good friends. (The custom of courtiers kissing a monarch's ring did not exist at this time.) Plutarch goes even further in suggesting that Hephaestion was Alexander's sexual partner when he uses the Greek word *philalexandros* to describe Hephaestion's relationship with the king. This translates directly as 'lover of Alexander'; while Alexander's other close friends are described with the word *philobasileus*, meaning simply 'a lover of the king'.[13]

Alexander's inconsolable grief upon Hephaestion's death also implies far more to their relationship than a close friendship. According to Arrian:

> Alexander flung himself upon his friend's body and lay there crying for the whole day. Even that night he lay stretched out upon the corpse, sobbing . . . For two whole days after Hephaestion's death, Alexander ate no food and paid no attention to his bodily needs, but lay on his bed crying uncontrollably.[14]

Arrian goes on to tell us that Alexander wanted the whole world to appreciate the similarity that he and Hephaestion bore to the mythical heroes Achilles and Patroclus, saying that, like Achilles, Alexander would 'rather have been the first to die, than live to suffer the pain of loss'.[15]

If everything else to suggest a homosexual relationship between Alexander and Hephaestion could be considered circumstantial, then the link that Alexander established between him and his friend and the two mythical heroes is virtual confirmation. When Alexander visited Troy in 334 BC, he and Hephaestion not only worshipped together at Achilles' tomb, but in the festivities that were staged in the city the two men played the parts of Achilles and Hephaestion. When Hephaestion died, Alexander even ordered a period of mourning which paralleled the funeral that Achilles had held for Patroclus in Homer's *Iliad*. The Greek playwright Aeschylus (525–456 BC) had composed a work about the Trojan Wars that was extremely popular by Alexander's time. Called the *Myrmidones*, it portrays the two heroes as lovers. This is summarised in a line from Achilles' speech when he laments over the dead body of Patroclus: 'Do these unblemished thighs that I worshipped and the showers of kisses you gave me now count for nothing.'[16] The famous Greek philosopher Plato (427–347 BC) wrote at length in his work, the *Symposium*, about the morals of the love affair Achilles is said to have had with Patroclus.[17] Achilles and Patroclus were not only said to have been lovers, they were the gay icons of the ancient world. The parallel Alexander continued to make between himself and Hephaestion and Achilles and Patroclus, well after there was any reason to portray himself as Achilles for political reasons (he had long abandoned the idea, in favour of being the mythical Hercules), plainly indicates that Alexander intended the world to know that he and Hephaestion were lovers.

The relationship must have broken down after Alexander met Barsine in 333 BC, as for many years Hephaestion was relegated to the sidelines. Hephaestion must eventually have come to accept the fact that he was no longer Alexander's lover, as in 327 BC he was the best man at Alexander and Roxanne's wedding. However, by the time they arrived in Susa, in 324 BC, the relationship seems to have been rekindled, as Alexander not only made Hephaestion his deputy, but also he spent more time with him than he did his women. Even on the wedding night when Alexander married Statira and Hephaestion married her sister Drypetis, the two men spent the night alone in Alexander's bedchamber.

Knowing how Hephaestion might have been tied up with the murder case, we are at last in the position to reconstruct a likely scenario of the tragic events.

In 327 BC Alexander and Roxanne fell in love. They married, and Roxanne became queen of the largest empire there had ever been. For three years Roxanne was the darling of the royal court, and when she returned to the west she imagined that with Alexander she would found the greatest dynasty the world had ever known. Sadly, her dreams were to be shattered. Suddenly, in Susa, not only did Alexander take a second wife, with whom he now intended to found his dynasty, he also revived his old love affair with Hephaestion and wanted the whole world to know. In the summer of 324 BC, Roxanne must have been devastated to watch the grand public spectacle of Alexander and Hephaestion jointly marrying Statira and her sister Drypetis. But to make matters worse, the two men spent the wedding night alone in Alexander's bedroom. This homosexual relationship may have been even more distressing and humiliating to Roxanne than Alexander's marriage to Statira. In the eyes of her people, it would have robbed her of her femininity. Remember, in July 329 BC, in Roxanne's homeland of Sogdiana, when one of Alexander's officers married a daughter of Spitamenes, the Sogdian leader, he continued a gay affair with his servant. Although this was acceptable in Greek culture, the Sogdians considered this to be the worst kind of insult. According to their customs, a homosexual relationship implied that the girl was an inadequate wife (there would have been no problem if the man had had an affair with another woman). The officer was killed by an angry mob; the girl, even though she was a tribal princess, was shunned by the entire community. Roxanne was already incensed by Alexander's marriage to Statira. His renewed and open affair with Hephaestion must have driven her mad.

Roxanne probably decided there and then that she would kill them all, and she knew of the means to do it – strychnine. Statira, however, was almost immediately sent on to Babylon with Meleager and his men. If she killed Alexander now, then Statira would almost certainly escape her clutches: she might be married and protected by Alexander's successor, whoever he may be. She would need to kill Statira the moment Alexander died, and she would have to be close to the girl when she poisoned him. Roxanne had to wait until she and Alexander reached Babylon. As a wise and astute man, Kalyana must have known just how furious Roxanne was. Perhaps he noticed that some of his strychnine fruit was missing, realised her intentions, and tried to dissuade her. Roxanne knew that if she was to succeed then Kalyana would have to die. If he had been poisoned with his own deadly fruit, he would know that there was no cure. Kalyana decided to end his own life according to the extraordinary Brahman tradition. Before dying, his last words were to warn Alexander that he would die in Babylon. Why he was not more specific is a mystery, but as a holy man he may have been bound by an oath of silence not to reveal what he had discovered in confidence. Alternatively, he may still have had compassion for the woman who poisoned him. If he told Alexander what he knew, or suspected, the chances were that she would be instantly killed. By cryptically warning Alexander that he would die in Babylon, perhaps he hoped to deter Roxanne from committing a mortal sin. If this was his intention, then he failed. When the army moved on to Media, and Roxanne went with them, the welcoming feast in Ecbatana gave her the opportunity to poison Hephaestion.

When they reached Babylon, because she was pregnant, Roxanne may originally have decided to wait until the baby was born before killing Alexander and his new wife. This would explain why she waited for a month. However, when the delegation returned from Siwa with the news that Hephaestion could be made a demigod, and Alexander held the most spectacular funeral for his dead lover, it may have been the final straw. At the feast that night, when Alexander proposed the toast to Hephaestion, saying that he would now be reunited with his dear friend in the afterlife, the incensed Roxanne may have decided that she could wait no longer for this to be. Somehow, Alexander survived this first attempt on his life, but when he recovered Roxanne poisoned him again. This time she made sure she gave him enough to succeed. Once he was dead, it took little persuasion to get Perdiccas to agree to Statira's death. Her bloodline was such a threat that he would probably have killed her anyway. But Roxanne did not want Statira executed, or beheaded quietly by a nameless guard. This time there was no reason to act clandestinely – Roxanne could take pleasure in extracting her final revenge by throttling the girl with her own hands.

When Perdiccas took power after Alexander's death, it was Arridaeus who became king in name. Roxanne and her newborn son, whom she named Aegus, were sent to Macedonia to live with Olympias. Here they stayed for eight years until Olympias was killed by Cassander. As Olympias had already murdered Arridaeus, Roxanne's son was crowned king with Cassander as his regent. The boy was given the throne name Alexander, after his father, and as Alexander IV he sat on the Macedonian throne. If this had been Roxanne's hope when she poisoned Alexander, then finally it had come to be. However, Aegus was king and Roxanne was queen mother for only a few brief weeks. Hoping to secure the throne for himself, Cassander had both of them quietly put to death. It was left to Diodorus to record their final epitaph.

> Cassander gave instructions to kill Roxanne and the king and to bury them in secret so that none could mourn at their graves . . . Now there was no one left to inherit the empire of Alexander the Great.[18]

When Roxanne died, the truth about Alexander's death went with her to her secret and long-forgotten grave. Only now, after 23 centuries, do we know that the greatest warrior who ever lived was finally brought down by a twenty-year-old girl.

SUMMARY OF CHAPTER SEVENTEEN
Alexander had been poisoned by strychnine, and only one of the eight suspects could have obtained it.

- The only place that strychnine could have been acquired by any of the suspects in Alexander's murder was the Punjab, which no one in Alexander entourage had visited until the spring of 326 BC. Indeed, until this time, no European is known to have visited India and even the Persians knew little about it. Alexander and Hephaestion both seem to have died of strychnine poisoning, which by the wildest stretch of the imagination cannot have been a coincidence. Neither could it have been an accident, as the substance was completely unknown in the west at this time.

- To have known about or obtained strychnine, the murderer had to have been someone who was with Alexander during the Indian campaign. This narrows the original field of eight suspects down to four – Meleager, Seleucus, Roxanne and Perdiccas. However, Meleager and Seleucus cannot possibly have murdered Alexander as they were completely unprepared to take advantage of his death.

- Perdiccas certainly had the motive to murder both Alexander and Hephaestion. And he did take power after Alexander's death. But if Perdiccas was the murderer, how did he acquire the strychnine? The *nux-vomica* tree is rare, even in the parts of India where it grows. The strychnine tree only grows at an elevation of over 400 metres and in moist rain forests, such as the Hindu temples of Nysa and Taxila, which were in the sub-tropical foothills of the Gandara Mountains. The tree does not grow in the lowland areas of the Indus Valley. When Alexander made the excursion to Nysa and Taxila in the spring of 326 BC, Perdiccas had been part of the advanced force building a bridge over the river Indus.

- The only suspect left who had visited the area where the strychnine tree grows was Roxanne. Roxanne's likely motive had been jealousy of Alexander's marriage to Statira, and she was also jealous of Hephaestion with whom Alexander seems to have had a homosexual affair. She had originally been considered a doubtful suspect as she was expecting Alexander's baby and would want him to remain alive until it was born. However, shortly after Alexander died, Roxanne murdered Statira by throttling her with her bare hands. This not only proves that Roxanne was capable of cold-blooded murder; but it also shows how furious she was. Perhaps she just couldn't wait.

- Roxanne is the only one of the eight original suspects with the motive, opportunity, *and* the means to have murdered Alexander. She was jealous to the point of frenzy, she was present on both occasions he was poisoned, and she – and she alone – was in the position to have directly obtained the murder weapon – the strychnine.

CHRONOLOGY OF KEY EVENTS

All dates given are BC

356	July	Birth of Alexander
338	August	Battle of Chaeronea
336	October	Murder of Philip and the accession of Alexander
334	May	Alexander lands in Asia Minor
		Alexander visits Troy
	June	Battle of Granicus
	Summer	Siege of Halicarnassus
	Autumn	Alexander in Gordium
333	April	Alexander leaves Gordium
	November	Battle of Issus
		Barsine and the Persian royal family captured
332	January	Siege of Tyre
	July	Fall of Tyre
	September–November	Siege of Gaza
	November	Alexander visits Jerusalem
	December	Persian governor of Egypt surrenders without a fight
331	January	Alexander in Memphis
	February	Alexander and Barsine visit the temple of Ammon at Siwa
	May	Alexander returns to Tyre
	October	Battle of Arbela
		Babylon surrenders without resistance
	December	Susa surrenders without resistance
330	January	Alexander in the Persian capital of Persepolis
	June	Alexander's army moves on to Ecbatana
	July	Death of Darius III

	December	Alexander in Prophthasia
		Philotas, Nicanor, and Parmenion executed
		Seleucus becomes commander of the Hypaspistes
329	January	Armies unite at Kapisa
	March	Alexander in Charikar
	May	Army crosses the Hindu Kush Mountains
	June	Fall of Bactra
		Bessus captured
		Alexander advances into Sogdiana
	July	Spitamenes leads revolt in Sogdiana
328	Winter	Nearchus in Bactra
	Summer	Alexander campaigns in Sogdiana
	Autumn	Alexander kills Clitus
	December	Spitamenes is captured
327	Spring	Capture of the Sogdian Rock
		Marriage of Alexander and Roxanne
	Summer	Death of Callisthenes
326	Winter	Hephaestion sent to construct a bridge over the Indus
		Alexander campaigns in the Gandara Mountains
	Spring	Alexander and Roxanne in Nysa
		Alexander and Roxanne in Taxila
	Summer	Defeat of Porus
		Alexander's infantry comes close to mutiny
	Autumn	Beginning of the journey down the Indus
325	August	Alexander in Patala
	September	Nearchus starts his voyage back west
	October	Crossing of the Gedrosian Desert
	December	Alexander's army reaches Pura
324	January	March to Persepolis
		Alexander crowned as king of Persia
		Execution of European governors
	March	Alexander meets with Nearchus in Susa
		Execution of thirteen infantry officers

		Purge of the Macedonian and Greek armies
	Summer	Hephaestion made vizier and cavalry commander
		Alexander honours Hephaestion and other officers
		Alexander marries Statira
		Meleager and Statira sent on to Babylon
		Death of Kalyana
	October	Alexander arrives at Ecbatana
		Death of Hephaestion
		Perdiccas becomes Alexander's deputy
		Zoroastrians pass death sentence on Alexander
323	May	Alexander enters Babylon
	1 June	Alexander's last banquet
	11 June	Death of Alexander
	Summer	Perdiccas secures the empire as regent to Arridaeus
		Roxanne murders Statira
		Death of Meleager
322	December	Theft of Alexander's body
321	Winter	War between Perdiccas, Antipater and Ptolemy
320	May	Perdiccas assassinated
319	Autumn	Death of Antipater
		Cassander becomes Arridaeus' regent in Europe
317		Olympias murders Arridaeus
315		Execution of Olympias
		Cassander murders Roxanne and her son
313	Autumn	Heracles king in Ionia
309		Death of Barsine and Heracles

BIBLIOGRAPHY AND TRANSLATIONS

Arrian, *Anabasis Alexandrou*, English trans. John Selby Watson, *The Campaigns of Alexander*, Bohn, London, 1860.

Adcock, Frank, *The Greek and Macedonian Art of War*, University of California Press, Berkeley, 1957.

Badian, E., *Studies in Greek and Roman History*, Barnes & Noble, New York, 1964.

Bevan, E.R., *The House of Seleucus*, Routledge, London, 1966.

Borza, Eugene N., *In the Shadow of Olympus: The Emergence of Macedon*, Princeton University Press, Princeton, 1990.

Borza, Eugene N., *Before Alexander: Constructing Early Macedonia*, Regina, Claremont, 1999.

Bosworth, A.B., *A Historical Commentary on Arrian's History of Alexander*, Oxford University Press, Oxford, 1980.

Bosworth, A.B., *Conquest and Empire: The Reign of Alexander the Great*, Cambridge University Press, Cambridge, 1988.

Bosworth, A.B., *Alexander and the East: The Tragedy of Triumph*, Oxford University Press, Oxford, 1996.

Bosworth, A.B. and Baynham, E.J. (Eds.), *Alexander the Great in Fact and Fiction*, Oxford University Press, Oxford, 2000.

Boyce, Mary (Ed.), *Textual Sources for the Study of Zoroastrianism*, University of Chicago Press, Chicago, 1990.

Burich, N., *Alexander the Great: A Bibliography*, Kent State University Press, Kent, 1979.

Burn, A.R., *Greece and Rome*, Scott, Foresman and Company, Glenview, 1965.

Carman, J. and Harding, A., *Ancient Warfare: Archaeological Perspectives*, Sutton, Stroud, 1999.

Carney, Elizabeth, *Women and Monarchy in Macedonia*, University of Oklahoma Press, Norman, 2000.

Cassius, Dionysius, *History of Rome*, Simon & Schuster, New York, 1988.

Cawkwell, G., *Philip of Macedon*, Faber, London, 1978.

Curtius, *Historiae Alexandri Magni*, English trans. Mole, D.M., *The History of Alexander*, Barnett, London, 1921.

Delbruck, H., *History of the Art of War: Warfare in Antiquity*, University of Nebraska Press, Lincoln, 1990.

Devlin, R.B., *History of the Aegean*, Palmer, New York, 1996.

Diodorus, *Bibliotheca Historica*, English trans. Mallins, D. *Diodorus' History*, Mumford & Brown, London, 1911.

Engels, D.W., *Alexander the Great and the Logistics of the Macedonian Army*, University of California Press, Berkeley, 1978.

Errington, R.M., *A History of Macedonia*, University of California Press, Berkeley, 1990.

Fraser, P.M., *Cities of Alexander the Great*, Oxford University Press, Oxford, 1996.

Fuller, J.F.C., *The Generalship of Alexander the Great*, Eyre & Spottiswoode, London, 1958.

Gaebel, Robert E., *Cavalry Operations in the Ancient Greek World*, University of Oklahoma Press, Norman, 2002.

Grant, R. and Grant, C. (Eds.), *Grant and Hack's Chemical Dictionary*, McGraw-Hill, New York, 1987.

Green, Peter, *Alexander of Macedon 356–323 BC: A Historical Biography*, University of California Press, Berkeley, 1991.

Green, Peter, *Alexander to Actium: The Historical Evolution of the Hellenistic Age*, University of California Press, Berkeley, 1990.

Habicht, Christian, *Athens from Alexander to Anthony*, Harvard University Press, Cambridge, 1997.

Hamilton, J.R., *Alexander the Great*, University of Pittsburgh Press, Pittsburgh, 1984.

Hammond, N.G.L., *Alexander the Great: King, Commander and Statesman*, Noyes, Park Ridge, 1980.

Hanson, V., *The Western Way of War: Infantry Battle in Classical Greece*, Oxford University Press, London, 1990.

Harrison, P. and Waites, G., *The Cassell Dictionary of Chemistry*, Cassell, London, 1998.

Heckel, W., *The Marshals of Alexander's Empire*, Routledge, London, 1992.

Heckel, W., *The Wars of Alexander the Great*, Routledge, London, 2003.

Heckel, W. and Yardley, J.C., *Alexander the Great: Historical Sources in Translation*, Blackwell, Malden, 2004.

Herodotus, *Historiae*, English trans. Aubrey de Selincourt, *The Histories*, Penguin, New York, 1996.

Historia Alexandri Magni, English trans. John Selby Watson, *The History of Alexander the Great*, Bohn, London, 1861.

Hodgson, Ernest (Ed.), *Dictionary of Toxicology*, Wiley, Somerset, N.J., 1997.

Hornblower, J., *Hieronymus of Cardia*, Oxford University Press, Oxford, 1981.

James, L.C. (Ed.), *The Grant Dictionary of Toxicology*, Grant and Sons, Los Angeles, 1989.

Josephus, *Jewish Antiquities*, English trans. William Whiston, Dalton, London, 1925.

Justinus, *Epitoma Historiarum Philippicarum Pompei Trogi*, English trans. John Selby Watson, *Epitome of the Philippic History of Pompeius Trogus*, Bohn, London, 1853.

Kemp, D.D., *The Environment Dictionary*, Routledge, London, 1998.

Klaasen, C.D. (Ed.), *Casarett and Doull's Toxicology: The Basic Science of Poisons*, McGraw-Hill, New York, 1996.

Lampe, Kenneth F. (Ed.), *AMA Handbook of Poisonous and Injurious Plants*, American Medical Association, Chicago, 1985.

Maynard, J., *The Death of Alexander Re-examined*, Daniels, London, 1972.

McNaught, A.D. and Wilkinson, A., *Compendium of Chemical Terminology*, Blackwell, Oxford, 1997.

O'Brien, J.M., *Alexander the Great: The Invisible Enemy*, Routledge, London, 1994.

Palmer, J., *The Army of Alexander the Great*, Brown, Exeter, 1989.

Pearson, L., *The Lost Histories of Alexander the Great*, Harvard University Press, Cambridge, 1948.

Pearson, L.I.C., *The Lost Histories of Alexander the Great*, Scholars Press, Chicago, 1983.

Plato's *Symposium*, English trans. Benardete, S., University of Chicago Press, Chicago, 2001.

Plutarch, *Bios Alexandrou*, English trans. John Dryden, *The Life of Alexander*, Harvard University Press, Cambridge, 1919.

Plutarch, *The Life of Artaxerxes*, English trans. John Dryden, Harvard University Press, Cambridge, 1919.

Robson, T.L., *Women in the Ancient World*, Davis, New York, 1989.

Sekunda, N., *The Army of Alexander the Great*, Osprey, London, 1984.

Stewart, A.F., *Faces of Power: Alexander's Image and Hellenistic Politics*, University of California Press, Berkeley, 1993.

Stoneman, R., *Alexander the Great*, Routledge, London, 1997.

Strabo, *Geographia*, English trans. Jones, Horace Leonard, *Strabo: Geography*, Harvard University Press, Cambridge, 1929.

Tarn, W.W., *Alexander the Great*, Beacon, Boston, 1956.

Timpson, B.E., *Tribal Religions of Ancient India*, Morgan Shield, New York, 1981.

Van der Leeuw, Charles, *Azerbaijan – A Quest for Identity*, St Martin's Press, New York, 1999.

Wilcken, U., *Alexander the Great*, MacVeagh, New York, 1932.

NOTES AND REFERENCES

CHAPTER ONE

1. Diodorus Siculus lived in the first century BC, during the time of Julius Caesar and Augustus. He wrote the forty-book *Bibliotheca Historica* (*The Library of History*), of which the first five and the twelfth to twentieth survive. The remaining work is usually referred to as the *Universal History* and the period of Alexander's reign is contained in books 16 and 17.

2. Plutarch was born around AD 46 in the Greek town of Chaeronea. Coming from a wealthy family, he studied philosophy in Athens. His *Bios Alexandrou* (*Life of Alexander*) is a collection of biographical essays that examine the virtues and vices of Alexander's reign.

3. Lucius Flavius Arrianus, or Arrian for short, was an important official in the Roman Empire and a personal friend of the Emperor Hadrian in the first half of the second century AD. As he served in the Roman army, his work on Alexander, the *Anabasis Alexandrou* (*The Campaigns of Alexander*) concentrates heavily on the military aspects of Alexander's life.

4. The *Historia Alexandri Magni* (*History of Alexander the Great*), or the *Historia* for short, was compiled by an unknown author in the Roman province of Dalmatia around AD 250. It is thought to be a copy of the work of an earlier Greek historian, Dionysius of Halicarnassus, who wrote during the reign of the Emperor Augustus. Dionysius' original no longer survives, but references in the *Historia* suggest that it was compiled from a variety of ancient sources, including the works of Alexander's contemporaries, Hieronymus of Cardia and Chares of Mytilene.

5. Marcus Junius Justinus, generally referred to as Justinus or simply Justin, was a Roman author who wrote around the year AD 190. His work on Alexander, the *Epitoma Historiarum Philippicarum Pompei Trogi* (*Epitome of the Philippic History of Pompeius Trogus*), was an abridged copy of the work of an earlier Roman historian, Gnaeus Pompeius Trogus, who wrote during the reign of the Emperor Augustus around the time of the birth of Christ. Apart from a few fragments, this original work no longer survives. Justinus' work, referred to as the *Philippic History* for short, is generally thought to be an accurate rendering of Trogus' original. Nothing is known of Justinus' personal life.

6. Diodorus, *Universal History*, 17: 115–116.
7. Arrian, *The Campaigns of Alexander*, 7: 24.
8. Plutarch, *The Life of Alexander*, vs. 79.
9. *Historia Alexandri Magni*, 13: 19.
10. Justinus, *Philippic History*, 12: 13.
11. *Historia*, 13: 21.
12. Diodorus, 17: 117.
13. Justinus, 12: 13.
14. Arrian, 7: 24.
15. Plutarch, vs. 79.
16. Bosworth and Baynham, *Alexander the Great in Fact and Fiction*, pp. 307–325.
17. Ibid.
18. Diodorus, 17: 117.
19. *Historia*, 13: 21.
20. Plutarch, vs. 79.
21. Arrian, 7: 25.
22. Plutarch, vs. 80.
23. *Historia*, 13: 22.
24. Plutarch, vs. 80.
25. *Historia*, 13: 22.
26. Plutarch, vs. 80.
27. Arrian, 7: 26.
28. *Historia*, 13: 23.
29. Justinus, 12: 17.
30. Plutarch, vs. 81.
31. Maynard, *The Death of Alexander Re-examined*.
32. Oldach, D.W. and Benitez, M.R., *Intestinal Bug Likely Killed Alexander The Great, University of Maryland Medical News*, June 1998.
33. *University of Newcastle-upon-Tyne Medical Dictionary*, Newcastle, 1999.
34. Ibid.
35. Justinus, 12: 13 & 16.
36. *Historia*, 13: 24.
37. Plutarch, vs. 81.
38. Ibid.
39. Justinus, 12: 14.
40. Plutarch, vs. 81.
41. Diodorus, 17: 118.
42. *Historia*, 13: 24.

CHAPTER TWO
1. Plutarch, vs. 81.
2. Quintus Curtius Rufus, or Curtius for short, was a Roman military commander who became a senator under Emperor Tiberius. Between AD 31 and 41, Curtius composed *The History of Alexander*, which was during the reign of Emperor Claudius.
3. Curtius, *The History of Alexander*, 9: 19.
4. Agency for Toxic Substances and Disease Registry (ATSDR), *Toxic Effects of Mercury Fact Sheet*, Washington, 1999.
5. The National Institute for Occupational Safety and Health (NIOSH), *Guide to Chemical Hazards*, Washington, 2002.
6. Ibid.
7. Department of Emergency Medicine, University of Southern California, Los Angeles, CA. *NLM Medical Encyclopedea*, Los Angeles, 2002.
8. Ibid.
9. *Historia*, 13: 21.
10. Justinus, 12: 13.
11. *The Wiley Dictionary of Toxicology*.
12. Ibid.
13. Ibid.
14. Ibid.
15. Ibid.
16. *Historia*, 13: 22.
17. *AMA Handbook of Poisonous and Injurious Plants*.
18. Plutarch, vs. 79.
19. *AMA*, see Belladonna.
20. Plutarch, vs. 80.
21. Arrian, 7: 26
22. *Historia*, 13: 23.
23. Justinus, 12: 17.

CHAPTER THREE
1. *Historia* 12: 17.
2. Plutarch, vs. 77.
3. *Book of Arda Viraf*, 1–17.
4. Boyce, Mary (Ed.), *Textual Sources for the Study of Zoroastrianism*.
5. *Historia*, 12: 18. Justinus, 12: 12.
6. Plutarch, vs. 77. Justinus, 12: 12. *Historia*, 12: 18.
7. Arrian, 7: 16.
8. Diodorus, 18: 114.
9. Diodorus, 17: 116.

10. Plutarch, vs. 79.
11. Ibid.
12. *Historia*, 13: 19.
13. Arrian, 7: 24–27. Justinus 12: 13–14. Plutarch, vs. 79–81.
14. Curtius, 8: 14 to 10: 10. *Historia*, 12: 20 to 13: 9.
15. Plutarch, vs. 81. Diodorus, 17: 118. Arrian, 7: 27. *Historia*, 13: 21.
16. Justinus, 12: 14.
17. *Historia*, 4: 11.
18. Plutarch, vs. 82.
19. Arrian, 4: 18–19.
20. Plutarch, vs. 82. *Historia*, 14: 4.
21. Justinus, 12: 10.
22. *Historia*, 8: 5.
23. Plutarch, vs. 21.
24. Justinus, 11: 10, 13: 2, 14: 6.
25. *Historia*, 13: 7.
26. Ibid., 13: 21.
27. Plutarch, vs. 53–54.
28. Curtius 10: 6.
29. Arrian, 4: 10 to 12: 5.
30. Justinus, 12: 11–12.
31. Delbruck, H., *History of the Art of War: Warfare in Antiquity*, pp. 36–40.
32. Bevan, E.R., *The House of Seleucus*.
33. *Historia*, 13: 20.

CHAPTER FOUR

1. Bosworth, A.B., *Conquest and Empire: The Reign of Alexander the Great*.
2. Justinus, 7: 9.
3. Ibid., 7: 5.
4. Ibid., 7: 1–6.
5. Diodorus, 16: 2.
6. Diodorus, bk. 16.
7. *Historia*, 1: 9.
8. Diodorus, bk. 16.
9. Sekunda, N., *The Army of Alexander the Great*.
10. Ibid.
11. *Historia*, 1: 11.
12. Diodorus, bk. 16.
13. Justinus, bk. 8.

14. Diodorus, bk. 16.
15. Plutarch, vs. 3.
16. Ibid., vs. 2.
17. Ibid., vs. 3.
18. Ibid.
19. Diodorus, 17: 5–6.
20. Justinus, bk. 8.
21. *Historia*, 2: 5.
22. Plutarch, vs. 6.
23. Diodorus, 16: 85.
24. Ibid., 16: 86.
25. Plutarch, vs. 8–9.
26. Ibid., vs. 9.
27. Plutarch, vs. 10.
28. Justinus, 9: 7. Plutarch, vs. 10.
29. Justinus, 9: 5.
30. Ibid., 11: 2.
31. Ibid., 9: 6.
32. Diodorus, 16: 94.
33. *Historia*, 3: 1.
34. Diodorus, 17: 2.
35. Justinus, 11: 2.
36. Plutarch, vs. 73.
37. Ibid., vs. 42.
38. Ibid., vs. 78.
39. Arrian, 4: 27.
40. Plutarch, vs. 81.
41. Justinus, 12: 14.

CHAPTER FIVE

1. Robson, T.L., *Women in the Ancient World*, pp. 103–108.
2. Ibid., pp. 39–48.
3. Plutarch, vs. 9.
4. Ibid., vs. 82.
5. Ibid., vs. 4.
6. Ibid., vs. 6.
7. Ibid., vs. 10.
8. Ibid., vs. 8.
9. Ibid., vs. 9.
10. Justinus, 9: 6.
11. Diodorus, 16: 93.

12. Plutarch, vs. 10.
13. Justinus, 9: 7.
14. Ibid.
15. Ibid.
16. Plutarch, vs. 11.
17. Plutarch, *Artaxerxex II*, vs. 5.
18. Arrian, 2: 14.
19. Diodorus, bk. 17.
20. Plutarch, vs. 15.
21. Euripides, *Trojan Women*.
22. Wood, Michael, *In Search of the Trojan War*.
23. *Historia*, 4: 6.
24. Plutarch, vs. 15.
25. Ibid, vs. 16.
26. Justinus, 11: 7.
27. Ibid.
28. Ibid., 11: 9.
29. Diodorus, 17: 34.
30. Ibid., 17: 35–36. Plutarch, vs. 24.
31. Plutarch, vs. 21–22.
32. Justinus, 11: 10.

CHAPTER SIX
1. Plutarch, vs. 21.
2. Ibid., vs. 22.
3. Ibid.
4. Ibid., vs. 21.
5. Ibid., vs. 22.
6. Ibid., vs. 24. *Historia*, 4: 18.
7. Arrian, 2: 14.
8. Burn, A.R., *Greece and Rome*, pp. 140–154.
9. Curtius, 4: 4.
10. *Historia*, 4: 18.
11. Curtius, 4: 6.
12. Josephus, *Jewish Antiquities*, 11: 317–345.
13. Arrian, 3: 2.
14. Plutarch, vs. 26.
15. *Historia*, 5: 9.
16. Arrian, 3: 3.
17. Justinus, 11: 11.
18. Ibid.

19. Ibid.
20. Diodorus, bk. 17.
21. Ibid.
22. Ibid., 17: 34.
23. Ibid., 17: 58.
24. Curtius, 5: 1.
25. Diodorus, 17: 65.
26. Ibid., 17: 67.
27. Ibid., 17: 68–71.
28. Arrian, 3: 21.
29. *Historia*, 13: 9.

CHAPTER SEVEN

1. Arrian, 3: 21–22.
2. Plutarch, vs. 47.
3. *Historia*, 6: 4.
4. Justinus, 11: 15.
5. Arrian, 3: 21–22.
6. Palmer, J., *The Army of Alexander the Great*, pp. 134–148.
7. Ibid., pp. 150–156.
8. Ibid.
9. Diodorus, 17: 75–81.
10. *Historia*, 6: 13.
11. Ibid., 6: 16.
12. Plutarch, vs. 52.
13. Ibid.
14. Ibid.
15. Ibid., vs. 53.
16. Ibid.
17. Ibid.
18. Justinus, 12: 5.
19. Ibid.
20. Diodorus, 17: 82.
21. *Historia*, 7: 5.
22. Curtius, 7: 4.
23. Ibid., 7: 5.
24. Ibid.
25. Curtius, 7: 6.
26. Ibid., 7: 7.
27. *Historia*, 7: 11.
28. Ibid., 7: 14.

29. Curtius, 7: 8.
30. *Historia*, 7: 16.
31. Ibid., 7: 18.
32. Justinus, 12: 6.
33. Plutarch, vs. 54.

CHAPTER EIGHT
1. Arrian, 4: 18–19.
2. Ibid., 4: 19.
3. Lucian's *Paintings*, vs. 7. English translation by Margaret Marshall.
4. *Historia*, 8: 7.
5. Ibid., 8: 13.
6. Diodorus, 17: 82.
7. Ibid., 17: 83–85.
8. Arrian, 5: 1.
9. *Historia*, 8: 17.
10. Philostratus, *Life of Apollonius*, 2: 8. English translation by Margaret Marshall.
11. *Historia*, 8: 18.
12. Timpson, B.E., *Tribal Religions of Ancient India*, pp. 73–88.
13. Diodorus, 17: 86.
14. *Historia*, 9: 2.
15. Ibid., 9: 4.
16. Ibid.
17. Strabo, *Geographia*, 15: 1.
18. *Historia*, 9: 6.
19. Plutarch, vs. 65.
20. Ibid.
21. Diodorus, 17: 87–88.
22. Justinus, 12: 8.
23. Plutarch, vs. 66.
24. Arrian, 7: 1.
25. Ibid., 5: 28.
26. Ibid., 5: 29.
27. Ibid., 5: 30.

CHAPTER NINE
1. *Historia*, 10: 2.
2. Palmer, *The Army of Alexander* . . . , p. 120.
3. *Historia*, 10: 2.
4. Arrian, 6: 18.

5. Plutarch, vs. 68.
6. Ibid.
7. Ibid., 71.
8. *Historia*, 10: 12.
9. Arrian, 6: 24–25.
10. Plutarch, vs. 69.
11. Ibid., vs. 71.
12. Arrian, 6: 26.
13. Curtius, 10: 5.
14. Ibid.
15. Arrian, 29: 1.
16. Plutarch, *The Life of Artaxerxes*, vs. 3.
17. Arrian, 4: 10.
18. Ibid., 4: 11.
19. Plutarch, vs. 58.
20. Ibid., vs. 63.
21. Arrian, 6: 27.
22. *Historia*, 11: 3.
23. Justinus, 12: 11.
24. Ibid., 12: 12.
25. Arrian, 7: 1.
26. Ibid., 7: 3.
27. Ibid., 7: 6.

CHAPTER TEN
1. Plutarch, vs. 21.
2. Ibid., vs. 32.
3. Ibid.
4. Curtius, 5: 1.
5. Ibid.
6. Ibid., 5: 2.
7. Ibid., 5: 3.
8. Diodorus, 17: 20.
9. Plutarch, vs. 41.
10. *Historia*, 6: 8.
11. Arrian, 7: 4–5.
12. Robson, *Women in the Ancient World*, pp. 83–89.

CHAPTER ELEVEN
1. Diodorus, 16: 94.
2. Arrian, 1: 22.

3. Diodorus, bk. 17.
4. Ibid.
5. *Historia*, 12: 9.
6. Ibid., 12: 11.
7. Justinus, 12: 12.
8. Plutarch, vs. 77.
9. Ibid.
10. Diodorus, 17: 114.
11. Arrian, 7: 9.
12. Ibid.
13. Plutarch, vs. 77.
14. Diodorus, 17: 114.
15. *Arda Viraf*, 1: 17.
16. *Historia*, 12: 10.
17. Ibid., 12: 11.
18. Herodotus, *Historiae*, 1: 140.
19. Strabo, *Geographia*, 15: 3.
20. Van der Leeuw, Charles, *Azerbaijan – A Quest for Identity*.
21. *Historia*, 4: 12.
22. Arrian, 7: 4.
23. Diodorus, 18: 7–8.
24. Justinus, 12: 13.
25. Ibid.
26. Ibid., 12: 12.
27. Arrian, 7: 9.
28. Diodorus, 17: 115.
29. Ibid.

CHAPTER TWELVE
1. Diodorus, 17: 114.
2. Justinus, 12: 15.
3. Ibid.
4. Curtius, 6: 10.
5. Justinus, 13: 2.
6. Curtius, 6: 10.
7. Justinus, 13: 2.
8. Curtius, 6: 10.
9. Justinus, 13: 2.
10. Curtius, 6: 10.
11. Ibid.
12. Justinus, 13: 3.

13. Ibid.
14. Ibid., 13: 4.
15. Ibid.
16. *Historia*, 14: 3.
17. Diodorus, 17: 118.
18. Plutarch, vs. 73.

CHAPTER THIRTEEN

1. Justinus, 13: 5.
2. Ibid.
3. Diodorus, 18: 7.
4. Ibid.
5. Justinus, 13: 6.
6. Curtius, 10: 9.
7. *Denkard*, 4: 17.
8. Justinus, 13: 6.
9. Ibid.
10. Ibid.
11. Diodorus, 18: 26–28.
12. Ibid. Curtius, 10: 10. *Historia*, 14: 7. Plutarch, vs. 76.
13. Diodorus, 18: 26–28.
14. Cassius, *History of Rome*, 75: 13.
15. Ibid.
16. Justinus, 13: 6.
17. Ibid., 13: 8.
18. Ibid., bk. 14.
19. Plutarch, vs. 82.
20. Diodorus, 17: 118.

CHAPTER FOURTEEN

1. Devlin, R.B., *History of the Aegean*, pp. 24–36.
2. Justinus, 14: 1–2.
3. Arrian, 2: 28.
4. *Historia*, 4: 1–2.
5. Diodorus, 17: 7.
6. *Historia*, 4: 18.
7. Devlin, pp. 41–44.
8. Arrian, 3: 21.
9. *Historia*, 7: 16.
10. Arrian, 7: 4–5.
11. Justinus, bk. 14.

12. Diodorus, 18: 48.
13. Ibid., 18: 49–50.
14. Ibid.
15. *Historia*, 14: 16.
16. Justinus, 15: 1.
17. Ibid., 15: 2.
18. Diodorus, bk. 20.

CHAPTER FIFTEEN
1. Curtius, 6: 10.
2. Plutarch, vs. 3.
3. Ibid., vs. 42.
4. Ibid., vs. 73.
5. Ibid.
6. Ibid.
7. Ibid., vs. 10.
8. Ibid., vs. 82.
9. Ibid., vs. 81.
10. Justinus, 12: 14.
11. Ibid., 13: 6.
12. Ibid.
13. Ibid., 14: 5.
14. Ibid.
15. Diodorus, 19: 11.
16. Ibid.
17. Ibid.
18. Justinus, 14: 6.
19. Ibid.
20. Ibid.

CHAPTER SIXTEEN
1. Curtius, 6: 10.
2. Justinus, 13: 2.
3. Curtius, 6: 10.
4. Plutarch, vs. 77.
5. *Historia*, 12: 11.
6. Justinus, 12: 12.
7. Plutarch, vs. 77.
8. *Historia*, 13: 23.
9. *NLM Medical Encyclopedia*, see Tetanus.
10. *Historia*, 13: 21.

11. Diodorus, 17: 117.
12. Justinus, 12: 13.
13. Diodorus, 17: 117.
14. Plutarch, vs. 79.
15. *Historia*, 13: 21.
16. Ibid., 13: 22.
17. Ibid.
18. Plutarch, vs. 80.
19. Justinus, 12: 17.
20. *Historia*, 13: 21.
21. Ibid., 13: 22.
22. *The Grant Dictionary of Toxicology*, see Strychnine.
23. *AMA Handbook of Poisonous and Injurious Plants*, see Nux Vomica.
24. Philostratus, *Life of Apollonius*, 2: 8.
25. Timpson, *Tribal Religions of Ancient India*, pp. 80–86.
26. Arrian, 7: 1.
27. *Historia*, 11: 3.

CHAPTER SEVENTEEN

1. Justinus, 13: 2.
2. Plutarch, vs. 82.
3. Arrian, 7: 23.
4. *Historia*, 8: 18.
5. Philostratus, *Life of Apollonius*, 2: 8.
6. *Historia*, 8: 17.
7. Ibid., 9: 2.
8. Arrian, 7: 1.
9. Plutarch, vs. 82.
10. Ibid., vs. 22.
11. Lucian's *Paintings*, vs. 7.
12. Plutarch, vs. 42.
13. Ibid., vs. 51.
14. Arrian, 7: 9.
15. Ibid.
16. Aeschylus, *Myrmidones*. English translation by Margaret Marshall.
17. Plato, *Symposium*, English translation by Seth Benardete, University of Chicago Press, Chicago, 2001.
18. Diodorus, 19: 105.

INDEX